ISRAEL
LAND OF PROMISE ▫ LAND OF PROPHECY

An informative travel adventure
by **GARY G. COHEN**
with special photo commentary
by **SALEM KIRBAN**

Published by SALEM KIRBAN, Inc., Kent Road, Huntingdon Valley, Pennsylvania, 19006. Copyright © 1974 by Salem Kirban. Printed in the United States of America. All rights reserved, including the right to reproduce this book or portions thereof in any form.

ISBN 0-912582-16-2
Library of Congress Catalog Card No. 74-77252

ABOUT THE AUTHOR

Gary G. Cohen is a professor at the Biblical School of Theology, Hatfield, Pennsylvania, where he has taught both Hebrew and Greek, as well as many other Biblical subjects.

Dr. Cohen's formal education has earned him the B.S., B.D., S.T.M., and TH.D. degrees, while his "informal" education had included flight training, the army chaplaincy, and trips to Israel.

This is Dr. Cohen's fifth book. He co-authored **REVELATION VISUALIZED** with Salem Kirban...and again, it is another change of pace from his previous writings.

This present work will take the reader on a trip across the towns of Israel...to share some of that land's laughter and tears...as well as its ancient history and prophesied glory.

ACKNOWLEDGMENTS

We are grateful for the cooperation of the following photographers for making available many of the pictures in this book:

L. Bozodulin	Arie Meiseles	Zev Radovan
Amnon Shpack	Ronnie Barkey	Aliza Auerbach
Asher Zohar	A.S. Barak	Leonard Schifter
Pinchas Koll	M. Simon	I.P.P.A. Ltd.
Y. Barzilay	I. Ben-Arieh	Barry Barber
Ralph Golomb	Bruce Heiman	

EXCERPTS from **ISRAEL, Land of Promise**

It was twilight and we could still read the Hebrew characters on the face of the stone...Its opening words read, "To the eternal memory."

chapter 2

* * *

As we touched and handled stones tooled two millenia ago we were driven backwards into the past as inside a time machine. chapter 3

* * *

At one time Herzl was prepared to bow to a British suggestion that Uganda in Africa become the New Zion for Jews, just as Salt Lake City has become the chosen New Zion of the Mormons. chapter 5

* * *

...the Bible points to a Satanically-inspired (not a God-inspired) persecution which will in the end drive Israel as a nation to cry out for her true God and Messiah. chapter 7

* * *

A mass suicide took place and Silva found only two women and five children alive. chapter 10

* * *

It began to snow and the guide told us that we were experiencing weather which came only once in fifteen years. chapter 11

* * *

The policy of the cruel Assyrian conquerors of Israel in 722 B.C. was to induce a forced population migration into all conquered lands. This policy led them to deport most of the Jews of the northern ten tribes into foreign countries. chapter 14

* * *

Emperor Hadrian desired to rebuild the city as a Roman city. He outlawed, because of the two revolts, all Jewish people from coming within ten miles of the city under pain of death. chapter 17

* * *

Above are some of the intriguing portions you will read in the book **ISRAEL, LAND OF PROMISE, LAND OF PROPHECY.**

DEDICATION

To **Dr. Richard Curry**
and to all those who love Israel

CONTENTS

	Preface	6
1	INTO THE CLOUDS	11
2	LOD, JOPPA, TEL AVIV	16
3	STOPPING AT CAESAREA	30
4	CARMEL, HAIFA, ACRE and HISTORY	35
5	HAIFA BAY, ANTI-SEMITISM and JUDGMENT	51
6	STANDING ON ARMAGEDDON	60
7	ISRAEL'S PROPHETIC FUTURE	73
8	ARRIVAL INTO TIBERIAS	94
9	TOURING NORTHERN GALILEE	99
10	GOLAN HEIGHTS and the GEOGRAPHY OF PALESTINE	115
11	THE LAKE, BETHSHAN and NAZARETH	135
12	CROSSING THE LAKE; EIN GEV; AND THE LIFE OF CHRIST	143
13	ROSH PINA, MAGDALA and CAPERNAUM	156
14	THE JOURNEY SOUTH (CANA, SAMARIA, SHECHEM, SHILOH)	166
15	WALKING THROUGH BIBLICAL JERUSALEM	184
16	JERUSALEM TODAY	206
17	INSIDE THE WALLS	221
18	THE ISRAEL MUSEUM and AFTER	227
19	SACRED PLACES IN JERUSALEM, BETHLEHEM, AND HEBRON	243
20	A DIP IN THE DEAD SEA and AN INVASION OF JERICHO	256
21	CROSSING THE OCEAN	279

PREFACE

This book is a primer on Bible history, theology, geography, archeology, prophecy, anti-semitism, and on the present day Middle East situation. It is a diary that alternates Bible study with eye-opening travel accounts. It will take you through Palestine as well as through some of the great teachings of the Scriptures. At times it will teach you; other times it will challenge you, make you want to pray, want to cry, or want to laugh until the tears run. In short, it will embark you on a modern pilgrimage, an ISRAEL SAFARI. Read with Bible and map beside you and let us begin.

Recently it was my privilege to tour the Holy Land with my good companion and fellow professor, the Rev. Robert J. Dunzweiler. This trip afforded us not only the precious opportunity to walk upon holy soil, the land of the Prophets, but it also gave us new insights in the fields of Biblical geography, history, archeology, and prophecy. It has been my desire by means of the written word to share the knowledge and pleasure acquired on this trip with those here at home.

Our world today has so many involved books flying at us that even the intellectual gets weary of reading complicated treatises. Thus, in order to inform a larger segment of the public, from teen-ager to Ph. D., it seemed best to write an account of my trip to the Holy Land, incorporating within it pertinent discussions of some of the various topics as they naturally arise as one walks through the Biblical sites.

Therefore, let us accomplish the above aims by following the pattern of the modern traveling study group wherein the students hear lectures, and have discussions while visiting abroad. Thus I invite you, the reader, to come with Professor Robert J. Dunzweiler and myself on a modern Holy Land Seminar. Gain six semester hours graduate credit for the mere price of this book, and travel through the land of the Bible. In addition to the travel the featured topics will include: Biblical Geography, History, and Archeology; Israel and Prophecy; and History of Modern Israel.

Be sure to follow our trip with a good MAP beside you. This will make the trip more profitable and enjoyable for you. Bring a Bible along so that you can look up and study the Scripture references which are periodically given.

We shall retrace the itinerary which Mr. Dunzweiler and I traveled in January 1968. Every time indication, air flight number, hotel name, hotel description, menu, and geographical, historical, and archaeological site description, et cetera, will be absolutely authentic just as Professor Dunzweiler and I experienced it. Even participation by guides, Arabs, Israelis, and missionaries will be authentic, according to the detailed day by day diary of the trip which I kept. Only the names and words of our traveling companions will be fictitious. By this I trust that the reader will be able, at least in some measure, to share in the thrilling experience of visiting the land of the Bible.

ITINERARY

Date:

January 7th. . . New York
January 8th. . . Madrid (Night: 4th—aboard plane)
January 9th. . . Athens (stopover)
               Lod
               Jaffa
               Tel Aviv (Nights: 9th & 10th—Hotel Dan)
January 11th. . . Caesarea
               Haifa (Nights: 11th & 12th—Dan Carmel Hotel)
               Mt. Carmel
January 12th. . . Acre
January 13th. . . Mount Megiddo
               Mount Tabor
               Tiberias (Nights: 13th through 17th—Hotel Ginton)

8 • ISRAEL Land of Promise, Land of Prophecy

January 14th . . . Caesarea-Philippi
                   Mount Hermon
                   Kuneitra
                   Golan Heights
January 15th . . . Lake Galilee
                   Beth Shan
                   Nazareth
January 16th . . . Ein Gev
January 17th . . . Rosh Pena
                   Magdala
                   Capernaum
                   Tel Hazor
January 18th . . . Cana
                   Mount Megiddo
                   Jenin (Beth Hagan)
                   Shomeron (Samaria)
                   Nablus (Shechem)
                   Mounts Ebal and Gerizim
                   Sychar
                   Shiloh
                   Jerusalem (Nights: 18th through 23rd—
                     King David Hotel)
January 22nd . . . Bethlehem
                   Hebron
January 23rd . . . Kal Ya
                   Dead Sea
                   Jericho
January 24th . . . Tel Aviv (Night: 24th—Hotel Dan)
January 25th . . . Athens
                   Geneva
                   New York

TERMS*

The cost of this travel seminar will be $699. This includes air transportation to and from the Holy Land, all lodging, three meals per day, all fees and honorariums. Private side

*If you went on a trip such as this, this is what the terms would be like.

journeys taken by individuals aside from the itinerary, as well as all expenses which incur therefrom, will be the individual's own responsibility. Accident or theft insurance is not included in the fee, but should be purchased privately by each person. The sponsors regret that they cannot assume any responsibility for accidents, bodily injuries, thefts, or other involvements which may occur. A deposit of $100 is due one month prior to departure. Because of certain non-refundable advance arrangements this cannot be returned in the event of a cancellation by the participant. Full payment is due 48 hours before departure; however, 12 or 24 month terms are available and quite reasonable.

Sincerely,
Holy Land Tours, Inc.

An Orientation to the Bible and to its land, ancient and modern, through an enlightening and entertaining modern tour.

by

Gary G. Cohen

Read this book and you will acquire a wealth of information about the Bible and Biblical backgrounds without the usual tedium of wading through a heavy textbook. You will want this volume to accompany you on your journey through Palestine whether you travel by plane or living room chair.

The chapter, "Walking Through Biblical Jerusalem," will teach you more on this subject than many a correspondence course. It alone is worth the price of this book.—The Publishers.

CHAPTER I

INTO THE CLOUDS

January 7th. Passers-by stared at me as I laid on the ground outside of the airport terminal. Perspiration covered my face as I realized that soon Professor Robert Dunzweiler, my co-host, and our seven tour companions would arrive. One passing lady gave a look of horror as her eyes beheld me lying face down on the cement. Yet, no one offered to help me up.

Alas—I had temporarily checked my small carry-on case in a locker and as I went to redeem it, my locker key fell in the sewer-drain outside the terminal building. In my joy at going to Israel I had flipped it into the air and...I missed my catch, and into the sewer it fell! The metal grate came off and by lying on the ground (wearing a good suit) I could just get my hands into the ice cold water 6 inches deep. Here systematically, in desperation, my hand went back and forth through the melted age old cigarette butts and sludge, feeling for the key amid the icy water. Time after time, because of freezing numbness I had to take my hand out of the water. Then, at last, I felt it...and raced to the locker...and then to Bob Dunzweiler and our companions.

Soon I was shaking Bob's clean warm hand...noting how wise and owlish my brilliant professor colleague appeared.

12 • ISRAEL Land of Promise, Land of Prophecy

Our companions who had signed up with Mr. Dunzweiler and myself for the tour were as follows: Mr. and Mrs. Arnold Escourt, he being a young student; Mr. Steven Reed, a commercial pilot, and his attractive and witty wife, Arlene; Dr. Gerald Schatz, the Headmaster of the Matthews School; Harold H. Fisher, an independent thinker and traveler; and Miss Barbara Miller, a fine girl with beautiful long black hair.

The route of our aerial voyage was New York to Lod Airport, Israel, with stopovers at Madrid and Athens. As departure time arrived, chatting vigorously and with great anticipation, we climbed aboard the huge TWA Boeing 707 Starstream four-engine jet liner. This was TWA Flight 904, departing New York at 6:15 p.m. E.S.T. Our scheduled flying time from J.F.K. to Madrid was six hours, and then after a one-hour respite, the flight from Madrid to Athens was anticipated as four more hours.

The capacity of our airship, in addition to its crew and the genial stewardesses, was 114 plus another 24 in the deluxe forward first class compartments. This made a total capacity of 138 in this highly attractive jet transport. I counted a total of 87 passengers aboard out of the possible 138 available seats, and for the first time in my life realized that scheduled airlines do not always fly with all of their potential tickets sold.

FORBIDDEN MADRID

The taxi, the roar down the runway, the lunge into the clouds in a high angle full power take-off, and we were airborne. Soon we were flying at 33,000 feet, six hours to Madrid. The stewardess demonstrated how we were to don the life jackets housed within each of our seats in the event of a forced landing in the ocean. As the stewardess put on the life vest the instructions came over the loud speaker first in English, and then it was repeated very quickly in French. Next the movie to be shown later that evening was described in English and then in Spanish. It was announced that while everyone could see the movie, it was necessary to pay $2.50 to rent an earphone headset in order to hear the sound.

Later, a steak dinner, filet mignon, was served at eight o'clock p.m.; it was delicious. Outside all was now dark and through the window one could barely make out the shape of the airfoil which held us aloft. At midnight while peering southeast from my window I noted an extremely bright sky object. Was it a planet or star? Perhaps a satellite? It was difficult to be certain from the limited view. My conclusion was that it most probably was Jupiter against the constellation Leo. I wanted to get a better look from another's window, but Professor Dunzweiler wisely cautioned me against awakening all of those already asleep. Since the safety of the craft did not on this occasion depend on the accuracy of my celestial navigation I abandoned further stellar observation for the night—to Mr. Dunzweiler's sigh of relief.

Bob and I whispered as we were hurled through the sky almost at Mach 1 toward Castilian country. At a time like this, 33,000 feet up, with the ocean rolling below and stars above, and with our eventual path from Philadelphia to Tel Aviv, Israel, taking us a distance of some 6,000 miles, we could only think of the words of Psalm 24:1 and 2:

> "The earth is the Lord's, and the fulness thereof; the world, and they that dwell therein. For he hath founded it upon the seas, and established it upon the floods."

We then drifted into sleep to the steady purr of the jet engines.

Our group with the other passengers were awakened by a female voice announcing that the Captain had asked everyone to straighten his chair and to fasten his safety belt as we were now making our final approach into the Madrid field. We could see the lights below amid the blackness. It was now January 5th, 1 a.m. Eastern Standard Time; 7 a.m. in Madrid. We could feel the pressure change on our ears as we lost altitude in our descent. The rumble of the wheels being lowered was followed by a quieter lowering of the flaps. With but one bounce we landed fairly smoothly. With the noise of the four engines reversing so as to reduce our ground speed quickly and the resultant tug of the deacceleration inertia we were all fully awake once more. The ocean had been crossed safely.

It was still fairly dark at the brink of dawn in Madrid. An airport bus drove us into the nearby terminal, and the ride was a chilly one to say the least. The airport shops were not yet open and the officer at the customs desk, wearing a blue uniform, informed us that the passengers en route to Athens on the one hour refueling stop were not permitted to leave the terminal building. On inquiry we were curtly told that we could not so much as walk outside the building to stroll the adjacent precincts of Madrid. This was true even though all of us had our passports on our persons. Ah well, the restaurant was open with its bar, which was of little value to us, and it was thrilling to hear natives converse in their rapid Spanish.

At the end of the hour an open bus via its frigid ride conveyed us to our majestic bird. In minutes we had again attained 33,000 feet, and the Captain explained that a new crew was now at the helm of the plane. He advised us to LOOK AT A MAP, and then pointed out that we would be flying over Barcelona, the leading Spanish seaport, and then we would pass over the Strait of Bonifacio, which divides the French isle of Corsica from the Italian island of Sardinia. Corsica would be on our left, with Elbe beyond, and Sardinia would be on our right. The flight, he proclaimed was to take three hours and fifty minutes, and breakfast was soon to be served. As we flew I noted on our map that from New York to Madrid had been 3600 air miles, and then from Madrid to Athens would be another 1500 air miles.

As we awaited our 8:30 a.m. Madrid time, breakfast, Bob Dunzweiler's unaltered watch showed that the time was 2:30 a.m. (in the morning) Eastern Standard Time. The coming breakfast felt more like a midnight snack, but the increasing dawn illuminated the *Spanish Daily News,* Spain's only English language paper which has a national circulation. We noted the large colorful headline on page 3, "Torero Receives Golden Ear." Out of the window, below, were many huge mountains and brown crags. The sun was seen lofting itself to our right front amid the cirrus and stratus clouds below.

Breakfast in the air for our party consisted of grapefruit, a cheese omelet on a slice of ham (this was not El Al), a roll and butter, a cake, and coffee. By the time we were finished we found ourselves over the Tyrrhenian Sea approaching Rome. Then in another couple of hours we began to glide into ancient Athens. After a fast descending half turn there in the blazing sunlight was the Acropolis in all her glory in the distance. As we rolled down the runway the Captain announced that the temperature was 39 degrees fahrenheit or 4 degrees centigrade. We climbed down the steps from the plane, and it was 11 a.m. Athens time (but 5 a.m. early morning by our Eastern Standard Time). We had traveled 5200 air miles from New York in ten hours of flying time plus an additional hour in Madrid. Now, at least, we were treading upon the land of the early democracies. Here at Athens Saul of Tarsus, of the tribe of Benjamin, preached his new religion of faith in His Messiah to the wise men of Greece.

Soon, in a few hours, we would step down upon Israel, the land from which Saul's religion came...the land of the ancient patriarchs, Abraham, Issac, and Jacob...the land of the prophets...and of the Bible.

CHAPTER II

LOD, JOPPA, TEL AVIV

It was still afternoon as we dismounted from our motor coach at the Athens airport. "Flight 704, Athens to Tel Aviv," came over the loud speaker in distinct feminine Anglo-Greco tones. Then to our dismay the voice intoned in somber timbre the announcement that Flight 704 was delayed, and that flight time would be at 5:50 p.m. rather than at the scheduled 3:30 p.m. time. Some moaned at this, others groaned, but I simply sat and waited, rising every ten minutes for a fresh tour of this not large aerodrome.

With joy we felt the movement of our plane as it leveled off out of its climb at 33,000 feet. We settle back in our seats for the short hop of 750 miles from Athens to Lod, Israel. The stewardess skipped our aisle by accident at beverage time, but Professor Dunzweiler was not above pursuing her down the plane's central corridor for the sake of a Seven-Up.

PLANE ON FIRE

Suddenly I noticed smoke to my immediate forward, and, fearing for the plane, I sprang up. The woman in the seat in front of me seemed to be staring our of her window toward the Number Three Engine of our Boeing 707. She looked horrified as smoke could now definitely be seen within the plane. She turned to me and in near panic said, "Pardon me, sir; but I've

Caesarea...founded by Herod the Great, the builder, who restored architectural grandeur to Palestine. Caesarea was the home of Cornelius in whose house Peter first preached to the Gentiles. Later it was the enforced residence of Paul where he preached before King Agrippa (Acts 23:31-26:32). In 66, a fight broke out between Jews and Greeks and ended with the slaughter of 20,000 Jews. The Crusaders made Caesarea their stronghold. In 1291, Moslems invaded the city and destroyed it.

18 • ISRAEL Land of Promise, Land of Prophecy

Air traffic is busy at Lod Airport, situated midway between Jerusalem and Tel Aviv.

Anxious faces of Israeli immigrants get their first glimpse of Israel.

The Jordan River, the border between Israel and Jordan.

20 • ISRAEL Land of Promise, Land of Prophecy

Women also serve. A typical Israeli soldier.

dropped my cigarette between the arm and cushion of this seat. It's starting to smoke; can you help?" . . . I frowned, and reaching forward with my foot to the cigarette now fallen to the floor, I tread it out. The stewardess now arrives and is informed as to what has transpired. I asked her if I would receive a certificate of commendation for having extinguished the fire in the plane. She shook her head negatively, and offered to shake my hand as an alternate commendation. We shook, and the affair was ended.

On our arrival at the Lod Airport I was a bit chagrined as the customs officials—a young, attractive girl with black hair and an older man in the aisle through which we passed—were more interested in conversing with each other than on noticing the newcomers. While not expecting a royal welcome, we were disappointed at not even being noticed.

Strolling casually about the airport we saw everywhere women soldiers and also male soldiers with automatic rifles strapped to their backs or in their hands. Uniformly the soldiers, male and female, appeared to be in their twenties.

Our party proceeded to the company that rented autos here at the air terminal. Professor Dunzweiler and myself were assigned a small vehicle, which, after a brief inspection, Mr. Dunzweiler pronounced to be of French make. Later on, his observation turned out to have a greater significance—but the reader will learn of this in a later chapter.

We then motored toward Tel Aviv, now discovering that Lod Airport is about twenty miles southeast of the city. It was twilight as we entered Jaffa, which is at Tel Aviv's southern tip. We still could see the famed lighthouse which stands upon the 116-foot rocky knoll of the city. Here the rocks jut out into the Mediterranean to form a small cape. Greek mythology cited these stones collectively "Andromeda's Rock" because it was here that she was supposed to have been chained when Perseus saved her from the sea monster. At this I looked up to hunt the sky for M31 which is the great spiral nebula galaxy in the constellation of Andromeda. It is the nearest galaxy to the earth, being some one and a half million light years distant. "The heavens declare the glory of God" (Psa. 19:1), thought I, peering upward. As the car bounced, I turned again to Jaffa.

YAFO

Suddenly the city, or better, the *town* of Jaffa arose to our eyes, filled with rubble-strewn hovels. We had reached the now narrow-streeted and darkened strip which became the "no man's land" between Jaffa and Tel Aviv in the Arab-Israeli conflict in 1948. Now twenty years later and the region still showed signs of the destructive gunfire that a score of years ago so marred it.

Modern English maps refer to this city as "Jaffa;" the Israelis cite it as "Yafo;" and our English Bibles name it as "Joppa." To this port, once Palestine's largest, came three thousand years ago (c. 969 B.C.) the Cedars of Lebanon for the construction of Solomon's Temple. From here, about twenty-eight centuries ago the Prophet Jonah departed in a boat bound for Tarshish on the first leg of his journey to preach repentance to that great city, Nineveh (Jon. 1:3).

The Apostle Peter was residing here at the house of one called Simon the Tanner when he saw the thrice-repeated vision of the unkosher animals proclaimed as now clean—teaching him that God through the Messiah was now declaring Gentiles to be clean (Acts 10:8-16). Then, after the vision had departed, to this city to find Peter came the emissaries of Cornelius, the Roman soldier. They delivered their message at Joppa that a pious Gentile wished to hear the good news of Peter's Messiah (Acts 10).

Yet again, it was here that in answer to Peter's prayer the Lord God demonstrated His approval of the faith proclaimed by the apostles by permitting Peter to raise Tabitha from the dead (Acts 9:36-43).

What tales could this city further relate! Through its streets rode the Turks; then came the Crusaders; in 1799 Napoleon besieged and conquered it; and yet here in 1948 Arabs and Israelis fought for it in the War of Independence.

We knew there was an artistic and built-up center in the mostly Arab occupied town of Joppa, but amid the narrow-laned streets with names in Hebrew letters it was hard to find our way. Over and over we drove through the same streets in no man's land seeking our exit, and it finally arrived, casting us into the unremitting sea of the maze called Tel Aviv.

LOST IN TEL AVIV

In Tel Aviv, a city which combines the most modern on and near its Rothschild Boulevard, with old and poor sections in other places, navigation is incredibly difficult. The city was begun only in 1909 as a Jewish suburb to the north of Jaffa, and now it is Israel's largest city, with a population of 500,000. Despite its beauteous coastal location and its center city skyscrapers, the concept of city planning was not introduced until relatively recently—the originators never dreamed of its present growth. Thus we soon found our party hopelessly lost amid the swirling and crisscrossing avenues of "Hill of Springtime" (the meaning of *Tel Aviv*). Finally, amid the street signs lettered in Hebrew we discovered Ben Yehuda Street and drove north upon it parallel to the nearby splashing Mediterranean. At last we had arrived at the destination's end, the Dan Hotel at 99 Hayarkon Street. We entered amid the rain which had recently begun to fall.

Here I must explain that while at the present moment I am young, hale, and hearty, and would happily abide on a tour which traveled in Class C hotels and thrived on a prospector's diet of sourdough and beans, this was impossible in the situation at hand. Due to health reasons, the physician had restricted Professor Dunzweiler to eating only well attested foods and to sleeping in draft-free rooms. Thus circumstances forced upon us the lot of lodging only at fine hotels with exquisite cuisines. Yet we all bore up well and I never heard a complaint against Mr. Dunzweiler on this account.

THE CONCIERGE SNARLS

When we entered the Dan Hotel our bags were whisked away from us. The concierge at the desk made us feel like somebodies when he snarled to a bellhop, "Take these people to their rooms." Then smiling at us he waved his hand ever so politely indicating that we were to follow. Professor Dunzweiler and myself declined the 72 lire a day room for the 55 lire per diem affair. This charge, the 55 lire daily, was for both of us (27.5 per person) for a beautiful room, private bath, and breakfast included. This came to about $8 per person per night in a truly deluxe hotel—and breakfast included! With taxes and other costs, we computed room and breakfast to total $9.30 per person.

Before our arrival, one American dollar equaled three Israeli lire or pounds. A recent devaluation, however, had occurred and now a dollar was equivalent to three and a half lire or three lire and fifty agorot. Thus we had gained, due to this devaluation of the local currency. Of course, we did not rejoice at their devaluation necessity; we would grant them stability of economy in preference to a mere short term gain by ourselves.

It should also be noted that Israel, unlike Italy or Greece, insisted that the tourist keep a money exchange ledger which had to have recorded upon it a signed record of every lire-for-dollars exchange made while visiting the country. We discovered also that imports were often taxed at a high rate. Israel was obviously not a wealthy country when compared with the United States. In fact, Israel's wealthiest appearances came universally at hotels which catered to visiting Americans. We noticed further that to the hotel room charge there was, as in the other European countries, an added charge for "service"—here it was ten percent. There was also an additional ten percent social welfare tax, but only Israelis had to pay this. It was thus more expensive for the native by ten percent to occupy a room in one of the hotels in his nation; yet many did.

As we strode toward the elevator which was to lift us to our rooms located on the seventh floor, I suddenly saw perhaps the largest lounge upon which my eyes ever had gazed. A ten-foot wide moat of water ran under a bridge amid the spacious sitting room of the hotel. This vista plus seeing the hotel's three or four restaurants long lived in my mind as the most luxurious of hotels. Professor Dunzweiler, philosophizing, declared, "It is better to stay in the cheapest room of the best hotel, than in the best room of a cheap hotel."

We awaken brightly on this Wednesday, *January 10th*. Looking out of the window of our seventh floor room one can see the Mediterranean below with its waves smashing against the shore line. Though called a "sea," it is essentially an ocean to the voyager. To the south along the coast the lighthouse of Joppa can be spied from our Tel Aviv window.

At breakfast we are greeted here and there by a *boker tov* ("good morning"). Professor Dunzweiler was discussing the Prophet Jonah at the meal, no doubt because of our proximity to Joppa, the Prophet's starting point for his eventful journey. This was a free day in Tel Aviv for our people, and they departed in various directions to see the city.

After the departure of our flock, my colleague leading the way, we walked to our auto. We were shocked to discover that the storm of the night had blown down a large dead tree and that it had collapsed immediately to the rear of our automobile. We rejoiced at having been spared the red tape which would no doubt have accompanied our having to report such a misfortune as a tree falling upon our rented car. After photographing the incident of the downed log, we launched out for the morning.

POTTERY DATING

Following lunch we went across the street from the Dan Hotel to a pottery shop that dealt exclusively in archeological finds. The lady in charge gave us a fine talk on pottery dating—as fine a talk as could be heard at the University of Pennsylvania Museum. She handed us a copy of the following pottery dating chart:

Byzantine Period	330-640 C.E. (same as A.D.)
Roman Period	63 B.C.E.-330 C.E.
Hellenistic Period	330-63 B.C.E. (same as B.C.)
Persian Period	586-330 B.C.E.
Iron Age II	930-586 B.C.E.
Iron Age I	1200-930 B.C.E.
Late Bronze Age	1500-1200 B.C.E.
Middle Bronze Age II	1850-1550 B.C.E.
Early Bronze Age	3100-1850 B.C.E.
Chalcolithic Age	4000-3100 B.C.E.

She explained that archeological levels once dug up could usually be dated by the shapes, designs, handles, spouts, paint, and paintings on the pottery vessels found and reconstructed. This was so because there were various unique pottery patterns to each civilization and time period. Because pottery broke easily and often, and because it was replaced with little effort, it was left buried in the rubble of numberless cities. Thus when archeologists during a "dig" discover at a certain level the presence of certain types of pottery remains and the absence of others, all things being equal, they can date that level according to charts comparing the pottery found with that which already has been positively dated and categorized.

It was Sir W. M. Flinders Petrie who in a summer expedition to Palestine in the early twentieth century discovered this phenomena of pottery and thus introduced the important pottery-dating tool. Sir Flinders at the same time discovered the significance of the "tel," and he informed the scholarly world that those abandoned, flat-topped, grassy hills scattered over Palestine were the remains of the ancient pre-Roman hill (*tel*) cities. These two discoveries, that of pottery dating and of the tel, were two of the most important ever made in Palestinian archeology, and the renowned Egyptologist Petrie made them both in one summer.

The charming lady thereupon displayed to us a bowl, almost, she said, five thousand years old. It was from the early bronze age. Next she showed us an object made of glass from the time of Christ. Iron decorative pieces and axe heads from 1000 B.C. were next exhibited.

MESSIANIC PROPHECY

We thanked her for her splendid lesson before we departed. Upon additional farewell conversation it came out that both Professor Dunzweiler and myself were seminary professors. This occasioned me to challenge her to receive a history lesson from us, just as we had from her. I gave her a copy of a short monograph by O. E. Phillips entitled, "Israel and the Messiah." It discussed some of the predicted characteristics of the Messiah which the Hebrew Old Testament prophets gave to us that we might recognize Him when He should appear. It was the Spirit of God speaking through these prophets that foretold the Messiah's coming.

The monograph listed the following characteristics of the coming Messiah as they were described years before by the Hebrew prophets:

1. He was to be born in Bethlehem (Micah 5:2).
2. He was to be God's anointed One (Psalm 2:2).
3. He was to be virgin born (Isaiah 7:14).
4. He was to be the seed of Abraham (Genesis 22:18).
5. He was to be of the Tribe of Judah (Genesis 49:10).
6. He was to be of the House of David (Isaiah 9:7).
7. He was to die for the sins of the world (Isaiah 53:3-9).
8. He was to be resurrected (Isaiah 53:10; Psalms 16:10; 22:22-31).
9. He was to go back to God until Israel would receive Him (Psalm 110:1,2; Hosea 5:15; Ezekiel 21:26,27).
10. At His return He will judge the nations (Psalm 2:8-11).
11. Jerusalem will be His throne (Jeremiah 3:17, 18).
12. Jerusalem will become an international city, the capital of the world, and the religious center of the earth (Zechariah 8:20-23).
13. All kings shall bow before Him (Psalm 72:7-11).
14. Israel will become like the Garden of Eden (Ezekiel 36:33-35).
15. Universal peace shall prevail over the earth (Isaiah 2:4).

We left with the prayerful hope that this woman might some day recognize her Messiah. Surely these prophecies written centuries before (Micah—700 B.C.; Isaiah—700 B.C.; Davidic Psalms—1000 B.C.; Jeremiah—600 B.C.; Ezekiel—600 B.C.; Zechariah—400 B.C.) prove the existence of a God who knows the future and that Jesus of Nazareth is indeed the Messiah of Israel and of all nations.

THE GRAY MONOLITH

We drove to Rothchild Boulevard in the heart of Tel Aviv. There we dismounted from our vehicle to see a large gray stone monument which was about ten feet long, eight feet high, and four feet thick. It was twilight and we could still read the Hebrew characters on the face of the stone. It explained in a touching way that it commemorated the fortieth year of Tel Aviv's existence. Its opening words read, *"Li-zachar aholam,"* which means, "To the eternal memory." It is difficult not to be moved by such words when they begin a narrative of gratitude for the sacrifice of those gone before.

STOPPED

On our way back to the Dan Hotel on Tel Aviv's Hayarkon Street which runs parallel to the Mediterranean coast, we found ourselves again lost. Professor Dunzweiler would ask the directions if the person we asked could speak German or Yiddish (which is oral German written in Hebrew letters); if they spoke Hebrew, I would inquire, *"Afo Re'hov Hayarkon?"* ("Where is Hayarkon Street?") In contrast to what we later found in Jerusalem, few in Tel Aviv seemed conversant in English.

At last a gentleman who spoke English said, "Go down the road three squares and turn left." At the end of two squares we abutted with a fork in the road! We stayed on the left . . . a whistle blew. A policeman rushed at us, and upon a closer inspection this one turned out to be an attractive policewoman of about eighteen to twenty years of age with jet black hair. Our pleasant surprise on seeing this officer to be a woman ceased instantaneously as she began to give us a tongue lashing in Hebrew. Her tone, her loudness, and her facial expressions and gestures mirrored an utter disgust for our error of driving down a one-way street. I started to give an explanation in English, and before I uttered a half dozen words she interrupted. "Oh, Americans!!! Go, go, go—down that way—but be more careful. Go, go, Americans, Americans!" The impression was received by us that going down one-way streets was typically American in her eyes, and that she desired to avoid the futility of a semi-Hebraic, semi-English dialogue on traffic regulations. It was difficult for us to drive away while trying to restrain our broad smiles. Yet we sorrowed for this beautiful young girl, for we felt that there was a message that she and multitudes like her needed to know.

That night at the hotel we could hardly escape the realization that the majority of the Americans here were so frequently the night-life-seeking tourist crowd. They contrasted so readily with the idealistic Israelis found on every street.

* * * * * *

CHAPTER III

STOPPING AT CAESAREA

Arising early on this *Thursday, January 11th*, promptly after our morning repast our entourage hastens northbound, toward Haifa. We have already made reservations to stay at Haifa's Dan Carmel Hotel for the nights of January 11th through the 17th, Thursday to Wednesday. Today's excursion will take us eighty-six kilometers northward along the excellent blacktop highway which runs parallel to the Mediterranean Sea. We will travel through the fertile citrus region known from Old Testament times as the Plain of Sharon.

As we depart Tel Aviv, after a brief disputation concerning the best route out of the city onto the Coastal Highway, we quickly find ourselves racing toward Haifa. Even though the month is January, the citrus trees—oranges, lemons, limes, grapefruits, tangerines—are luxuriant green and in fruit. We are in the period of the early rain. This period usually commences in November and lasts through the month of January, with December and January producing the strongest rainfalls of the year. This is the rain which follows the seedtime and which nurtures the early growth of the crops. The latter rains fall from March to May, when the crops are in maturity, and these are lighter than the former waterings.

Trees in verdant foliage, more orange and lemon groves, bus stops, and hitchhikers are the constant visual fare imbibed by us as we migrate to higher latitude.

Stopping At Caesarea • 31

Having traversed two-thirds of our route for this day, we spy a sign which informs us that the ancient city of Caesarea may be reached by a movement of two kilometers west at the next crossroad. We elect to take it and within seconds are braking our vehicle at the city named for Caesar. Our party dismounts.

LITTLE ROME

Prof. Dunzweiler: "We are now standing in *Caesarea*, a city, according to my map, located at thirty-two degrees, thirty minutes north latitude, and thirty-four degrees, fifty-five minutes longitude east of Greenwich. Herod the Great constructed this city at the location formerly called 'Strato's Tower.' He erected the city from 25 to 12 B.C., naming it in honor of his patron, Caesar Augustus. He made it the Roman capital of the land of Judea which it remained throughout the lifetimes of Christ and the Apostle Paul. As you can see, it is right on the Mediterranean Sea, being some thirty-two miles north of Joppa. Some have styled it 'Little Rome' because of its beauty and majestic white stone buildings.

"In New Testament times it also was a great seaport and commercial center, lying on the great road between the commercial capital, Tyre, and Egypt. Josephus spoke of its massive harbor, and underwater exploration in 1960 confirmed his descriptions. This Caesarea must not be confused with Caesarea Philippi, the latter being an entirely different city far to the north beyond the Lake of Galilee.

"This Caesarea, wherein we now stand, was the home of Philip the Evangelist, and the Apostle Paul visited him here (Act 21:8). In New Testament times one must picture the recently built Caesarea as a Roman island in the midst of a Hebrew and Samaritan sea. Thus it is not strange that Cornelius, the soldier who was the first gentile convert to the new faith, being a Roman, should be dwelling in the city of Caesarea (Acts 10:1).

"So also, when Paul in A.D. 58 was arrested by the Romans in Jerusalem—the religious leaders wrongly accusing him of having taken a non-Jew into the Temple—we discover that the Roman captain sends him for safe keeping to Caesarea (Acts 23:23). The Roman Captain, Claudius Lysias, having obtained knowledge of a Jewish assassination plot against Paul, realized at once that Paul as a Roman citizen would be safest in Caesarea, the Roman city (Acts 23).

"Here Felix the Roman Governor resided, and here Paul remained awaiting trial for two entire years (Acts 24:47). The Governor, in this case, wanted to please the religious leaders in Jerusalem, so he kept Paul, the great Apostle, a prisoner in this very city in which we stand this day for two long years until the accession of Porcius Festus as Governor and Paul's subsequent appeal that his trial should be heard at Rome before Caesar (Acts 24:27; 25:1, 11-12). It was in this city that Paul witnessed of his faith in Christ to the patron of the Jews, King Agrippa, and to his queen, Bernice—fulfilling the prophecy made by the Lord to Ananias that Paul would testify of Christ before 'the Gentiles and kings' (Acts 9:15)."

Barbara: "Paul spent two years imprisoned here? Did that bring his preaching to a halt?"

Prof. Dunzweiler: "No, it did not. In fact, Paul, speaking of this imprisonment of two years here at Caesarea, and of its continuation while he awaited his appeal before Caesar in Rome for two *additional* years, (Acts 24:27; 28:30), said:

" *'But I would ye should understand, brethren, that the things which happened unto me have fallen out rather unto the furtherance of the gospel; so that my bonds in Christ (that is, the chains which he wore around his wrists because of his testimony in Jerusalem that Jesus was the Messiah) are manifest in all the palace, and in all other places; and many of the brethren in the Lord, waxing*

Stopping At Caesarea • 33

confident by my bonds are much more bold to speak the word without fear' (Phil. 1:12-14.)"

Prof. Cohen: "Here in Caesarea in A.D. 66, twenty thousand Jewish people were killed, and the Jewish rebellion against Rome burst forth. Here in 639 A.D. came the Arabs; in 1101 the Crusaders; in 1187 the Arabs again under Saladin; and in 1228 the Christians in the Sixth Crusade. From the 14th to 16th centuries the Ottoman Turks dominated this area. The Turkish government then ruled until the First World War and the British accession of power. This lasted until 1948, when Israel was declared to be an independent state."

BARBED WIRE

At this we began to walk about. We had arrived after the time for collecting a fee to enter the ruins, and the elderly Arab collector, being about to leave, smiled and waved us to enter free. The walls and the chief buildings had been destroyed by the Arab Sultan Bibars of Egypt at c. 1256 A.D. (Egyptian rulers have not been Egyptians since Alexander the Great's conquests in 336-323 B.C.)

The statuary of Roman emperors and leaders which we now beheld were done in intricate detail, yet they now had a chief fault. This was that they were uniformly headless. This was no accident, for the heads were in like manner absent from the figures at the Theater of Dionysius by the Acropolis. The Islamic Turkish forces had centuries ago beheaded these in accordance with their belief that such violated the commandment, "Thou shalt not make unto thee any graven image" (Exod. 20:4).

As we touched and handled stones tooled two millenia ago we were driven backwards into the past as inside a time machine. We walked upon the still-standing ramparts and fortifications of Crusader days, including stone arches which spanned Crusader streets. Much of these were still standing. Even much of the massive walls and of the moat stood firm, but some of the approximately fifteen-feet-thick walls had fallen. Each large stone we walked upon in the paved streets and squares spoke of having been handled and rehandled by hands from Herod's day through the times of the Crusaders until our own season. Here was a fortified city along the sea which still spoke through its magnificent statuary and pillars of a mighty day not so long past. An amazing sight was the moat constructed by the Crusaders of the Middle Ages. Also, their windows, eight feet wide on the outside and three inches wide on the inside, designed for shooting arrows, were astoundingly fascinating.

We then walked to the Theater of Herod, and its condition, somewhat restored, was superb. It was all of stone, essentially a semicircle, and it is used for festive occasions even today by Israel. Paul may well have sat on this seat, or in that, during his two-year detention here—for as a Roman citizen awaiting trial he would have had considerable liberty (Acts 28:30).

Before departing we were informed that a new modern hotel is nearby, and that modern Caesarea is the site of Israel's *only* golf course. At this we take our leave, feeling within that we have here today once again touched Rome and the Bible both at Caesarea.

It is dark as we depart. I wished to get inside the Theater of Herod but it is locked up behind a high fence. I think of climbing it, but a triple row of rolled barbed wire says, "No." Climbing into our auto, I spy above us in the sky a cluster of stars which looks quite familiar. The group includes the following exotic names: Alcyone, Asterope, Celaeno, Electra, Maia, Merope, and Taygeta—the seven sisters—with Pleione, their mother, and Atlas, their father. These are the Pleiades spoken of in Job 9:9 and 38:31, an open cluster, located in the constellation, Taurus the Bull. Six stars can be seen easily at a glance on a good night by one who has 20/20 vision, yet a telescope can see at least 250 stars. One can see, I realize, the same stars as those seen in America when he or she stands in Europe or the Near East.

Our car door shuts, and we sprint in the darkness toward Haifa, the car leaping in excitement as we go. We have been where kings, crusaders, and apostles have stood—Caesarea. May we be as Paul, willing ourselves to be bound as prisoners for the sake of the truth of God.

CHAPTER IV

CARMEL, HAIFA, ACRE, AND HISTORY

It is still Thursday, *January 11th*, but the evening is now well spent and even twilight begins to fade into utter blackness as we drive in a northerly vector. We are still on the coastal plain of Sharon, but as we cover the thirty-five kilometers from Caesarea to Haifa, even in the darkening light, one can see high hills and mountains at our sides.

On a map of Palestine, if one goes along the seacoast to the same latitude as the lower tip of the Sea of Galilee, he will observe a projection of land that pushes itself here into the Mediterranean. This is the location of Mt. Carmel, an extenuated peak of some ten to fifteen kilometers summit which runs northwest to southeast. On the northwesterly slopes of this ranging mount is the city of Haifa. It is reputed to be Israel's most beautiful city, and it easily lives up to this name.

We had reached Haifa, but needed to locate the Dan Carmel Hotel. I stopped at a petrol station and asked for the usual, "Ninety-two octane benzine." The Arabic merchant was kindly, but could not understand my request for directions. A customer nearby, who also appeared to be Arabic, did understand my Hebrew when I said, *"Apho malon Dan Carmel?"* (Where is Hotel Dan Carmel?) After a minute of words and motions it was clear that we were to follow until our rescuer would point that we were to turn right as he went straight.

This worked well and we were on the slopes of Carmel, rising with each moment. It was pitch dark now, but some children were out walking alone. (Women hitchhikers traveling alone everywhere in Israel also testify to the expense of autos, and to the general fact that it was safer in Israel at night than in the United States. I asked many who spoke English about this, and they all affirmed it to be so. No one had heard of any hitchhiker robberies or attacks to their recollections). The children directed us, and in three minutes our cars pulled into the luxurious Dan Carmel—a mountainside paradise which stand on the haunts once paced upon by that mighty prophet Elijah. Arrows direct our vehicle to the underground parking facility, and from there an elevator whisks us to the lobby.

The Dan Carmel is on the north slope of Mount Carmel, near the crest, and we are assigned rooms on the north side. We are still in the off season and paying the identical rate that we paid in the Hotel Dan of Tel Aviv. This was arranged because both of these hotels are in a chain of four hotels composed of the Hotel Dan in Tel Aviv, the Dan Carmel in Haifa, the King David Hotel in Jerusalem, and the Accadia in Herzlia. So, despite our modest rates, our room has its own private bath and balcony; it is of exquisite decor, and its view is the most enchanting that I have ever seen, with its perfect overlook upon the Bay of Haifa directly outside our window beyond the slope.

HOLY GROUND

Before retiring Professor Dunzweiler remarked to our group that tonight we were camping upon holy ground, for God here manifested Himself in a mighty way. It was on these slopes that Elijah had his contest with the priests of Baal, and, although these priests prayed earnestly for many hours slashing themselves with knives, showing their sincerity, yet their prayers received no answer and there was no god Baal to kindle miraculously the offering which they had placed on the altar. Yet when Elijah prayed, though the altar had been soaked three times with water, God heard Elijah's prayer and

Israel accepts all types of immigrants!

38 • ISRAEL Land of Promise, Land of Prophecy

This tranquil scene in Israel reflects some of the beauty of the land.

Sunset over Haifa.

An Arab prays in a mosque in Acre, one of the oldest cities in the world. It was known in Old Testament times as Accho (Judges 1: 31). It is nine miles north of Haifa.

Moonlight over Haifa bay. Haifa is Israel's second largest city and is the center of the country's heavy industry. Located at the meeting place of mountain, valley and sea, it climbs the slopes of lovely Mount Carmel.

Haifa harbor is equipped to handle 2,500,000 tons of cargo a year and is the home base of Israel's navy and merchant fleet. Haifa bay is the site of oil refineries, glass and textile works, and chemical industries.

Israeli women soldiers check their automatic weapons. Women serve in the armed forces for 2 years; men, 3 years.

Bridge over Suez Canal erected by Israelis during Yom Kippur War in 1973.

miraculously sent fire from Heaven to consume the burnt offering (1 Kings 18). Through this miraculous sign and others performed by Elijah and Elisha at about the year 900 B.C. the nation of Israel, which had come to be almost wholly polluted at this time by the Canaanite fertility cult worship of Baal, was graciously called back to the worship of the one true God, Jehovah (or as they may have pronounced it, "Yahweh"). Elijah had the 450 false prophets of Baal slain. Sadly enough, as in Elijah's day, today religious false prophets who deny the Bible fill the earth.

I added that it was upon this mount that Elijah had prayed for rain to end the three-and-a-half-year drought which was drying up Israel and causing famine as a judgment against the sins of the nation and of her king Ahab (1 Kings 18).

> "The effectual fervent prayer of a righteous man availeth much. Elijah was a man subject to like passions as we are, and he prayed earnestly that it might not rain: and it rained not on the earth by the space of three years and six months. And he prayed again, and the heaven gave rain, and the earth brought forth her fruit." (Jas. 5:16-18).

Yes, here was a place where God had answered prayer.

Prof. Dunzweiler: "It was on Mt. Carmel that God answered Elisha's prayer and raised from the dead the son of the Shunammite woman (2 Kings 4:18-37).

"It was here on Mt. Carmel that, after David had protected Nabal's flocks of sheep, Nabal railed against David and would not give David's soldiers even one sheep for food. Then when David was coming to avenge himself by force, Abigail, a godly woman, brought David sheep for food from her husband Nabal's flock and prevented David from shedding Nabal's blood. Later, when evil Nabal died, David sent for Abigail and made her his wife (1 Sam. 25). This, too, came to pass where we lodge tonight."

THE DAUGHTER

At this, our brief discussion closed. We strolled to the gift shop and noted that the two ladies in charge were closing for the night. As they put their shop to bed they engaged us in conversation, and one related to us the following touching story which shows the spirit which rose to meet the crisis of the Six Day War of June 6-11, 1967.

After the first saleslady told us that she came to Israel from Holland in 1939, the second declared that she immigrated only three and a half years ago from Canada. The second lady went on to say that her second husband had then died and had bequeathed to her a small piece of property in Israel which he at one time had purchased. She decided to attempt to start a new life, and thought that a new country was the place to commence it. So she and her fifteen-year-old daughter left Toronto and came to Haifa to begin again. She related that while this was fine for her, her fifteen-year-old daughter hated and despised the move. She spoke English, and Canada was her home, and all of her friends were Canadians. There were some awful scenes with bitter tears between mother and daughter, but against her will the daughter was simply forced to accompany her mother to the struggling new land where another tongue was spoken.

The woman continued, describing the fact that after they had been in Israel but three years, hostilities threatened to break out, in May, 1967. The Canadian Consulate wrote to the mother advising that she and her daughter, still Canadian citizens, ought to leave Israel and return to the safety of Canada. She decided to leave the decision to her daughter who was now eighteen. Her daughter had been dragged to this land under protest; should she also have to risk her life under protest? She said that she went to her daughter and stated that, with the invasion and death lurking, they could now return to Canada if she, the daughter, wished. Her daughter replied, "Oh, Mama, how can you ask me that question? We cannot leave Israel!" This was a tender moment.

I told the two salesladies that in Luke 21:24, Jesus had spoken of a future day when Jerusalem would again belong to the Jews. He said, "And Jerusalem shall be trodden down of the Gentiles, until the times of the Gentiles be fulfilled." He as the Messiah knew that the city then in Roman domination would some day again be put in the hands of the Israelites. That day has come, I said, and now we may expect God to begin to deal with national Israel again so as to fulfill all of His words prophesied concerning them. The women listened eagerly. How we hoped that they too might see that Jesus is the Messiah not of the Gentiles only, nor of the Jews only. He died for all who will turn to Him in repentance and faith, both of the Jews and of the Gentiles. It began to rain and the wind howled as we retired on this mountaintop.

CARMEL EXPEDITION

January 12th, Friday. Before lunch we constituted an expedition to Carmel's summit and our motor safari departed from our station. The trees, both broadleaved hardwoods and evergreen softwoods, are still green in January here in Haifa. In fact, the grass and the entire area was green. As we drove, Professor Dunzweiler and I laughed at the supposed argument against Christ's birth being in December on the grounds that shepherds could not have been outdoors with their flocks in that month. We laughed because the country was green and cool, but not cold, and animals were seen frequently and continually. The Scriptures do not give us the month of Christ's birth nor even the year, though study has shown that it must have been between the years of 4 to 6 B.C., since we now are certain that Herod died in 4 B.C. It occurred probably in the fall or early winter, but the assertion that shepherds could not possibly be outdoors with their flocks in late December is an argument composed by someone in a Chicago flat and convincing only to one in a New York apartment.

Carmel's mount is 1638 feet high, running northwest to southeast, with the sea at its foot. Its summit ridge runs about ten miles, and we soon abandoned the idea that we could casually locate the exact spot whereupon Elijah had his contest with the priests of Baal. The summit was a long expanse and at its southern end we came to an Arab village. It was called Issfiya, and it was obviously economically poor.

The people looked kindly at us, and, though we could not speak to them, the members of our party tried to smile at them.

Our entire company was forced into a lengthy delay for the sake of Professor Dunzweiler's avid desire to secure a perfect stone from the top of Mt. Carmel. After, I should estimate, an examination of perhaps forty billion stones, Mr. D. settled for about a dozen gems to his particular liking. Then, being advised of their weight and of possible objection by the border authorities, he consented to part with the larger ones of his collection. He dropped about four of these one by one, grimacing with each drop in a painful contortion.

As we proceeded to return we saw more Arabs. Many of the women were veiled, men rode upon donkeys, and many sat around, no doubt without work. We observed one plowing a rock-filled field with a wooden plow. (Many fields in Israel are either rock-filled or they have been manually cleared of their rocks.)

We next did some driving about Haifa, and, though it had its more desolate spots near part of the waterfront, the city on the whole was quite pleasant and attractive. It was much like the American suburbs of many cities. The large Roman Catholic Carmelite monastery was here and some hotels. The houses were clean and well kept, but yet modest. One did not see sprawling mansions here as one would in America if he looked. Here in Israel's second largest city by population, 225,000, and its first seaport for the last thirty-five years, we saw beauty from its bay to its mountain. We also visited the golden-domed Temple of Bahai on Carmel's north slope. Who would have believed that on the mount where Elijah fought the false prophets a world temple of unity would stand? We could not enter, for it was not yet 3 p.m. We then returned to Molon Dan Carmel for our midday repast.

ACRE'S TREACHEROUS REEF

In the afternoon we drove to "Atikah Ako," and "Acre" of Crusader fame, which is another city along the Mediterranean coast twenty-one kilometers north of Haifa. It is a great walled citadel which has been named, "The Fortress to Many Empires." A young hitchhiking Israeli soldier pointed us to it, and its mammoth fortifications bedazzled our eyes.

Dr. Cohen: "In Old Testament times, in the days of the judges (c. 1400-1000 B.C.) this city was named, 'Accho' (Jud. 1: 31). In the New Testament, however, it was known by its Greek name, *'Ptolemais.'* When returning to Jerusalem at the end of the Third Missionary Journey (c. A.D. 58), the Apostle Paul stopped at the port of Tyre and then by boat 'came to Ptolemais, and saluted the brethern, and abode with them one day' (Acts 21: 7). From Ptolemais he next sailed to Caesarea, and from there to Jerusalem.

"The present name of this location, 'Acre,' comes from the epoch of the Crusaders (12th and 13th centuries) when the Knights Hospitallers of St. John took the city and dubbed it, 'St. John of Acre'—the latter portion of the name reaching back to the pre-Christian nomen of 'Accho.'

"Ako is listed as a principal city in the pre-Christian writings of the Assyrians and the Egyptians, as well as being mentioned in the Old Testament in Judges 1:31. The city apparently withstood the attacks of the Hebrew tribe of Asher in the period of the Judges (1400-1000 B.C.; Jud. 1:31), and a millennium later it held out against the forces of the valiant and pious Simon Maccabeus in the 2nd century B.C. The city fell to the tidal wave of humanity which descended upon it during the First Crusade when the Genoese fleet came up against it (1096-99 A.D.). Later in the 12th century Saladin defeated the Christians and captured Acre, but Richard the Lion-Hearted and Philip II of France recaptured it for Christendom during the Third Crusade (1187-1193 A.D.). Then for a century the Christians owned it until it succumbed fully and finally to Moslem hands. All told, the city has stood against at least seventeen sieges.

"In modern days, the Jewish Resistance Organization executed one of the most astounding escapes of this era when in the 1948 struggle for independence it loosed the many captive Jews caught illegally entering the country from the British citadel prison of Acre. From there you can see the prison building in the center of Old Acre where we now stand, surrounded by all of these immense walls. It is now utilized for a mental sanitarium. This escape story is told in the book, *Exodus*."

We now began to survey the walls of the city. Dr. Schatz observed, "These walls are about eight feet thick!" Professor Dunzweiler inched his way prone across a wall and I became fearful of his safety. "Eight or nine feet to my estimate," he declared with the assurance of a man who had just read the vernier scale on his micrometer. He then pointed to the gigantic black rocks out in the water just outside the city's massive walls. Their flat tops extended about thirty meters out to sea treacherously hidden by only a few inches of water. It was clear that no ship could get close enough to the walls even to set loose its men, for it would be dashed in pieces by these jagged stones before getting close enough to release its human cargo of invaders.

Next we gazed at the sight of the stone walls and the deep moat, now dry, which surrounded the city on its landward bounds. This was a true fortified city from antiquity as described in the story books. It was spectacular, yet quite real.

As we again returned we drove spellbound and aghast, for history was alive and true here in the Holy Land.

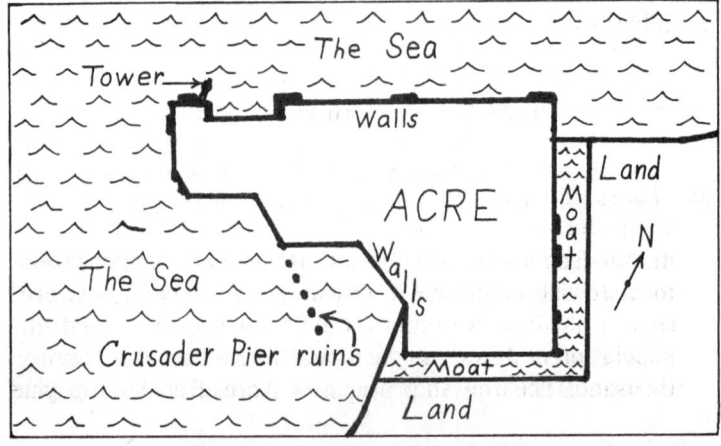

CHAPTER V

HAIFA BAY, ANTI-SEMITISM, AND JUDGMENT

It still being Friday, *January 12th,* after supper our group heard some accounts of the happenings that had occurred in the now serenely pacific Haifa Harbor outside of our hotel. It was not easy to lend credence to these events when our eyes beheld these blue waters bedecked in festive regalia with the jewels of shimmering ship lights floating silently upon its moonlit Sea of Tranquility. The lady of the gift shop who had come to the country in 1939 told of what she recalled. This led to Harold Fisher's questioning of Mr. Arnold Escourt who chimed in with a lengthy narration of some history. The account ran as follows, with the young Mr. Escourt speaking, while from time to time referring to *Fodor's Modern Guide to Israel, 1967-68*:

THE BALFOUR DECLARATION

Mr. Escourt: "The struggle of Haifa Bay was precipitated in the modern age first, perhaps, by *Theodor Herzl's* writings in 1896. Eager ears were awaiting this word, and the quest for a Jewish homeland in Palestine was started. At about 1900, 4000 Jewish settlers went into Palestine and the population of Jews was then over a quarter of a hundred thousand. The Jewish people now planned to buy up land from the Arab Turkish owners in Palestine and to settle there. At one time Herzl was prepared to bow to a British suggestion that Uganda in Africa become the New Zion for the Jews, just as Salt Lake City had become the chosen New Zion of the Mormons. The persecuted Jews of Russia and Europe, however, would only be satisfied with setting their feet on Palestinian soil.

"In the final score of years of the 19th century and the fourteen years of the next prior to the Great War a hundred thousand Jews reached Palestine. In 1917 *Lord Balfour* and the British Government declared their pledge to 'use their best endeavors to facilitate the establishment in Palestine of a national homeland for the Jewish people.' Balfour's picture with the date 1917 and the words, 'A national homeland for the Jewish people,' today appear on Israeli medallions issued by the government. By 1922 the League of Nations approved a *Palestinian Mandate* which called upon Britain to order Palestine politically, administratively, and economically so as to 'secure the establishment of the Jewish national home' and 'facilitate Jewish immigration.'

"The early 1930's saw Jewish cries for partnership with the Palestinian Arabic world meeting little acceptance. Raids and death came to pass, and increasing difficulty was now the rule. By 1936 His Majesty's Royal Commission decreed that the Jewish State must be limited to but one-twentieth of the initial deposition. Then in 1939 at the start of World War II when Arab oil looked toward the Nazi-Japanese Axis, the *British White Paper* declared its decision that Jewish immigration ought to be limited to 75,000 over a five-year period. This was an open attempt to live up to their commitments to the Zionists while at the same time appeasing Arab oil interests at a crucial moment in British history. As restrictions increased Winston Churchill with some conservatives and all of the Laborites denounced in Parliament the findings of the White Paper. These findings and the regulatory restrictions which followed them, it was continually maintained, denied the performance of what

His Majesty's government had publicly pledged, and this at a time when growing Nazi persecution of German Jews made a refuge for them mandatory and humane."

Mr. Escourt (continuing): "This brings us to Haifa Harbor. The fires of Europe began raging out of control, and Jews fortunate enough to escape Hitler boarded boats for the homeland haven in Israel of which they had heard. The boats reached Haifa Harbor only to have their desperate and homeless occupants told the same words which echoed in Jewish ears throughout the Middle Ages when many *so-called* (but false) Christians confiscated their money and lands and with clubs drove them out of country after country without pity. James in the New Testament (chap. 2) denounces those people who profess to be true but by their works show themselves to love neither God nor man.

WEEPING ON THE MOUNTAIN

"Thus the Jews in those boats out on Haifa's Bay—their faith in *fallen* humanity near restored at the sight of Carmel's crest—heard the words, 'No entrance; the quota, the quota; papers are necessary...' But their papers had been burned while often still in the pockets of their loved ones and children! So came the desperation of the *Exodus* to Haifa Harbor. From 1939 on Jews wept on this mountain of Carmel for their kindred out on the bay who were so near and yet so far away. One of the ladies of the gift shop has just confirmed the truth of this statement. Thus the vessel called the *Struma* was shipwrecked here with only one life escaping out of 764. The *Patria* blew up right in the harbor here with 250 'illegal immigrants' dying out of 1,080 on board while the hills of Galilee are still today chiefly empty with no man to till their slopes. The people of Haifa could only let their tears, which already had left stains on Russian and European lands, run down the side of Carmel to mingle with those falling from off the railings of the forbidden ships waiting out in the harbor.

"Then in November 29, 1947, the United Nations voted to end the British Mandate, and to make Palestine a federal state with Arab and Jewish divisions. With this, on May 14, 1948, the British left their protectorate, and, despite a U.N. Commission, the Jews and Arabs were left to fight it out. On that same day David Ben Gurion declared *Israel's independence*, and Haifa's Harbor was opened to the distressed Jews of Europe and Russia as tears of joy now began to dilute the pools of past sorrows in Haifian waters. Let us think of these events as we now look out over these still waters."

WHY DID THEY SUFFER?

Mrs. Florence Escourt: "Professor Cohen, why did these things happen to the Jewish people?"

Prof. Cohen: "To answer you Biblically, let me refer you to the passage of Isaiah 5:1-7. In this section of the Bible God calls Israel His special vineyard. God is the farmer, Israel is the vineyard, and the fruit of this vineyard was to be righteousness and uprightness. God explains that He did everything possible to cause this vineyard to grow well and to yield its proper fruit. He even built a wall around it; that is, He gave Israel His special divine *protection* as well as giving to her His care. Yet God, the Farmer, says of Israel His vineyard, that, after all of His care and protection, when He went to find fruits of righteousness all He could find were fruits of wickedness. His vineyard, Israel, did not wish to please Him, therefore He decided in His sovereignty as the One who owned the vineyard to let it grow wild just as it itself wished. So He removed the hedge and the wall which was the divine protection which had surrounded Israel, and this permitted the wicked animals all around to enter the vineyard and devour it. He also permitted thorns and thistles to grow from within without weeding them out.

"Do you see? When Israel rejected God and preferred the ways of the sinful men of this world, after God did everything He could for the nation through a period of centuries, He *removed His protection* (the hedge and the wall which He had erected around Israel) and the evil beasts of the nations began to enter and to carry away Israel captive. Thus the Assyrians carried away captive the Northern Kingdom, Israel, when it destroyed Samaria in 721 B.C.; thus the Babylonians carried away captive the Southern Kingdom, Judah, for seventy years (c. 605-535 B.C.) and destroyed Jerusalem and the first temple in 586 B.C.; thus also when the nation had rejected its Messiah and after an additional forty years of grace had not repented nor turned to Him, the Romans came and in 70 A.D. destroyed Jerusalem and the second temple leaving a million dead and carrying away another hundred thousand.

THE ANTI-JEW LAWS

"It has thus continued. In the 7th century A.D. came the Spanish anti-Jewish laws; the Crusaders amassed a record of Jewish butcheries and burnings which few can believe; in 1215 A.D. the Fourth Lateran Council under Pope Innocent III passed more anti-Jewish laws; and the Vienna Church Synod in 1267 dressed the Jews of Europe in pointed caps and with red and yellow wheels on their breasts and backs so that they could be spotted more easily. Henry III and his followers in England in the second half of the 13th century confiscated Jewish property (1230), sold their taxation rights (1255), massacred 1500 in London on Easter week of 1264, and expelled them from England in 1290. So also they were expelled from France by Charles VI on the Day of Atonement in 1394. In the 14th century, after the Black Plague had slain twenty-five million in Europe—perhaps a third of the population—the Jews were blamed and murdered by the mobs by the thousands (1800 in Strasbourg; 6,000 in Mayence; 3,000 in Erfurt; etc.). Then in 1480 came the Spanish Inquisition and in 1492 the Jews were expelled from Spain with their property stolen—many of them to die like animals on the high seas, in flight, and as slaves. In 1496 Pope Alexander VI entitled Ferdinand and his queen as 'Catholic Sovereigns,' listing their expulsion of the Jews among their accomplishments. What more shall we say concerning the *pogrom* Jewish persecutions in Russia of recent centuries, and of Hitler's beastial genocide of the six million, including 200,000 Jewish children? Yet still the fires of anti-Semitism burn within the breasts of the wicked throughout the world."

IS THE BIBLE ANTI-SEMITIC?

Harold Fisher: "This incident, or rather Bible passage, which you quoted at the start of your remarks, Isaiah 5:1-7, is that from the New Testament? And also, doesn't that passage as you have used it teach that Bible believers ought to be anti-Semitic, which attitude you yourself admit to be a wrong one?"

Prof. Cohen: "On your first question, Isaiah 5:1-7 is not from the New Testament at all; it is from the *Haftorah*, from the Old Testament Prophets. Thus the divine assertion of Israel's sinfulness (not of every Jew, of course, for Isaiah himself was a *justified* Jew who trusted in God) comes from one of Israel's holy prophets. In fact, this truth is taught continually by the *Old* Testament prophets; for example, by Isaiah 1; Jeremiah 5; Ezekiel 5; Amos 4-6; Daniel 9:3-16; 2 Chronicles 36:12-21; etc.

"On your second question, 'Should Bible believers be anti-Semitic?' let me declare that the answer is an unequivocal, No!"

Harold Fisher: "Aren't you contradicting yourself? You say that Bible believers should not be anti-Semitic, but before you stated that you believed that it was God's sovereign purpose that Israel should have its walls torn down and that it should suffer for its sins."

Prof. Dunzweiler: "The answer here lies in separating on the one hand (1) a divinely announced prophecy of coming judgment for sin from (2) a direct commission to someone giving him authority to carry out the prophesied judgment."

"Let me illustrate this. Compare Genesis 9:6 with Genesis

3:16-17. In Genesis 9:6, God says, 'Whoso sheddeth man's blood, *by man* shall his blood be shed.' Here God not only announces that the punishment for murder is to be capital punishment, death; but here God *also* names mankind, that is, human government, as the one who is to carry out the death sentence upon the murderer. Thus God says, '*By man*' shall the murderer's blood be shed.

"However, contrast this with Genesis 3:16,17, where God states that as a penalty for Adam and Eve's sin women are to have pain in childbirth and that thorns and thistles were to grow up when man cultivated the ground. *Here God announces a prophetic judgment without commissioning any human being or human beings to execute this divine judgment.* Thus it has indeed come to pass that a woman has pain in childbirth, but we are not obliged to make sure that she has plenty of pain. In fact, to do so would be sinful. So also, the soil does yield thorns and weeds, but we are not commanded to make certain that weeds grow.

"*This is the case with the judgment of Israel.* Moses himself prophesied in Deuteronomy 28: 25,63-67, and especially verse 29, that Israel would sin greatly and would be scattered among all of the nations of the earth as a judgment for this; *but nowhere does the Bible in either the Old Testament or the New Testament call upon the rank and file of believers in God to carry out God's judgments on Israel. In fact, the very opposite is the case.* In Isaiah 10:5-19 God calls the wicked nation of Assyria 'the rod of mine anger' and his 'axe,' and He explains that He has called *wicked* Assyria, an idolatrous nation, to be His rod for punishing Israel. He then proclaims that he will next destroy Assyria for her sins which included her high-handed despoiling of Israel. So has it ever been. When Israel sinned against God and chose not to have God as her protector, God took down His divine wall of protection and the *wicked* nations brought to pass His prophesied judgment. Then God destroyed these wicked nations in turn for their cruel attacks upon Israel.

"So it has been with Assyria, Babylon, Persia, Spain, and Nazi Germany; and so it will be with all who persecute the Jews. Thus in God's unsearchableness He executes all of His decrees. He makes the wrath of man to praise Him (Psa. 76:10). He at the same time also fulfills His promise to Abraham (the father of the Jews), viz., 'I will bless them that bless thee, and curse him that curseth thee' (Gen. 12:3) by then destroying the persecutors of the Jews."

IS THE NEW TESTAMENT ANTI-SEMITIC?

Barbara Miller: "Tell me, is the New Testament anti-Semitic?"

Prof. Dunzweiler: "No. It is not anti-Semitic despite the fact that it correctly records the part played by the Jewish leaders in the time of Christ in demanding that the Roman authorities crucify Christ. Christ Himself was a Jew, a son of Abraham, and a son of David from the Tribe of *Judah* (Matt. 1:1-3). The twelve apostles were all Jews for all of the Hebrews were called 'Jews' as a general term after the deportation of the Northern Kingdom of Israel by Assyria in 721 B.C., which left only *Judah* in the south—from which we get the word 'Jew.' And out of the twenty-seven books of the New Testament, all but two, Luke and Acts, were written by Jews.

"Christ Himself in Matthew 23:37-39, after having strongly condemned the sinfulness of the Pharisee sect of Jewry, said that He would have gathered Jerusalem to Himself as a hen gathers her chicks but *they* would not come to Him. Yet even here He speaks of His future return when Israel will say, 'Blessed is he that cometh in the name of the Lord.' From the cross He said, 'Father, forgive them; for they know not what they do' (Luke 23:34). And Paul in Romans 9:1-3 and 10:1 wishes himself to be accursed from God if this could save Israel. Paul in Romans 1:16 thusly declares, 'I am not ashamed of the gospel of Christ: for it is the power of God unto salvation to every one that believeth; to the Jew first, and also to the Greek.' "

Haifa Bay, Anti-Semitism and Judgment • 59

Barbara: "I'm satisfied. But why do so many Christians speak against the Jews?"

Prof. Dunzweiler: "For one thing I do not believe that many real believers in Christ do this. Those who persecuted the Jews acted so opposite to the teachings of Christ that we may declare them not to have been Christians at all—despite any claims on their part to the contrary. As James teaches in the New Testament, that faith which yields no good works is a dead and a useless faith (Jas. 2:17).

"Also some have been persuaded by Hitler-like, Satanic stories (Rev. 12) that the Jews are Khazars, or that they alone are behind the Communist conspiracy, and that the Jews plans to take over the world (as the Protocols of Zion, a proven forgery, claim). Some say that the Jews rob everyone of their money (though in the Middle Ages the Jews were denied almost every occupation save moneylending and commerce, and they were expelled from country after country with their possessions confiscated—thus showing the real regal thieves). But, Barbara, as with other people, some Jewish people have done real evil, not thinking of the effects on their people, and they have brought to all ill will. However, we must love Germans despite a Hitler, and we must love Jews despite a Judas, for Christ was a Jew from the Tribe of Judah."

Barbara: "Professor, what of Israel's future? Has she hope?"

Prof. Dunzweiler: "She has a glorious hope. We will discuss Israel's future within the next few days. Do you remember our discussion on Romans 9-11? All Israel will yet be saved. However, there will be a period of great birth pangs before she is ready to say, 'Blessed is he that comes in the name of the Lord' " (Matt. 22-39; Rom. 11:26).

As we retired I peered out of the window onto Haifa Bay, and my mind went back . . . and then forward to that coming future day . . .

CHAPTER VI

STANDING ON ARMAGEDDON

As we passed the desk on the bright and brisk morning of Saturday, *January 13th*, Professor Dunzweiler reminded me that we had asked the concierge at the desk on the previous morning if he would see that reservations were made for our group in the Dan Hotel of Jerusalem. The hotel was called the King David and we desired accomodations for January 16th to the 23rd. We inquired and the concierge gave us the following copy of a teletyped conversation which had transpired between the Dan Carmel Hotel in Haifa (DANOTEL HA) and the King David Hotel in Jerusalem (KINDOTEL JM).

• 61

Israeli soldiers at lonely desert outpost during Yom Kippur War.

62 • ISRAEL Land of Promise, Land of Prophecy

Panorama of desert shows carnage of Yom Kippur War of 1973. Israel lost over 2400 dead. This toll in a country of 3.1 million persons is comparable to the United States losing 168,000 combat dead. (The U.S. lost approximately 50,000 in Vietnam).

Israeli women soldiers march in review during 25th Anniversary celebration in Jerusalem.

Israeli army jeep in a convoy at sunset.

64 • ISRAEL Land of Promise, Land of Prophecy

Army radio operator

Technician, Weismann Institute

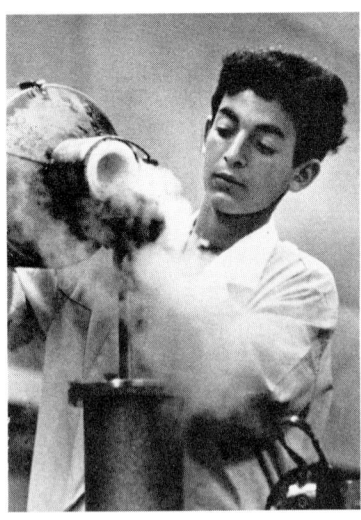

Silversmith near Lod

Typical Kibbutz couple.

SOME OF THE FACES OF ISRAEL

9.55   12.1.68

R DANOTEL HA
ATTENTION RESERVATIONS:
PLEASE RESERVE FOUR DOUBLE
ROOMS STANDART OR ECONOMY
FOR MR. DUNZWEILER AND MR.
COHEN AS FROM 16.1 TO
23.1
PLEASE CONFIRM***********

R KINDOTEL JM

MMT PLS

ON THE 17/1 WE
ARE FULLY BOKED
SO ONLY AS FROM
THE 18/1 I CAN
CONFIRM IT*

PLEASE DO SOMETHING!***

SORRY I CANT
THROW THE PEO-
PLES OUT*

MOM PLEASE
WILL CALL YOU BACK LATER
YOUR NAME PLEASE*********

OK NANNET HERE J*

OK THANKS SALEM HERE BIBI

R DANOTEL HA

R KINDOTEL JM

We laughed as we solved the code-like riddles of the above message. The discussion was obviously conducted in English instead of Hebrew. Our party agreed that the simplest way to handle the situation was for us to stay in Tiberias for one extra day and then to move to Jerusalem on the 18th instead of the 17th as we had previously planned. No one's feelings were hurt and all was fine.

We had observed that last night shoes were placed outside of the doors. We concluded that this must be an Israeli practice which has a connection with the Sabbath ("Shabat") day which starts at sundown Friday and which lasts until sundown Saturday. When the waiter told Professor Dunzweiler that the hotel did not scramble eggs on *Shabat*, we concluded that our deduction on the shoe matter must be correct. It was only when we spoke to an Israeli in Tiberias that we were informed that the hotel chambermaids cleaned the shoes, and that the practice had nothing at all to do with the Sabbath.

GHOST SHIP

Driving out from the underground parking area of the Dan Carmel we determined to get on the main road at Haifa Bay. Then we designed to drive southeast for 33 kilometers to Mt. Megiddo, and from there we would head northeast some 42 kilometers to Tiberias on the Lake of Galilee—stopping en route at Mt. Tabor.

Upon making our connection with the thruway road at the north of Haifa, at the bay, we began our race toward Megiddo. Suddenly an old ship, but not a small one, jumped before us on the road. It obviously was an exhibit or a memorial of some type, as it was now permanently moored in concrete to the land beside the highway and it had a sign in front of it. We drove near and parked the car on a knoll, and then came to investigate. The ship was a small transport with two decks above the hull. It was perhaps a hundred feet long, but it was far from a luxury vessel. The sign before it was written only in Hebrew which said, *"Anet hamafelim 'Af-al-pe-can.'"* We surmised that this was one of the refugee ships, and wondered whether its human cargo had reached its intended goal, or whether this ship was salvaged from the sea bottom nearby.

THE CAVE

From our map we comprehended our proximity to Elijah's cave. We asked a middle class looking man its whereabouts and he called his eleven-year-old son. The man, who spoke English as did the son, said that it was only about a half kilometer away and that his son would get into our auto and direct us. With that he bade us adieu and went into the house leaving the boy with us. This shocked me because in America we tell our children never, never, under any circumstances, to get into a car with a stranger. Here, however, incident after incident showed that this was not so. There is apparently more of a help-one-another spirit here because of the nation's difficulties, and crimes of violence occur much less frequently than they do in the United States—not speaking, of course, of the border problems with Jordan and Syria.

The boy had us stop our cars, and guided us up the path upon Carmel's slope. After about an eighty-foot climb, we arrived at the cave which I estimated to be about fifteen meters deep, ten across, and four high. This is a rough estimate, however, because we were not permitted in. The little boy snapped his fingers and said, "We may not go in today; I forgot. It is Shabat" (Sabbath). I handed the lad a pound (28 cents) for his trouble, and told him that the Professor and I were teachers in a school that believed that Jesus was the Messiah of Israel. He nodded and said, "On *Pasach* (Passover) Elijah comes before the Messiah." His reference was to Malachi 4:5, 6 which one living down the street from Elijah's cave should surely know. On this Jesus said, "Elijah is indeed come, and they have done unto him whatsoever they pleased, as it is written of him" (Mark 9:13). Jesus referred, of course, to His forerunner, the Prophet John the Baptist, and to Herod's having thrown him into prison and killed him. The lad smiled broadly and waved vigorously as we departed on our way now to Megiddo's peak.

ARMAGEDDON

Thirty-three kilometers southwest of Haifa we reached Tel Megiddo or "Hill-mound Megiddo."

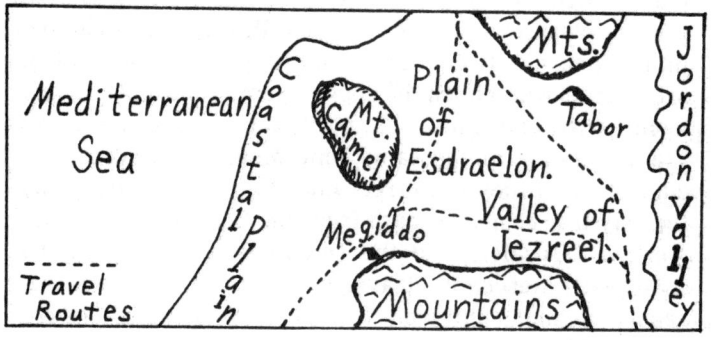

The *tel* had the same shape as all of the *tels* or city-hill-mounds, sloping sides with a flat top. Beneath the *tel* there was a small museum and a store which sold slides of Israel, souvenirs, and food. It was manned by a friendly Arab keeper, his wife, their son, the son's wife, two small children, and two cute white Scotty puppies. The married son had a cast on his foot, but all were well and cheerful looking. After securing some refreshments, the temperature being cool and the wind quite brisk, we paid the fee and were permitted to walk to the mound and to ascend it via its winding but not long road. The wind blew hard, but all northern Palestine, it seemed, could be seen from here. It was January, but the trees were green and full.

Prof. Cohen: "We are now standing atop Tel Megiddo which is also the famed 'Armageddon' (Rev. 16:16). Beside this mount is the great East-West valley across Israel where the final battle of this age is to be fought, according to the Bible. 'Ar' or more properly, *'Har,'* in Hebrew means 'mountain;' and 'Megiddo' means 'place of troops.' Thus 'Armageddon' in the Hebrew simply means 'Mount Megiddo' or 'Mountain of Troops' which is precisely where you are today standing.

"Observe our location on this blue and white map placed here by the government. Megiddo stands at the crucial intersection of the two great Palestinian trade and military routes. It commands the mountain pass east of Mt. Carmel whereupon the ancient armies marched to and from Egypt and Asia. This north and south route is the Via Maris. Yet at the same time Megiddo stands at the edge of the Valley of Jezreel mountain divide which was the only true *east-west* path from the Coastal Plain in the West to Jerusalem and the Jordan River Valley in the southeast. Merchant, traveler, and general with his armies coming south from Europe or Asia by way of the Coastal Plain roads could only get to Jerusalem easily by traversing this Esdraelon-Megiddo-Jezreel valley.

"Since all knew that northern invaders would inevitably pass by Mt. Megiddo on their way to Jerusalem by this south-easterly route, if time afforded them the opportunity, they would make haste to arrive here first and to position their own forces most favorably in the high regions. Thus battle after battle through the centuries has been fought in this 'Valley of Megiddo' or 'Armageddon' and this city, when properly fortified, becomes the key to the door between Jerusalem to the south and to Syria, Europe, and Asia to the north. At the same time it stands watch over Asia-Egypt invasions. Can you see its importance?

"Because of the fact that the city upon this mound is the military key to Isreal each nation in power through the ages who wished to dominate Palestine has attempted to capture Megiddo, and then to supply it amply with troops and supplies so that it would serve as their own strong frontier outpost to secure Jerusalem and the territories below. Thus this fortress city, built on a ten-acre mound only 70 feet higher than the surrounding flat plain—imagine it as a thimble standing in the southwest portion of a path between two books which represent mountains —has been the scene of great Biblical and post-Biblical battles. Here Barak and Gideon of the Book of Judges were victorious with God's help; here Saul and King Josiah were defeated; and here the Maccabees fought off Antiochus IV Epiphanes between the times of the Old and New Testaments. Megiddo was conquered successively by Egyptians, Canaanites, Israelites, Philistines, Assyrians, Persians, Greeks, and Romans.

"In 1918 it was here that Allenby in command of the Allied forces won the decisive battle of Northern Palestine and thus secured it from the Turks. He later, when a title was offered him by the British Crown, took the dub of 'Viscount Allenby of Megiddo.' It is interesting that the first bombs dropped by the Syrian Air Force in the June, 1967, War were dropped here in the crucial Valley of Armageddon.

"Thus it is not so strange that the Bible declares that in the last days of this era, when Antichrist—the wicked world Fuehrer—brings down his land armies to destroy

Jerusalem, as his multitudes are assembled in their grand bivouac here in this valley, Christ Himself shall appear in his glory and destroy the Antichrist and his armies (Rev. 16:16; 14:14-20; 19:11-20:3; Isa. 63:1-6; Joel 3:1-17; Zech. 12:9-14; Ezek. 39:17-29).

"As you can plainly see from our vantage point here, the flatlands of this valley will have no difficulty in holding the multitudes upon multitudes of the invading evil hordes which the Bible says will assemble here for that yet future final battle against Jerusalem (Joel 3:1-17, etc.). Can you see that gradually rising mountain out there in the northeast? That is Mt. Tabor, and it is about 25 kilometers, or 15.5 miles away, and the land between here and there is relatively flat, generally uninhabited, and able and waiting to hold the men of that final immense army."

TWENTY LEVELS

Steve Reed: "It is obvious that much archaeological work has been done here. Could you say a word on this?"

Prof. Cohen: "Professor Dunzweiler?"

Prof. Dunzweiler: "All right. Interestingly enough Edwin Robinson, the famed Near Eastern geographer and archaeologist, stood here in 1838. Then it was known as Hill or *Tel el-Mutesellim*. Robinson wrote in his diary while here the words, 'I wonder where Megiddo could have been!' Since then this *tel* has been identified as ancient Megiddo, and it has been excavated in 1903-5 by Gottlieb Schumacher of Germany, by C. S. Fisher in 1925-27, by P.L.O. Guy from 1927-35, and G. Loud in the 1935-39 prewar years. These last three expeditions were all under the auspices of J.H. Breasted of the Oriental Institute of Chicago. Then Yigael Yadin and the Department of Antiquities worked this mound from 1958 to 1960.

"As we walk we can see some of the chief sights. Twenty occupational levels have been uncovered in the various 'digs,' going back to about the time of the building of the great Pyramids, 2700 B.C. Over there is the Southeast Temple site dating back perhaps into the third millennium B.C. You can see the steps which go up to the round altar which has been unearthed from its mud covering. Here upon this 'high place' which faces east to meet the rising sun the ancient Canaanite peoples worshiped the sun, and then as the years went by their Baal fertility-cult gods. In the tenth century B.C. Solomon rebuilt Megiddo and restored its walls so as to take advantage of its key military location. Over there you can see the remainder of his giant stables for the horses for his chariots (1 Kings 9:19). Yonder see that gaping hole. It is the grain storage silo of the eighth century B.C. Israelite King, Jeroboam II.

"Next we shall walk through the underground water tunnel on the western portion of the *tel*. Here we shall descend 120 feet below the surface of the mound by 157 steps carved in the stone. Then we traverse 300 feet laterally through a tunnel now lit up by electric lights. Finally we will climb up another 47 steps and we come to the site of the ancient water well. All of this is underground, mind you, dug out of the rock in the twelfth century B.C. What an engineering marvel for those times! Thus when a siege was upon Megiddo, possibly by a superior army passing through from Egypt to Asia, the city could hold out within its huge walls for an indefinite time because it had its own internally concealed water supply. Four centuries later when Jeroboam II added his giant grain storage pit, an immense supply of grain was also on hand for emergencies and lengthy sieges."

We separated, each going his own way pursuing his own interests. Everywhere blue and white signs described some temple, or house, or building now in ruins. Often the novice archaeologist had to look at the seemingly senseless ruins over and over, comparing them with the diagrams on the blue and white signs, in order to be convinced that Solomon's Temple or some other earlier or later construction relic was actually before him. If one at random switched every sign, few would notice this at all. Professor Dunzweiler again and again walked through the fascinating water tunnel, looking like a Roman general who had just taken the city and now for the first time comprehended how it was that his foes could do without additional water for so long a time.

Leaving the *tel* we went to the attractive museum beside it. Our admission tickets had already paid the fee. The museum was small, and there was no one there but our party. Apparently tourists did not overly often pass this way. The chief item of the diminutive museum was a model of Megiddo's city as it appeared in the period after Solomon had restored it—high walls all around the circular mound, with large and ornate castle to the south end. The huge stables and the multitowered fortified entrance to the city were at its north with many barracks for soldiers, houses, and other structures—all in white and stunningly beautiful.

I marveled at the pottery fragments that were jutting out of the mud and rock sides of the elevated hill city by the tens of thousands. I had thought that one would probably never be so lucky as to chance upon even one pottery fragment from the ancient world; yet here they were in masses and masses everywhere for the taking. The world of history and the Bible struck one here as being very real. I shut my eyes and, like Walter Middy, I awakened living here in Solomon's day guarding the great mountain openings to the land of Israel for our wise king. Suddenly Prof. Dunzweiler nudged me and my dream left me. He asked if we were going to eat lunch here. I nodded while removing my Solomonic armor. We ate here, and I had chocolate-covered sugar wafers and tea, having had a hearty breakfast previously.

CHAPTER VII

ISRAEL'S PROPHETIC FUTURE

After lunch was devoured, it yet being Saturday, *January 13th*, we retraced our steps to the summit of the *tel*. Our party sat down on the northern observation point behind a clump of trees. Mt. Tabor lofted itself in the distance as our seminar hour of the day was about to be conducted behind this windbreak. I distributed a talk which was mimeographed on several pages of pink paper. I explained its substance paragraph by paragraph. The full text of the talk, however, is as follows:

ISRAEL'S PROPHETIC FUTURE

The Six-Day War and Prophecy

The Six-Day War which took place on June 6-11, 1967, has reawakened interest among many in Bible prophecy, especially as it concerns Israel. The Lord in Luke 21:24 had said, "And Jerusalem shall be trodden down of the Gentiles (i.e., by the nations), until the times of the Gentiles be fulfilled." That is, almost two thousand years ago, while standing in a Jerusalem which was about to reject Him officially, a Jerusalem then dominated, "trodden down" by the Romans, Christ saw Jerusalem's future. He saw the city's catastrophic fall and devastation in A.D. 70 to the Roman siege under Titus when almost a million perished of disease and starvation within its walls, while another hundred thousand were taken captive to Rome while Jerusalem burned (Luke 21:12-24). Yet He saw beyond this even to the consummation of this age. One of the things that He saw, as shown in the verse quoted above (Luke 21:24), was a time when Jerusalem would not be "trodden down by the nations"—that is, a time when the Jews themselves would again own and dominate this city. The events of June 6-11, 1967, I believe, fulfill this verse. The amazement at this fulfillment has turned multitudes to their Bibles for a fuller study of the prophecies which surround Israel and the end of this age.

Is is an indisputable fact that ancient Jerusalem, the Old City with its walls rebuilt, did not officially or truly belong to Israel as its governing nation since the time of Christ until the June 6-11, 1967 war. Anyone who today has the privilege of walking through this city will see with his or her own eyes that Jerusalem is in fact *not* now being trodden down by the nations, but that it now belongs to Israel. Their Parliament Building rises prominently in the midst of New Jerusalem and their soldiers and their guides occupy without hindrance the Old City with the Chasidim Orthodox Jews pursuing the Old Testament Sabbath and reciting their endless multitudes of prayers at the Wailing Wall.

Midnight Pancakes

In the light of Israel's now owning Jerusalem, what is the present situation today with regard to prophecy? Let me answer this by a story about pancakes. Once last year a little girl three years of age awakened her father at about *midnight** and asked him to wake up her mother so that her mother could cook some pancakes. The father told the little one that it was useless to get Mother up because with the lights out, it being midnight, he was almost certain that Mother would not consent. Of course, he could not be absolutely sure, for maybe Mother would jump up, say, "Mmmmm, that sounds fine," and race down the stairs to cook pancakes. This, however, did not seem probable. This is what the situation looked like

*This was my daughter, Caralee.

concerning God's fulfilling His prophecies concerning the restoration of Israel in the Middle Ages. He, of course, could have fulfilled them then if He in His sovereignty so desired, yet outwardly, like the midnight request for pancakes, with the Jews scattered without prospect of regathering, the time did not appear to have arrived—the "Times of the Gentiles" were still very much present with the world.

Yet, however, on the following morning after the father talked to his wife, he pointed his daughter to pancake batter being ready in the kitchen, syrup being on the table, the griddle being hot, and it being breakfast time. Now it appeared that the time for pancakes had at last arrived. Yet, here, too, Mother may have said that she was merely testing another recipe, and that the menu for the morning was cold cereal as usual. This is the prophetic situation of today with regard to Israel: a national Jewish state in existence since 1948; the old city of Jerusalem now in possession of Israel since June 6-11, 1967; the temple area controlled by the Israeli government despite the Mosque of Omar's presence; and trouble in the Middle East which sees no solution yet in sight—and which may be the precipitating cause which will yet bring Antichrist with armies from all nations to Palestine (Joel 3). It seems as if the batter is being now prepared in the kitchen of the nations, and that the griddle is being heated.

With this in mind, let us now examine the four main prophetic themes that the Bible show yet to lie in the path of this nation, Israel.

I. Persecution

God will some day accomplish all of His purpose for Israel and that nation shall yet be saved; that is, the elect remnant (Rom. 9:27; 11:26). We shall see this more fully later, but for now, however, let it be said that the Bible points to a Satanically-inspired (not a God-inspired) persecution which will in the end drive Israel as a nation to cry out for her true God and Messiah.

Jeremiah 30:7 declares, "Alas! for that day is great, so that none is like it: it is even the time of Jacob's (i.e., Israel's) trouble, but he shall be saved out of it." When one reads the context of this verse, especially Jeremiah 30:4-11, he sees that Jeremiah the prophet is speaking in the midst of the calamities that face Israel at about 606 B.C. Here the people have forsaken their God and the Babylonians are about to take Judah away captive for the seventy-year period (c. 605 B.C. to 535 B.C.—with Jerusalem itself destroyed in 586 B.C.). In the midst of this trouble Jeremiah prophetically sees ahead to the final period of "Jacob's trouble" (30:7) which would be consummated in the last days, and which would conclude with Israel being free forever from the yoke of foreign governments (30:8), and with Israel serving the true Messiah who would sit on David's throne (30:9). In fact, this passage yields the outline for Israel's future: I. Persecution (30:7); II. Deliverance (30:8); III. Conversion (30:9); and IV. Restoration (30:10).

Jeremiah 30:8 says, "In that day," i.e., the day of Israel's trouble—when it is persecuted by the nations—God will "break his yoke from off thy neck, . . . and strangers shall no more serve themselves of him." Then verse 9 goes on to speak of Israel's conversion to their true God and Messiah. These things have never yet come to pass! Following the Babylonian captivity which was impending at Jeremiah's day there was *neither* national conversion *nor* full restoration such as these verses describe. When the Babylonian Empire fell to the invading Persian hordes and Cyrus the Persian gave his edict (c. 537 B.C.) permitting the Jews to return to their homeland, only a token number actually returned to Jerusalem under Zerubbabel (c. 536; Ezra 1-6). In the return under Ezra some eighty years later and then under Nehemiah ten years after that, only some of the Jews came back to Jerusalem (Ezra 7-10; Nehemiah 1-13). The Jews were still dispersed and scattered, according to Moses' prophecy in Deuteronomy 28:25, 37, 49, 63-67, after the trouble that faced them from Babylon in Jeremiah's day and they remain so even to this day. Plainly the prophecy of Jeremiah 30:7-11 has not yet been fulfilled. The time of "Jacob's trouble" (Jer. 30:7), with the Israelite deliverance, conversion, and restoration following, has never yet been realized. "Troubles" they have had, yes, and countless ones, but their final time of trouble is still ahead.

a. Russia to Invade Palestine (Ezek. 38:1-39:16)*

In fact, before the final period of world trouble spoken of in Jeremiah 30:7-10 reaches its end, the Old Testament prophet Ezekiel, writing about 550 to 600 years before Christ, tells of a time when RUSSIA WILL INVADE PALESTINE ONLY TO HAVE HER INVADING ARMIES MIRACULOUSLY DESTROYED. This astounding prophecy is given amid Ezekiel chapters 37-39, which deal chiefly with the theme of the eventual restoration of Israel. While the interpretation of some of the details of this prophecy is yet uncertain and debated, let the reader examine these chapters for himself and he will see that the main thrust of the prophecy is quite clear. Israel shall eventually be restored, but before this God shall deliver them miraculously from an invasion by armies from the region which we now call RUSSIA. Ezekiel called her Gog and said that she came from the NORTH (38:1-6; 39:1-2).

When will this happen? No one knows exactly when, except that it shall occur "after many days . . . in the latter years" (38:8). It shall come to pass at a time when "my people of Israel dwelleth safely" (38:14), and when Israel has to some measure been returned to the land of Palestine and has acquired some degree of wealth (38:11-13). This prophecy has *never* been fulfilled; but it could come to pass now in our own day when Jews are once again back in Israel and prospering. The fact that Russia is agitated against Israel and has set its face against this land for evil makes the fulfillment of these predictions a not so unlikely thing as it was in former days. In fact, before the Six-Day War of June 1967, one could not really say that Israel was actually back in her ancient land, for the segment of land owned by Jordan *west* of the Jordan River was the precise area which the Israelites under Joshua had conquered. The area taken by Israel in the previous 1948 struggle was outside of this central portion; it was the land added to the realm by David and Solomon. Only since June, 1967, has the stage been completely set for this dramatic act in God's prophetic Holy War drama of the ages.

Soviets Mobilized for Mideast
7 Divisions Readied Last October, Reports Say

By MURREY MARDER
Washington Post Service

WASHINGTON — The Soviet Union is reported boasting that it mobilized seven Russian divisions to fight for Egypt last October.

The published reports, now circulating across the Middle East, cannot be independently authenticated. If verified, they would be the first Soviet admission of what the United States charged was happening, resulting in the American global military alert the night of Oct. 24-25, during the Arab-Israeli war.

At the time, the Soviet Union accused the United States of openly moving closer to the United States, to the dismay of the Soviet Union.

The Soviet Union, in turn, is appealing over the head of Egyptian President Anwar Sadat to try to demonstrate that it has been loyal to Arab nationalism.

Much of what is being said on both sides "has the ring of authenticity to it" and basically "is credible" when compared with information known to American intelligence, U. S. sources said Wednesday.

However, "this is a propaganda brawl" between the Russians and the Sadat regime, a special noted to "a number of Egyptian official and political personalities."

Vinogradov is now the Soviet ambassador in Geneva for the Middle East peace talks.

The As Safir article came to the attention of officials in Washington when it was reprinted next day by the Beirut newspaper An Nida, which American sources say is a Communist organ supporting the line of the Soviet Communist Party. An Nida said, "As Safir has obtained an important document which contains the Soviet Union's views and what happened during the October war," which began on Oct. 6, 1973.

Its account of the October alert, attributed to Vinogradov is as follows:

"In the early hours of 20 October, at exactly 6:300, President Sadat contacted me and asked me to convey an urgent message on the situation to Brezhnev (Soviet Communist Party chief Leonid L. Brezhnev) and ask him to intervene to achieve an immediate cease-fire.

"(As I learned later, Syria did not want to have a cease-fire at that time because it was on the verge of launching its big counteroffensive.)

"I contacted Moscow. The director of the office informed me that Comrade Brezhnev had gone to bed only one hour before and that he could not wake him up. I asked him to wake him up on my responsibility. I informed Brezhnev of the situation as explained by President Sadat and of his request.

"The Soviet leaders immediately issued a decision for a partial alert of the Soviet forces. Seven Soviet military divisions were mobilized and put on the ready to be taken to fight on the Egyptian front. In fact, an advance group arrived in Cairo."

b. Israel's Final Tribulation

Let us now return to that *final* period of persecution upon Israel, "Jacob's trouble," which before we noted that *Jeremiah* 30:7-10 spoke of—and this is *not* identical to Russia's end-time invasion of Israel though that *may* occur during this period (or it may occur prior to it). *Daniel* 12:1 speaks of this same end-time persecution of Israel:

". . . and there shall be a time of trouble, such as never was since there was a nation even to that same time: and at that time thy people (Daniel's people, Israel; cf. Dan. 7:5-19, 20, 24) shall be delivered, every one that shall be found written in the book."

Daniel here shows that it will begin as the most fearful persecution in history and that it will be followed by national Israel at last being delivered. This is manifestly the same account as in Jeremiah. Today, as we look back, it could only point to Hitler's Satanic mass murder or to one yet to come. Since the Jews were not delivered as Jeremiah and Daniel describe after World War II, as the need for the June 1967, War testified, this time of persecution and subsequent deliverance must lie still ahead.

In *Matthew* 24:21 the same prophetic story is repeated, viz., "For then shall be great tribulation, such as was not since the beginning of the world to this time, no, nor never shall be." National Israel is again the primary subject to this tribulation. This is shown by the previous verse, Matthew 24:20, "But pray ye that your flight be not in the winter, *neither on the sabbath day"* (emphasis mine). Here in Matthew 24:15 the Lord has told of the Antichrist's committing of the "abomination of desolation" in the middle of the seven-year period (Dan. 9:27, 2 Thess. 2:3,4), and He is telling those in Judea to flee for their lives (Matt. 24:15-22). The fact that He says that they should actually pray that their flight from the persecuting Antichrist should not occur on the Sabbath can only point to His addressing at least these remarks primarily to the elect Jews of the end-time.** Today on the Sabbath Jerusalem comes to a halt and one cannot even get gasoline for his car. A flight from this city on such a day would run into unimaginable complications.

**Although Luke 21:12-24 speaks of the events of the fall of Jerusalem in 70 A.D., these events of Matthew 24:15-22 were never fulfilled then. Titus, the Roman general, was superstitiously afraid of the Temple. Josephus who was his aide tells us this. Titus neither committed the "abomination of desolation" of Matthew 24:15 nor did he proclaim himself to be this world's only god in the Temple as the Antichrist will yet do (2 Thess. 2:3-4).

Revelation 12 is a chapter which speaks of this same future persecution of Israel. Here a dragon is seen persecuting a woman who is rescued by God. The dragon is plainly Satan (Rev. 12:9) who will accomplish his final attack against Israel through the Antichrist, who is the "beast" (Greek, "wild beast") of Revelation 13:1-10. That the woman of Revelation 12:1 is Israel is seen by comparing her sun, moon, and twelve stars with Joseph's dream of Genesis 37:9-10. There in Genesis by a dream of the same sun, moon, and twelve stars (eleven plus Joseph who is the twelfth) the incipient nation of Israel is portrayed as: Jacob, the sun; Rachel, the moon; and the twelve tribes as the stars.

Daniel 9:27 shows that the "abomination of desolation" will be committed by the Antichrist *at the midpoint of the seven-year Tribulation Period*. Christ, in Matthew 24:15, declares that this act by Antichrist is the signal for all of the remnant who will turn to Him to flee from Jerusalem and Judea, for the persecution then starting will continue until His appearance at the end of the remaining three and a half years (Matt. 24:15-31). So, too, Revelation 12 fits perfectly with this, for in both verses 6 and 14 it is asserted that this final anti-Israel persecution will last for exactly three and one-half years. (The 1260 days of Rev. 12:6 equal three and a half years with 30 days to the month; and the time, dual-times, and a half of a time of Rev. 12:14 also equals 3 1/2 years.)

What then is the prophetic picture here? It is that in the last days Israel is to face fierce persecution. Who will be the agent causing this persecution? Answer: From Revelation 12 it is clear that the Dragon, Satan, is the one who wishes to destroy this nation in order to foil God's prophesied purposes, in the latter days, of reclaiming and restoring her. Who finally rescues Israel? Answer: Revelation 12:6 shows that it is God who prepares her a hiding place. So, too, Matthew 24:22 shows that for the elect's sake God shortens this persecution by Christ's appearance of Revelation 19:11-20:3. Why? Answer: Revelation 7:1-8, and many other passages, some of which we shall later look at, show that in the end-time God will finally have His way with this stiff-necked nation and He shall seal His elect and they shall turn to the true God in their coming midnight hour and to their Messiah, none other than our blessed Lord and Saviour, Jesus Christ. What is the lesson here for any Christian who for one reason or another is inclined toward anti-Semitism? Answer: Revelation 12 shows that Satan is the one who wishes to destroy Israel and the Jews, and it is God who shall yet save Israel. Can there be any explanation to justify a Christian's standing in Satan's corner? The answer is, "No."

II. Deliverance

The above discussion brings us to this next point. The Bible not only clearly pictures the coming awful hour of Jacob's persecution, but it also unequivocally announces her subsequent rescue—and that by the Lord Himself.

Plain of Esdraelon where the Battle of Armageddon will be fought. This is often referred to as the Valley of Jezreel. It has been the scene of endless wars...the Pharoahs of Egypt, the Hittites, Israelites, Philistines, Assyrians, Syrians, Persians, Greeks, Romans, Crusaders, Turks and even the British under Lord Allenby during the first World War in 1918 fought here.

The Sea of Galilee and the city of Tiberias. Tiberias was built around 20 A.D. by Herod Antipas as his new capital. Magdala (Matthew 15:39), the home of Mary Magdalene, was situated three miles to the north.

SABRA is now a term used to designate Israeli-born Jews. Sabra is a fruit of cactus plant which is prickly outside and sweet inside. Such a term suggests the strength and protectiveness of the nation as well as the character of its individuals.

84 • ISRAEL Land of Promise, Land of Prophecy

Mount Tabor rises on the northeastern area of the Plain of Esdraelon. It is believed by many to be the scene of the Transfiguration of Christ. See Matthew 17:1.

• 85

Members of the Israeli "Society for Protection of Nature" explore the Dead Sea desert canyons.

86 • ISRAEL   Land of Promise, Land of Prophecy

A Bedouin girl in the Sinai desert. Whenever in public Bedouin women must be kept veiled. Bedouins are of the Islamic faith and claim Ishmael as their ancestor.

Arab and camel rest on Jericho road.

88 • ISRAEL   Land of Promise, Land of Prophecy

This remarkable photograph taken from Mt. Nebo shows the Dead Sea in the foregound and the Promised Land as Moses may have witnessed it over 3000 years ago.

Thus Jeremiah 30:7-11 not only proclaims "Jacob's trouble," but it also announces, "But he shall be saved out of it ... I will break his yoke from off thy neck .. lo, I will save thee from afar ... and Jacob shall return, and shall be in rest, and be quiet, and none shall make him afraid." As has been said above, this has not yet happened, and anyone who thinks that Jacob is now at rest and quiet and unafraid has, as another once said in a World War II context, fallen asleep upon both his Bible and his newspaper.

Daniel 12:1, after speaking of the end time trouble of Israel which would surpass the great persecutions of all previous history, adds, "And at that time thy people (Daniel's people, Israel) shall be delivered, every one that shall be found written in the book." So, too, Revelation 12:6,14-16 shows that the fleeing woman, Israel, will be rescued at the end. Matthew 24:21-31 likewise shows that God will intervene for the elect's sake. "Except those days should be shortened, there should no flesh be saved" (v. 22) must mean that, if God allowed the persecution to run its natural course, all of the elect, and perhaps all of mankind, would be consumed. Instead, God shortens the period of persecution by His coming to destroy the Antichrist and his armies which are gathered for some diabolical reason at this time in Palestine, in the Jezreel Valley and its environs—that is, at Armageddon (Rev. 19:11-20:3; 16:13-16; 14:14-20; Joel 3:1,2, 9-17; Isa. 63:1-6; Zech. 12:9). Note these many references here cited, and there are more, and see that this teaching that Israel shall be threatened with annihilation in the end-time, suffer its greatest hour of persecution, and then be rescued by none other than God Almighty is a major theme of Biblical prophecy. Let no one think that this doctrine is a result of the twisting of one obscure verse; but let all see that it is a constant theme of the Bible played over and over by the prophetic strands. It will come to pass. Israel shall be saved by Jehovah, by Christ at His appearance at the end of the Tribulation Period.

We here now stand on top of "Armageddon," which in the Hebrew is "Har (Mount) Megiddio (Place of Troops)." Looking northeast, Mt. Tabor, the probable site of the transfiguration of our Lord, can be seen; and in between these two famous locations lies fifteen and a half miles of relatively flat land which is the strategic military land pass of Israel. Allenby in 1918 won his decisive victory here for the British and was given the title, "Viscount Allenby of Megiddo." Here there is room for the prophetic hordes of Antichrist's land armies to be gathered together at the end of the seven-year Tribulation for the final attempt to thwart God's will for Israel, the Battle of Armageddon (Rev. 16:12-16). And here, through the 1,600 stadia of Revelation 14:20, a distance of 184 miles stretching from Bozrah in the South (Isa. 63:1) through Jerusalem and Armageddon to Tyre in the north, the Lord Jesus will slay in judgment the hosts of the Antichrist's armies when He shall be revealed from Heaven at the end of the Tribulation (Isa. 63:1-6; Rev. 19:11-20:3). There is much room for armies to bivouac here, the land is empty and open; there is consternation today over Israel with Russia, Communist China, Egypt, and Syria still desiring to see Israel destroyed and breathing threats. Perhaps it shall be soon? The griddle is hot. The persecution will come, but so will the deliverance!

III. Conversion

By this time some may be saying, "Yes, it is clear in prophecy that Israel is yet to be persecuted and then to be delivered by God, but how can God rescue Israel when Israel still rejects her Messiah? There is only one way of salvation and that is through the one Christ; therefore, on what grounds can the Lord desire to save Israel if she continues to reject Jesus?"

It is in answer to this question that we come now to our third main point. The answer lies simply in this, Israel at the end-time will turn to Christ as her Saviour and Messiah. Thus God rescues her, for many Jews alive during that generation when "these things begin to come to pass" are elect according to the foreknowledge of God (Matt. 24:22). They will certainly turn to Christ. That this conversion of Israel's latter day remnant is true and that it is taught in the Bible can be seen from the particulars which follow.

Zechariah 12:10 reads,

"And I will pour upon the house of David, and upon the inhabitants of Jerusalem, the spirit of grace and supplications: and they shall look upon me whom they have pierced, and they shall mourn for him, as one mourneth for his only son, and shall be in bitterness for him, as one that is in bitterness for his firstborn."

Here clearly the house of David and Jerusalem, Israel, is seen at last turning to Jesus as their Messiah. They "look upon" Jesus *"whom they have pierced"* (emphasis mine) in the "look" of conversion and trust. Then as they see Him in His true divinity and humanity, with His hands punctured by the wounds of Calvary even for their sins, they turn to mourning. They "mourn" as they at last have their eyelids opened by the outpouring of God's "spirit of grace and supplications" for they now see that this Jesus whom they and their nation has so long rejected is in reality their true Saviour as well as the Saviour of all who call upon His name (Rom. 10:13).

When shall this be? The verse previous to this one declares it—Zechariah 12:9, "And it shall come to pass in that day, that I will seek to destroy all the nations that come against Jerusalem." Here again, as before, we see that the prophetic focus is on the events of the final days of the age when the Antichrist and his armies from many nations come against Israel to persecute and to destroy. It is at this time that God will give His deliverance when all see that sinful mankind cannot save. The remnant of the Jews left alive will suddenly be rescued from certain annihilation (Matt. 24:22) by Christ's appearance. He will then save Israel from the final Satanic attack upon them (Joel 3:2; Rev. 19:11-20:3), and then "they shall look upon me (Christ) whom they have pierced" (Zech. 12:10). Oh, the irony of it all; but oh, the grace of God in it! The one "despised and rejected" by Israel for these many centuries (Isa. 53:3) is the very one who shall save them in the end not only from their assailants but also from their sins; for, "in that day there shall be a fountain opened to the house of David and to the inhabitants of Jerusalem for sin and for uncleanness" (Zech. 13:1). It is then that Paul's words of Romans 11:26 will have their complete fulfillment, "And so all Israel shall be saved."

IV. Restoration

We have thus far seen the first three steps of God's prophetic program for Israel: Persecution, Deliverance, and Conversion. It is now needful to complete this prophetic stairway with its final step, Israel's Restoration.

Many people, as they have gazed at the prophetic utterances of Israel's restoration, have sought to explain them away, for how could this people be again exalted by God when they daily turn their backs upon the Saviour who only can save both Jew and Greek from the guilt and pollution of sin (Rom. 3:9; 10:12)? Some, the British-Israelite advocates, have said that when we read that Israel will be blessed in the last days we should substitute the words "Britain and America" for the word "Israel." The amillennialists (who believe that the millennial kingdom of Isaiah 11 and Revelation 20 is *now*, and that Satan is *now* in prison so that he cannot *now* deceive the nations, Rev. 20:3—which is manifestly false despite their erudite explanations) say that the church has inherited all of national Israel's blessings and that God is done with Israel forever. Therefore, they say that we should substitute the words "Christian Church" for "Israel" in the restoration prophecies. All these, however, are wrong.

God has a special program for Israel which will in the end yield a restored nation; for, ". . . as touching election, they (Israel) are beloved for the fathers' sakes" (that is, because of God's covenant with Abraham, Isaac, and Jacob, Gen. 12:1-3; 17: 4-8). "For the gifts and calling of God are without repentance;; (that is, God doesn't change His mind when He decrees an unconditional covenant, and though national disobedience, as in the case of Israel, may delay the divine bestowal of His covenant blessings on the nation, eventually in God's time they will indeed be bestowed fully.) Romans 11:28-29.

Thus we see that for the fulfillment of God's promises to Abraham and the fathers, God in His sovereign plan will in the end restore Israel by grace. The fires of persecution will cause them at last to forsake their trust in their own selves and in their fellow man, and, looking away from sinful man, they will scream in desperation for God. God will hear their cries and

Christ will deliver them, and they shall look upon him "whom they have pierced" and be converted to Jesus. At this time God will now fulfill His word and accomplish His eternal purposes toward the nation. He will restore them. So we read:

> "Yea, many people and strong nations shall come to seek the Lord of hosts in Jerusalem, and to pray before the Lord. Thus saith the Lord of hosts; In those days it shall come to pass, that ten men shall take hold of all languages of the nations, even shall take hold of the skirt of him that is a Jew, saying, We will go with you: for we have heard that God is with you" *(Zech. 8:22, 23)*.
>
> "Behold, the days come, saith the Lord, that I will raise unto David a righteous Branch, and a King shall reign and prosper, and shall execute judgment and justice in the earth. In his days Judah shall be saved, and Israel shall dwell safely: and this is his name whereby he shall be called, THE LORD OUR RIGHTEOUSNESS. Therefore, behold, the days come, saith the Lord, that they shall no more say, The Lord liveth, which brought up the children of Israel out of the land of Egypt; but, The Lord liveth, which brought up and which led the seed of the house of Israel out of the north country, and from all countries whither I had driven them; and they shall dwell in their own land" *(Jer. 23:5-8)*.

Read Isaiah 62:1-7; Joel 3:15-21; and countless other passages. The story of the restoration of Israel is not built on one verse; it is a theme played over and over again in the Bible. It will come to pass, the the Lord will be glorified in it.

* * * * * *

The paper having been delivered, after another hour of inspecting the *tel*, we again took up our positions in our vehicles. We were moving at a rate of eighty-five kilometers per hour at a compass azimuth of sixty degrees, aiming for Tiberias via Mt. Tabor. As we drove across the Jezreel Valley's width we could only think of that great coming day of the Lord which would have its climactic conflict here at Armageddon.

CHAPTER VIII

ARRIVAL INTO TIBERIAS

While we were en route, it still being the afternoon of Saturday, *January 13th* we gave a lift to a nineteen-year-old Israeli soldier who pledged that he would direct us to Mt. Tabor and Tiberias. After ten kilometers going northeast from Megiddo we drove through Afula. Then after an additional thirteen the soldier advised us to "Bo smola" ("Go left"). It seemed that he was taking us short of our goal of Mt. Tabor—for interrogation or customs, perhaps? As we motored on, it soon became apparent that we were taking a back road into the mountain. At the conclusion of five more kilometers we were at the foot of the gradually sloping Tabor which rose 1929 feet above the surroundings.

EYEWITNESSES OF HIS MAJESTY

We glided slowly up the twisting and winding mountain-side road. It was at a steep incline and frightening. It was much like the sharp climb up to the mountain of the big redwood trees at Sequoia National Park in California. To make a slip of the wheel would at times have meant to have the car and its passengers plunge down the mountain. As we reached the top it seemed like the Grand Canyon of the Colorado or like Moro Rock at Sequoia near Mt. Whitney. I would have guessed that we were ten thousand feet up rather than two thousand. The height of Tabor cannot be apprehended by seeing it from afar when it appears to be merely a big hill because of its lack of crags and pointed intrusions. Once atop, its height is dazzling to the eyes, and all of Galilee and the surrounding country can be seen on a clear day.

This is the isolated mountain—high, and in Galilee—that traditionally has been identified as the site of Christ's transfiguration. His body and garments glowed with a celestial light, Moses and Elijah appeared with Him, and the voice from Heaven came from a cloud and said, "This is my beloved Son, here him" (Mark 9:1-13).

Some have suggested that the transfiguration may have occurred on the southern slopes of Hermon. This is put forth because, after Peter's famed confession of Christ at Caesarea-Philippi (Matt. 16:13-28) which is at Hermon's foot, six days later the transfiguration took place on a high mountain in the Galilee region (Matt. 17:1). But six days is more than ample to walk from Caesarea-Philippi to Mt. Tabor! It could have happened at either place.

The Apostle Peter wrote the following words which spoke of that transfiguration scene that took place on the high mountain years ago. He declared near the close of his life the following words which I read to our group as we stood on Tabor's summit:

> "Yea, I think if meet, as long as I am in this tabernacle, to stir you up by putting you in remembrance; knowing that shortly I must put off this my tabernacle, even as our Lord Jesus Christ hath shewed me. Moreover I will endeavour that ye may be able after my decease to have these things always in remembrance. For we have not followed cunningly devised fables, when we made known unto you the power and coming of our Lord Jesus Christ, but were eyewitnesses of his majesty. For he received from God the Father honour and glory, when there came such a voice to him from the excellent glory, This is my beloved Son, in whom I am well pleased. And this voice which came from heaven we heard, when we were with him in the holy mount" *(2 Pet. 1:13-18).*

Barbara: "That is most interesting, especially since he claims that he and the other disciples of Jesus have not 'followed cunningly devised fables,' for this is exactly what they are accused of by those who disbelieve the New Testament accounts."

Dr. Cohen: "Yes, and the word for 'fables' in the Greek is *muthois,* that is, 'myths.' Peter is saying that the apostolic preaching that Jesus actually was the Son of God, the Messiah, was not a collection of cleverly planned myths; but, on the contrary, he along with James and John were on this mount when the transfiguration took place and when the voice from Heaven attested to the truth of Jesus' Messiahship."

At this we peered off of the mountain top and felt tremendously isolated from the world beneath as we beheld its kingdoms below. We began to examine the elaborate and quite large monastery chapel and building complex which was here hidden in the sky from prying eyes beneath. Suddenly a monk in his early forties came out of a door, and before someone could say, "We cannot speak Hebrew too well yet"—"or Latin,"—the scarlet-sacked cleric said, "Hello; Americans, aren't you? I'm from Canada."

As we drove on to Tiberias, saving our visit to nearby Nazareth for another day, I mused that the last leg of our journey of this day was to be about 30 kilometers according to our map. Yet we were low in gas, or rather "benzine," and I was becoming somewhat alarmed. Since I was driving I decided not to mention this to Professor Dunzweiler who had begun now to sleep. Why should I advertise my negligence? If we ran out of gas it would be known by all soon enough.

We dropped off our soldier, after telling him that Professor Dunzweiler and I were "Nazarenes" (*"Natzarot"*) as this name, and not that of "Christian," is the name whereby the Israeli soldiers recognize our faith. Our saying this made me think of Matthew 2:23, "He shall be called a Nazarene." Jesus was a Nazarene not only because he was reared in the town of Nazareth, but also as a further fulfillment of Isaiah 11:1 which speaks of the Messiah. Isaiah 11:1 says that the Messiah shall be the "Branch" (that is, a young shoot; in Hebrew, a *natzer*— "Nazarene") which comes from the roots of Jesse; that is, from the lineage of David who was the son of Jesse. Jesus was this *natzer* from the Tribe of Judah, the seed of Jesse, the seed of David (Matt. 1:1,3,6).

STRANGER IN TIBERIAS

It was pitch dark as we entered Tiberias. As we sped in on a road of low elevation, in the dark our eyes were all at once greeted by lights from the houses situated on the hill section of the town. As we watched the lights above us shine as a beacon, we were reminded of Christ's words of Matthew 5:14, "A city that is set on a hill cannot be hid."

I rejoiced to be promptly directed to a benzine station, and the Arab manager was most pleasant. Minutes later we were unpacking and readying ourselves for the 7:30 p.m. supper at our new headquarters, the Molon Ginton ("Hotel Little-Garden") of Tiberias. This hotel, although quite adequate and nice, was not the fancy spacious affair that the Tel Aviv Dan or the Dan Carmel were. We were now out of the big city tourist areas, and in the more rural region of Galilee. Yet this was the season when the Israelis came to Tiberias for its warm mineral baths, and the smallness of the hotel enabled us to meet the Israelis. We were no longer surrounded by fellow American tourists.

Suddenly, a knock came at the door of the room which Professor Dunzweiler and I shared. I opened the door and an attractive strange Arab girl was standing there saying in chopped English that she had something for us. International intrigue? No, merely two oranges from the hotel management. She was an employee and each night each guest was given a piece of fruit to chew upon at his or her leisure. The elaborate hotels did not do this, thought we, as we eyed the fruit for our late night snack.

After supper our party was busily engaged in purchasing wooden camels from the hotel gift shop for friends in the States. Mr. Dunzweiler showed me a wooden camel, a carved and varnished brown indigenous beast, for which he paid ten dollars in American money. He explained to me that it would be well worth the money when cherished and prized later back home in America.

We went to bed in Tiberias with moonlit Lake Galilee magically shimmering through our window with tremulous lights upon her now gentle waves. Alas, was it true? We were in Galilee concerning which Isaiah, the Hebrew prophet, seven hundred years before Christ, foresaw that ". . . in Galilee of the nations. The people that walked in darkness have seen a great light: they that dwell in the land of the shadow of death, upon them hath the light shined" (Isa. 9:1,2). Yes, it was here twenty centuries ago that the Messiah manifested himself as He began to show Himself and His self-authenticating words and works to a world perishing in sin.

CHAPTER IX

TOURING NORTHERN GALILEE

Sunday morning *January 14th* made its exciting debut. Breakfast was early and it was served in a dining room that held about one hundred people, rather than in a spacious aircraft carrier type sprawling room which held almost a thousand as in the Tel Aviv Dan. Nevertheless, here, too, the order of the day was a buffet bonanza of sour creams and all types of raw and smoked fish. Orange juice was the starter and coffee the finale. For me and most of the others this was the local color for which we craved. Professor Dunzweiler, however, summoned a waiter and whispered to him that scrambled eggs were what he craved, along with a dish which when named was greeted by an incredulous grimace of ignorance upon the waiter's face—Cream of Wheat! The Cream of Wheat was at once dropped from the discussion, and Mr. Dunzweiler put pressure upon the waiter to deliver the eggs. The waiter obliged and all were content.

After our own Sunday services, our group, with lunches packed for us by Molon Ginton, waited in the lobby to depart on a guided bus tour of "Galilee and the Golon Heights." Soon the tour's guide enters the hotel and after cheerily greeting the desk clerk in a Hebrew exchange, motions for us to follow. He, the guide, is an Israeli young man of about thirty—thin, bony, and with boundless exuberance for his land and country. He wears a red, white, and blue wool knit hat which gave him a fitting seafaring look (though I would not myself wear that hat unless playing the role of a young have-no-care). Regrettably, Professor Dunzweiler was taken ill this morning and was not with us on this tour.

RABBINICAL TIBERIAS

The bus motors away from our hotel, and now begins to roll into the heart of Tiberias much like a multiengined jet taxis to the main runway. Our guide is speaking now Hebrew and now English, and it is immediately obvious that many Israelis and few Americans are on board. It is explained that much of the territory covered in today's tour has just been captured in the June 1967 War, and therefore, the majority of the Israelis aboard who live in the South have never seen it any more than have we Americans.

The stores of Tiberias are crowded next to one another and they vary from those run by poor people to those run by middle class entrepreneurs. Arab and Israeli are both seen. The town is small and easily capable of being surveyed entirely by foot. Soon we pass the various sites of the graves of famed rabbis. Moses Maimonides of the 12th century A.D. who coined the "modern" thirteen principles of Jewish Faith, though born in Spain, lies here. Rabbi Yohanaan Ben Zakai, who petitioned the Roman Conqueror Titus in the first century A.D. to spare the city's center of learning is interred here, as is Rabbi Akiba who declared in 132 A.D., upon the initiation of Bar-Kochba's revolt against Rome, that Shimon Bar-Kochba was the Messiah of the Jews.

The guide explained that Tiberias was built by Herod Antipas (ruled 4 B.C. to 44 A.D.), King of Galilee and Perea, son of Herod the Great. The city was named in honor of the Roman Emperor Tiberias (ruled 14-37 A.D.). After the Roman destruction of Jerusalem in A.D. 70 the seat of Judaism with its Sanhedrin, "Court of Seventy," was moved northward to Tiberias. When Hadrian, the Roman Emperor, in c. 135 A.D. permanently banned the Jews from Jerusalem because of the Bar-Kochba revolt—following so soon in the wake of the 69-70 A.D. revolt which resulted in Jerusalem's utter devastation by the Romans—Tiberias' place of importance was secured.

Then in the second century A.D. the rabbis declared that for the Jews the name of the city was to be henceforth not "Tiberias," named for a pagan emperor, but it was to be "Tiveria" or "Good spirit"—the exact original meaning of the last word being uncertain.

AROUND THE LAKE

Our vehicle is now racing north along the west bank of the Sea of Galilee. Our encirclement of the lake will be clockwise with a penetration into northern Israel that will take us forty kilometers north of the upper edge of the water. The water body so famous for Christ's deeds upon it and around it has two names from antiquity. "Sea of Galilee" and "Lake Kinneret" (Chinnereth) are these names. The name "Kinneret" comes from the Hebrew *Kinnor* which means "lute"; that is, the lake is shaped like the main section of this pear-like, guitar-like stringed instrument. Its waves are the strings!

The water here is fresh, the elevation 686 feet *below* sea level, the main delicacy is St. Peter's Fish, and the size of the lake is approximately today eight miles east by west and fourteen miles north by south. The waters off Mt. Hermon to the north fill it and it pours its blue-green liquid into the Jordan to its south. An aqueduct channel is seen by us beside the lake so as to remove a stream of mineral water from entering the fresh Kinneret. It is sailed to the Tiberian baths and from there released into the Jordan's murky, brownish liquid. Other aqueducts take the fresh Galilean waters and by-pass the more mineralized and muddy Jordan as well as the Dead Sea, and this fresh water from this northern lake is let loose in the Negev to the south so as to make those deserts miles away to bloom as gardens.

The traditional Mount of the Beatitudes was pointed out by our guide. It was a still-green, large, grassy knoll by Lake Galilee's northwest sector. It was adjacent to the site of ancient Capernaum on the Lake. Here—or possible if this location is wrong, on another nearby hill—Christ fed the five thousand (John 6). This miracle of the feeding of the five thousand is the only miracle of Christ's ministry, except for

His resurrection from the dead, which is recorded in all four of the Gospel accounts. Here He showed Himself by His miraculous multiplication of the fish to be able to create animal cells instantaneously. Thus He not only displayed His divine powers, but here He also once and for all demonstrated to both unbelievers and doubting Christians, who wondered with reference to the original creation, that animals could have been instantaneously brought forth. One looks today at the knoll for signs of the miraculous; but alas, without Christ standing upon it, it now appears to be just another hill.

ROCKS

The hillsides, mountainsides, and fields are covered with huge to medium-sized surface boulders. Rocks, rocks, rocks; stones, stones, stones! I have never seen so many. One must see it to believe (or must one?). Our guide explained that Galilee is covered with basalt, an igneous gray and black rock, and dolomite, a magnesium carbonate-rich limestone-marble. It is thought that a volcanic eruption once covered this area with these rocks to a two-to-three-mile depth. With these rocks everywhere the Arab farmers have generally cleared a field and used the rocks to fence off parcels of land. Later, we saw some Arab farmers who were attemtping to plant and to plow in between the rocks lying upon the land. With the average diameter of the rocks being about a foot and with their being everywhere in such numerous amounts, this practice seemed short-sighted and destined to yield only the barest of crops. The guide said that a kibbutz settlement in Galilee took about seven years to clear adequately a rock field so that it could be fully planted.

Christ, in John 10, spoke of the sheepfold which was a stone enclosure for keeping the sheep safe from the wolves at night. Here before us everywhere we could see rock fences which were often so high that it was difficult to ascertain whether they were sheepfold type revetments to enclose animals at night or merely fences built high merely to dispose of the rocks. Obviously, for any who had animals they would suffice. One who knew John 10 could not but think, as we drove by the endless rock enclosures, of Jesus' description of the good shepherd entering the sheepfold in the morning, calling his sheep by name, and having his sheep follow him. Surely this was the perfect picture of Christ's entering the world, calling His elect to Him by the external preaching of the Gospel and the internal call of the Spirit, having His own recognize that He was the true Messiah of God, and then following Him (cf. Rom. 8:29,30).

I CANNOT BELIEVE MY EARS

The bus strikes a cavity in the road, and I am jarred into listening again to the voice of the guide. It is now raining. From my map I judge that we are about to go by Lake Huleh, that three-mile-in-diameter little lake also known as the "waters of Merom" in Joshua 11:5-7. I am excited with anticipation of seeing this so slight map object which for years I have taken pride to point out whenever sketching a map of the Holy Land. The guide speaks and I cannot believe my ears. The Israeli government has drained the lake dry in order to use its area for planting. The draining took place between 1957 and 1961, and now only a tiny memorial pond remains. The guide continues that the Jordanian government has accused Israel of planning to do likewise with Lake Kinneret, but he denies it vigorously. The bus moves on as I sit sullen in disbelief—Lake Huleh-gone! I feel it to have been a blunder with regard to preserving historical locations despite the guide's assurances of the tremendous and needed production yields. I frown as we zoom further northward in the now dense rain.

TEL HAZOR

The bus now stops at an artificial mound hill, a *tel*, which lies fourteen miles due north of the Sea of Galilee. This is Tel Hazor which was initially excavated in modern times. This was done in 1955 on an initial "dig" directed by Yigael Yadin for the Hebrew University of Jerusalem. Until 1955 it was a scrubcovered hill with a flat top.

Hazor's mound from above is shaped like a footprint with its east-west length being 600 meters and its north-south width 200 meters. It is forty meters high, its sides slope steeply, and in area it comprehends twenty-five acres.

Most of the antique cities of Palestine are not named in the Egyptian, Palestinian, or Mesopotamian pre-Biblical writings. Hazor, however, is. In the Egyptian Execration Texts, inscribed over 1800 years before Christ, Hazor is listed as one of the potential enemies of Egypt.

My head turns as Arnold Escourt hands me the booklet, "Hazor," printed by the National Parks Authority. Since copies were at the moment short, he offers to read aloud the brief section called, "Hazor in the Bible."

Arnold: "It is, however, from the Bible that Hazor is seen to have been a key city of high stragic value. This emerges particularly from the references in the Book of Joshua and the Deborah prose narrative in Judges. The victory of Joshua by the 'waters of Merom' marks, according to the Bible, a decisive phase in the conquest of Northern Canaan. Following this battle, the Bible tells us 'And Joshua at that time turned back and took Hazor and smote the king thereof with the sword . . . and he burnt Hazor with fire' (Joshua 11:1-13). And in Judges 4:2 we read, 'And the Lord sold them into the hand of Jabin king of Canaan, that reigned in Hazor; the captain of whose host was Sisera . . .' "Two later Biblical passages make mention of Hazor. Solomon rebuilt 'Hazor, and Megiddo, and Gezer' (Kings 9:15), the three strategic cities dominating the plains of Huleh . . . And in 2 Kings 15:29 there is a report of the conquest of Hazor by Tiglath-pileser III, king of Assyria. "Nearly six hundred years later, in 147 B.C.E., Jonathan the Hasmonean fought against Demetrius 'in the plain of Hazor' (1 Maccabees 11:63)."

Dr. Cohen: "I see from the last page of the guidebook that the archeological excavations here have unearthed twenty-one city strata with the occupations going from the 27th century B.C. Early Bronze Age, when the three great pyramids

Mt. of Beatitudes. Site of the Sermon on the Mount (Matthew 5:1-12).

Minister of Defense, Moshe Dayan, chatting with Arabs crossing Allenby Bridge. This bridge links Israel with Jordan.

A Hasidic Jew, this little boy proudly sports his father's fur hat.

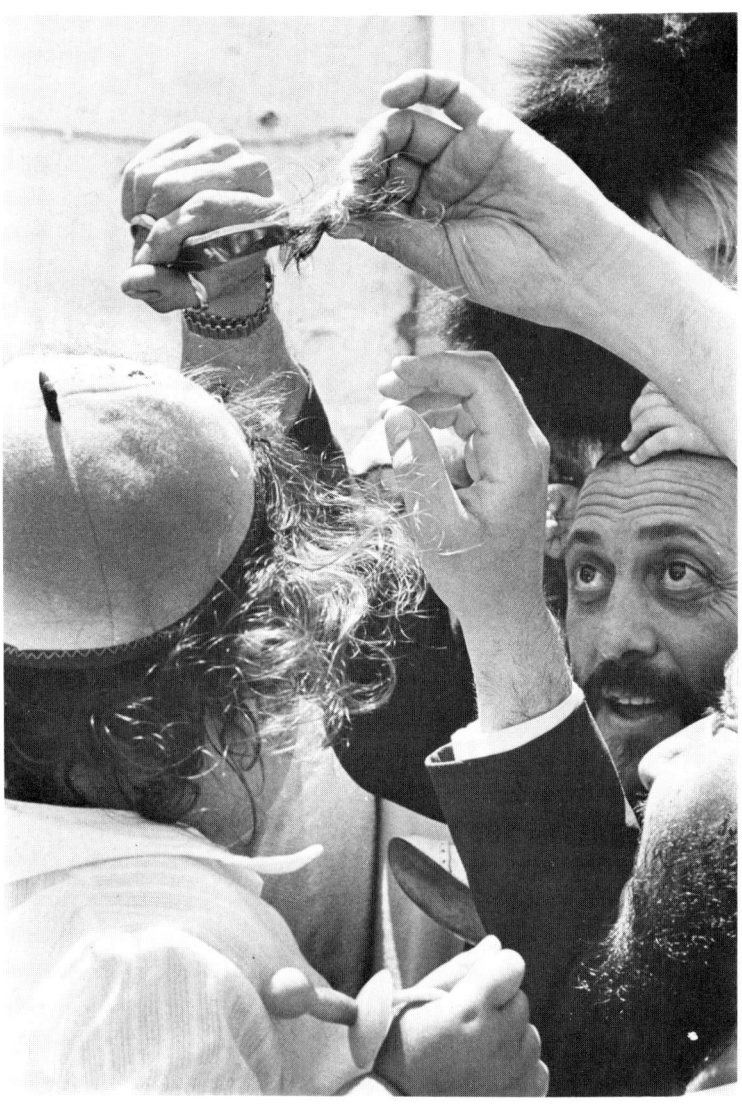

The Lag b'Omer celebration of cutting the hair off. This Jewish festival commemorates the unsuccessful revolt by Simon Barchocheba against the Romans in the 2nd century A.D.

were built, to the second century, B.C., the Hellenistic Period, when Greek culture dominated."

THE KIBBUTZ

After Tel Hazor we mount the bus and in minutes we have covered the less than two miles distance to the north which brings us to Kibbutz Ayelet Hashahar. The Hazor Museum is located here and is maintained by this kibbutz. Our guide explains that a kibbutz is a collective farm or settlement. He takes special pains, it seems, to explain to all of us in the bus that it is not Communistic. He declares that the kibbutz is privately owned, and privately self-governed—in contrast to the Communistic and socialistic scheme of government ownership and management. In the case of a kibbutz: a group of refugees or young Israelis, who wish to see their country develop, receive a plot of land which is given to them by the government. If they will farm it for five years, more or less, it is theirs. They run everything and elect their own officers. Most kibbutzim put much energy into land reclamation and farming, but many run restaurants and other enterprises. They see that schooling is provided for the children and housing for the families. Each of these collectives, however, differs from the others. It is estimated that the kibbutzim around Lake Galilee and to its immediate south contain about 10,000 people at present. The guide concludes in quick Hebrew, and I gather that he is telling the natives that he has just explained to the Americans what a kibbutz is. There is pleasant laughter at the end of his words, but my Hebrew is too limited to follow the jokes.

We leave the bus and are pointed toward the restaurant run by this kibbutz. As we walk, our guide says: "A restaurant like this produces for the people here a means of acquiring hard cash in between their farm crop harvests. This is very essential." I sat at a table with two fellows, one nineteen and the other twenty-three, both from Canada. They were sporting beards of great prominence and I felt I was back in the ancient world. Both were most cordial and we had an interesting chat as they explained how they had taken a year off from their schooling and were touring Europe and the Near East, in their words, "on a shoestring." They had spent the previous month in Turkey. They looked and sounded authentic. When the modest bill came for our cake and coffee, on my seeing their discussing agarot—akin to our pennies, I volunteered to pay their check.

Northbound again, Lebanon was now only five miles to our left. The guide began again. "It is green," he asserted, "all year long here in Upper Galilee. Here there is snow perhaps once per year; and today in January through the drizzle all looks green."

Great pointed hills are all around. Citrus groves planted here seven years before are today thriving. The guide is now telling us that to our left are the Mountains of Naphtali. That tribe inhabited this region north of the Sea of Galilee and upon the west bank of the Upper Jordan River. Between the peaks lie flat plains—level as those of Indiana.

Now the guide is telling us with roaring enthusiasm of the new development city to the left of our bus. It is called, "Kiryat Shmona," or "Suburb of the Eight," he explains,"for here eight men were martyred for Israel." "Here new immigrants are developing the land. Look there, and you will see two new textile factories—cotton." From my map I note that Kiryat Shmona is thirty-five miles north of Lake Kinneret.

170 LOST

Barbara: "What are we stopping for? There is nothing here, at least on my side of the bus."
Passenger: "A girl on this side of the bus is getting on!"

Sure enough, a fifteen-year-old girl climbed aboard. The guide, who apparently was the Vehicle Commander, spoke to her in Hebrew for a minute, smiled, and motioned her to sit down, saying, "Cain, cain" ("Yes, yes"). The guide begins again informing us that Kibbutz Daphne, mentioned in the book, *Exodus*, is to our left. He adds that the events of the

Exodus which described this kibbutz did not actually in fact apply to it, but rather the name was used.

We have now been driving west for about eight miles and we are pointed to our right to Tel el-Fahar. The guide laments: "Here at Tel el-Fahar during the Six-Day War, June 6-11, 1967, 170 Jewish boys were lost. This was the largest number of Israeli soldiers lost in any one engagement during the war." He goes on, alternating English with Hebrew.

Guide: "We are now crossing into former Syrian territory. We have almost reached the present northern extremity of Israeli territory and for about nine miles, since Kiryat Shmona, we have been moving eastward. The Israelis here have not seen this territory any more than you Americans. It is newly conquered, so those from Tel Aviv and Jerusalem are seeing it along with you for the first time. Look over there. That is a Syrian tank wrecked, and its twisted metal tells you the story."

"*Anachnu bonu . . .*"

ON THE ROCK IN THE RAIN

Our location being thirty miles north of Lake Galilee, we are in the territory of the Tribe of Dan. Tel Dan, the *tel* of the ancient northernmost city of Israel, is within two miles. The bus screeches to a halt. The rain has increased and the flats behind us are flooded with brown water rolling over them. We are now at Banias Water Fall and three miles to the northeast is the city of Banias or "Caesarea Philippi." Here the water flows from Mt. Hermon's melting snows. It flows through Banias and then down to these falls providing the Jordan with one-third of that river's water. This southerly flowing Banias River is the most eastern source of the Jordan, and today from the heavy rains blanketing this entire vicinity the river has become a raging torrential stream that looks like the swift-flowing Colorado. We left the bus and stood in the oozing and sinking mud under the rain showers in order to see the falls. The guide yelled to be heard above the falls and the downpouring rain. "Here," he screamed, "the river begins to make a sharp descent as it empties into the lower Jordan. Remember, the surface of Lake Galilee is six hundred feet below sea level."

A short ride in our tour bus brought us to the site of Banias. The Banias River flowed by, but from our location it here looked more like a stream than a river. The city sat at the southern foot of that giant, Mount Hermon, and in Old Testament times it was the location of a shrine to Baal; that is, "Baal-hermon" ("Master-of-Mt.-Hermon"). Judges 3:3 and 1 Chronicles 5:23 refer to it. Later in the Inter-Testament Period, the first four centuries B.C., the Greeks converted the place into a shrine for their god of nature, Pan ("All"). Hence they called it *Panias*. The modern name, Banias, is obviously a slur of *Panias*.

In 20 B.C. Herod the Great erected a white marble temple at this site and dedicated it to his patron, the emperor, Augustus Caesar. When Herod the Great then died in 4 B.C., his son, Herod Philip, acquired the territory called "The Fifth Province," which lay east of Galilee and the Jordan. This acquisition comprised one-third of Herod the Great's domain and it included Panias. Herod Philip increased the size of the city, improved it, and beautified it, naming it "Caesarea" in honor of the now reigning Tiberias Caesar. However, to separate it from the well-known Roman seaport on the coast also called "Caesarea," the explanatory nomen was added to this one, viz., "Philippi," that is, "Caesarea Philippi," "The Caesarea of (Herod) Philip."

The rain was fierce, and the guide laughingly said that if anyone wished to run out in the rain to the solid rock mount which was the Caesarea Philippi ancient worship shrine, then that person could run out in the rain and all would wait. I recalled that here it was that Christ said to Peter, "Thou are Peter, and upon this rock I shall build my church" (Matt. 16). This was a pivotal point in Christ's ministry, and I determined to stand on what might have been the very spot where upon the Lord stood when He made this pronouncement. All watched as

I started to run the seventy-five yards to the shrine.

The shrine was a solid rock in the general shape of a *tel*. Across its base the water of the Banias River poured from right to left, dropping for a small falls after passing two-thirds of the rock intrusion. At the upper left there were some graves or shrines with two crosses easily visible. At the lower right a path crossed the water and led up into a large cave with a smaller one immediately to its right. These caves were the Grotto of Pan. I finally succeeded in reaching the caves and I entered the grotto. All of the apostles at once could have spent the night here with room to spare. Some of the rocks in this cave, on its floor, were boulders as large as a man in height.

"UPON THIS ROCK"

As I stood in this mountain or large hill of rock, with rock extrusions jutting forth everywhere, my mind raced back to the Biblical situation surrounding this site (Matt. 16:13-21). I sat and recalled that during the third year of Christ's ministry, "the Year of Opposition," many had deserted Him at the culmination of the events recounted in John 6 (when Christ refused the wish of the Galilean masses that He become a political bread-providing revolutionary king). With the crowds of Galilee now largely gone and the religious authorities growing daily in enmity toward Jesus, it seemed to the disciples that their Master had missed the crest of the political tide. "Why didn't He accept the crown after He had fed the five thousand?" (John 6.) Even the disciples were yet looking for a messiah like Bar Kochvah who was to lead an anti-Roman revolt a century later. Now without the crowds the little band went north. Finally when they had at last reached here, Caesarea Philippi, Christ led them into a deeper faith. He here began to teach them plainly that He was soon to be crucified for the sins of the world at Jerusalem and then rise again (Matt. 16:21). It was essential that they again at this point be persuaded that despite the recent departure of the crowds of Galilee He was still truly the Messiah.

> When Jesus came into the coasts of Caesarea Philippi, he asked his disciples, saying, Whom do men say that I the Son of

man am? And they said, Some say that thou art John the Baptist: some, Elias; and others, Jeremias, or one of the prophets. He saith unto them, But whom say ye that I am? And Simon Peter answered and said, Thou art the Christ, the Son of the Living God. And Jesus answered and said unto him, Blessed art thou, Simon Bar-jona: for flesh and blood hath not revealed it unto thee, but my Father which is in heaven. And I say also unto thee, That thou art Peter (Greek: *petros,* "rock-boulder"), and upon this rock (*petra,* "rock-shelf"—upon which men construct houses, Matt. 7:24,25) I will build my church; and the gates of hell shall not prevail against it.

What is the rock upon which Christ will build His congregation? It is not Peter. Why? Because (1) Christ called Simon by the name "Rock-boulder" (*Petros*—Peter), but He said that He would build His congregation on "this rock-shelf" *(Petra)*; and (2) Peter, though here a real boulder in faith, is immediately after his confession shown by Christ not to be a solid immovable rock-shelf, for Peter declares that Christ shall not go to the cross, and Jesus answers him with, "Get thee behind me, Satan . . ." (Matt. 16:21-24). Peter also denied the Lord thrice despite his contrary boast.

Who or what is the rock-shelf then upon which Christ's congregation shall be built? Answer: It is Christ Himself. Why? Because the aim of this entire discussion was Christ's desire to clarify His disciples in their knowledge and faith in His Person and Work. Thus the final declaration by Him which obviously concludes this discourse must be related to the initial quest. The quest was not to learn the true nature of Peter; it was to reveal who Jesus was. So 1 Corinthians 10:4 likewise declares, "And that Rock was Christ."

* * * *

The rain was now slightly abating, and I dashed from the cave toward the bus. My fellow passengers looked incredulous as I re-entered. Some admired my intrepitude; others only stared quizzically. The bus started again as the guide patted me on the back. I was glad that I had done it. I was now wetter than the others but one doesn't get to Caesarea Philippi every day.

CHAPTER X

GOLAN HEIGHTS AND THE GEOGRAPHY OF PALESTINE

It now being about eleven o'clock in the morning still *January 14th,* our bus was rolling east from Banias to Masada, a distance of ten kilometers, upon the not straight road. As we drove, the guide explained that the Arab people pronounce "b" for "p" , and thus the ancient name of *Panias* has become over the recent years "Banias." He said, "Without desrespect, listen and you will hear the Arabs say, 'Blease' although those who have mastered their English in school may not do this."

The guide now explains that we are leaving the Banias-Masada road for a northern excursion upon the foot of Mt. Hermon.

Guide: "On a clear day Mt. Hermon with its snow-capped peak, 9232 feet into the air, is visible from the Lake of Galilee. From our present vicinity of Dan and Caesarea Philippi, about thirty miles north of Kinneret, Mount Hermon runs for about forty miles north-northeast. It is on the border between Lebanon to its west and Syria to its east, and it is the highest of the Anti-Lebanon Mountains. It is a long ranging mount which in itself is a mountain range.

"Israel took the southern heights of Hermon to make sure that the Syrian artillery shelling from here would be stopped.

"The Mediterrannean and Jerusalem Pines are still green here on this part of Hermon."

I mentioned to those near me that Mt. Hermon was possibly the actual scene of the transfiguration since it occurred on a high mount six days after Peter's confession at Caesarea-Philippi, which is at Hermon's foot (Matt. 16:13-17:13). Then after walking about on Hermon for a short period, there being snow on its ground, we board the bus which then rushes us to Masada.

We soon arrive at Masada which is thirty miles north of Lake Galilee. (We are *not* at the famous Masada which is forty air miles south of Jerusalem and three miles west of the Dead Sea. This latter one inspired the motto of the Israeli commemoration coin, "Masada shall not fall again." In the second century B.C. Judas Maccabee had erected a stronghold there, and later Herod the Great built this great rock mesa into a fortress. In 70 A.D., after Jerusalem fell to the Romans, 967 zealots—men, women, and children—fled to Masada's rock sanctuary (*metzuda* means "citadel") and held out there against the Roman Tenth Legion commanded by Silva until 73 A.D., when Silva fired the walls by means of having built a ramp up to them. A mass suicide took place, and Silva found only two women and five children alive. These had hidden. The awful sight caused Silva to spare the seven, and from these Josephus recorded the account.)

The northern Masada where we are is a Druse village. Druses are non-Moslem Arabs who practice their own secret religion. Some of them are in the Israeli army, and they are identifiable by the army uniform with a flowing Arab head covering. The Druses broke from the Moslems in the 16th century, declares our guide.

FLOODED KUNEITRA

Snow is now falling as we move southeast along the fourteen-kilometer road from Masada to Kuneitra. We are now riding upon the Golan Heights, which is the name for the cliffs and mountains to the immediate northeast of Lake Galilee. All of the trees are green, and they sprout out amid the

Golan Heights and the Geography Of Palestine • 117

white blanket of snow now covering all of the earth. It is readily apparent as we drive that the guide and the Israelis spying out this land for the first time are quite elated as they ride upon this new territory taken in the recent June, 1967, War. They are bubbling with joy at each new sight.

As we proceed to Kuneitra the snow has somehow vanished and again it is the rain which drops. The rain water running to the left side of our road parallels the road and has made its own swift river eight to ten feet wide, and occasionally the plains beside us are flooded. The guide intones that the road which we are crossing leads to Damascus which is forty-five miles to the north-northeast. He recounts that in the June, 1967, War the Israeli army desired to reach Damascus to bring back the two thousand Damascus Jews to Israel, but, however, because of the United Nations Commission they did not go through with this plan. They did, he continued to narrate, accomplish their prime task of seizing about twenty miles of Syrian land in order to provide a buffer zone against Syrian heavy artillery fire.

We are driving down the middle of the wide Mississippi River, it appears, as I survey the flats before Kuneitra now covered entirely with the brown muddied rain water. On our bus one can imagine himself sailing down a river on a boat.

At last, we arrive at Kibbutz Golan where we are to partake of lunch. This kibbutz was begun in July, 1967, in an effort to locate Israelis on the newly acquired land. We eat lunch in the restaurant of the kibbutz. It is obvious that this is a relatively new project as all of the people are young, in their teens, twenties, or thirties. Everything looks like the first day of camp with repairs and improvements needed everywhere. The young men and girls were smiles and seriousness both at once.

Upon someone's asking why these have come, our guide answers boldly and vigorously, "Because Israel needs a settlement here; and because they have a hope of making money also." We ate and talked. The prices were very low and everyone seemed willing to share with anyone. The bathroom was composed of a tiled floor with an opening where a receptacle shaped like a toilet bowl should fit on top; yet there was no bowl and it did not look as if one was to be put there—as the floor was perfectly tiled with inch by inch tiles.

As we motor southeast everywhere the fields are separated here by walls made of piled rocks gathered from the fields. Here the walls are generally about three feet high. They enclose lots about 100 by 200 feet, walled on all four sides. Near houses the stone walls run higher and mortar work is evident. These are animal enclosures, property dividers, and private yards. Such walls cover the landscape everywhere here in "Golani." I try to grasp the number of rocks and as I muse, seemingly in the distance the voice of our bus leader is urging, "Here live Moslems from Calcutta called, 'Circasans.' "

THE RESCUE OPERATION

An army truck in front of us has lost its right rear wheel amid the pouring rain, and our bus is giving the stranded Israeli soldiers a lift. They pile in with packs on their backs and submachine guns in their hands. One sits beside me. We have not traveled a quarter of a mile but a ruckus has developed. The discussion is in Hebrew, with our guide and the soldiers alternating. The soldiers are getting off the bus and each turns as he steps out of the door to make a remark in Hebrew to our guide and to the bus driver. The soldiers want to go in another direction from our route, and the bus driver and guide have apparently said, "No." Our guide is now yelling, and in answer to one soldier's remark, our guide is reciting his own military record. The rain is dashing down, it is cold, and some of the soldiers do not look well dressed. I recall my own past miseries bivouacking in snow. I can't see why the bus cannot take the troops at least to a shelter. I, however, could not follow all of the "Hevreet" (Hebrew) discussion—but our guide's war record was lengthy. The soldiers were now sloshing in the rain yelling epithets as we departed. Roughly translating the gist of them, they were saying, "Stupid...stupid! Why did you pick us up in the first place? We were better off waiting in the damaged truck because at least there we were dry...Why did you pick us up? So you could take us away from our dry truck only to let us off in this awful rain?..So you could laugh?..Stupid fellow...

Golan Heights and the Geography Of Palestine • 119

You are not Israeli...If you were such a good soldier you would know better...The Arabs shot away your brains... Stupid...He was no soldier...Stupid!"

Syrian trucks destroyed by the Israeli Air Force are on the sides of the road and often seen as we drive south parallel to the Upper Jordan above Kinneret Lake with the river ten to fifteen miles to our right (west). My shoes and socks have become soaked from the sundry stoppings, and my feet are desperately cold now. I realize that it is just seven months since the cessation of the hostilities of the June 6-11, 1967 War, though border incidents come daily, and Ezekiel 39:14 comes to mind. This passage tells that it will take seven months for the burying of the bones by Israel of the destroyed northern invading force of Gog (Russia). When that invasion, prophesied in Ezekiel 38:1-39:16 takes place, just as now outside of my bus window, after seven months the debris of war will still be evident. Tanks, trucks, and cars wrecked in the war and mangled entirely steadily mark our pathway.

We are approaching Fik which is a town five miles east of Lake Galilee. Roughly, if you draw a line going east and west through the middle of the Lake, on the west (left, on a map with north at the top) you have Tiberias on the shore line, and on the east five miles from the water you locate Fik. If you continue on six miles to the east you meet the Yarmouk River which here divides Syria to the north from Jordan to the south. Today Fik and the additional six-mile stretch to the Yarmouk River is in Israel's possession; before the June, 1967 War, of course, this land and that of the Golon Heights east of the Lake was entirely in Syrian-Jordanian dominion.

EAST GALILEE'S GOLAN CLIFFS

Our view, as we speed south-still slightly north of Fikis rock walls, a house here and there, and Israeli army camps. These Golan Heights are a vast rock-filled desolate lifted plain crying for a million settlers. The elevation, said our guide, of the Upper Golan Heights north of the Yarmouk River beside Syria varies from 6500 to 1800 feet above sea level; and Lower Golani south of the Yarmouk beside the nation of Jordan goes from 2100 to 900 feet.

With Lake Galilee's waters 600 feet below sea level and Golan so high in cliffs which stand to the edge of the lake, one can quickly understand the account of Matthew 8:28-34. Here in the territory of the Gergasenes, just to the right of our bus, near the edge of the lake, this took place. Taking Lake Galilee as a clock, with 12 to the north, this would place Gergasa at the 3, near Fik. There at Christ's presence there was a remarkable and unique manifestation of the supernatural world. Two men possessed of demons came out of the tombs and the demons in them said to Christ, "What have we to do with thee, Jesus, thou Son of God? art thou come hither to torment us before the time?...If thou cast us out, suffer us to go away into the herd of swine." Christ said to them, "Go," and the great herd of swine "ran violently down a steep place into the sea, and perished in the waters" (Matt. 8:29-32). Here the Golon Heights run up to the edge of Lake Galilee and then they fall off in sharp precipices. The cliffs drop into the Lake suddenly and one can visualize the swine running westward, and then, when the land was no more, plunging down into the water below.

Were the demons real? Yes. Why do I think so? I think that they were permitted by the Divine Governor of the Universe to be especially active and manifest when the Son of God walked upon the earth. Thus we read of things not commonly experienced today. Also, Christ's life and words everywhere testified that He only uttered the absolute truth (John 14:6). When Christ entered into *conversations* with the demons He left us with the incontrovertible impression that they really existed. He did not deceive us. And here on Golani's cliffs their helplessness before His majesty, their malignity, and their true existence were all manifested.

THE DECAPOLIS CITIES

We are pulling into Fik. One person in our bus is pointing to a lone donkey, very young, standing abandoned near the now evacuated Syrian-Jordanian army camp. Because of the 1967 War, Fik is now a desolate void. Only six miles into the new

Israel territory it is much too close for raiders to be a place to raise a family. Now another person is standing and pointing through the windows on the right. Here Lake Galilee is in perfect view. It is surrounded by mountains, except for a slight breach to the south where it pours into the Jordan. It can be well pictured by one pouring some light blue liquid, perhaps diluted blueberry juice, into a cereal bowl. The sides of the bowl represent the mountains and the central liquid the lake. The lake is exquisitely beautiful and tranquil in appearance, deceptively so. It is a living optical illusion, for the mountains on all sides make it look so small that one could throw a stone across it or yell to a friend on the other side, but yet it is eight by fifteen miles, and, despite its appearance, those mountains are far away across those waves and the voice crying to the other side will never be heard. Here our hearts leap as we think of the wondrous signs that Christ did on this lake.

The rain is dropping sparsely now. Our bus empties as we stop south of Fik to walk through a Syrian army underground bunker. It slept four on metal beds, although the mattresses are now utter rags. Mud floors. Such hidden underground burrows are everywhere in this region east of the Lake. Would that they will not be used again, but men are again already crying out words of hate and breathing out threats.

Before us now stands one of the towns of the Decapolis (Greek for "Ten Cities") which originally were ten Greek colonial cities occupied at first in 200 B.C., all but one being east of the Jordan. They were named, according to Pliny: Scythopolis (Beit Shean or Bethshan, the one west of Jordan), Pella, Dion, Gerasa, Philadelphia, Gadara, Raphana, Kanatha, Hippos, and Damascus. The town we stand at is Hippos, or, as per our guide, "Epospolis." One can note how the hippos("horse" in Greek, as *hippo potamus* or "horse-of-the-river") has come to be "Epos" with "polis," the word for "city," added. It is here, some suggest, that the herd of swine plunged off of Golan's cliffs.

Here in Golani the hills, or mountains, are huge and the valleys are deep chasms dropping down into another world below. Thousands and thousands, not hundreds and hundreds, of rock fences divide the patched fields into a fifty-meter grid pattern. Now, adjacent to us are the ruins of a Russian manufactured K-34 tank beside a double row of yard-cubicle concrete anti-tank barriers.

YARMOUK CHASMS SOUTH OF THE LAKE

We are now about four miles east of the southern tip of Lake Tiberias (Kinneret, Galilee) and below we can see the lake waters rushing into and filling the Jordan River. To our left, east of the Jordan, lies the Yarmouk River Valley. This valley is immense, beyond anything imagined. Here the heights of the mountains and the depths of the valleys are an indescribable sight. At every new twist of our bus along this winding road a new gorge is revealed gouged deeply into mother earth. The plunges down are fatal precipices and the ride has become breath-taking and spectacular. Some of our passengers look white with fright. The Yarmouk Valley, cutting its way southwestward in its hurry to join the Jordan seven miles below the Lake, is cliff-lined like the Grand Canyon, only not as deep. The walls, however, especially those on the eastern side, are sheer drops. The Yarmouk Irrigation Canal and the rich banana fields of its valley, Israeli and Jordanian, are before us.

Israeli armed guards are posted here on the road at every half mile. At last we are crossing the Jordan and it is here the greenest water that I have ever seen. In fact, until now, except for paintings, I do not recall ever having actually seen bright light green water, but it is real, and it is matchless.

From the Jordan intercept at the south tip of the Lake of Galilee it is but ten kilometers north to the city of Tiberias which was our starting point. As we drive we behold that it is raining on the Lake. Storms rise suddenly on this water, and we recall Christ's stilling the winds and the waves (Matt. 8:23-27). "But the men marvelled, saying, What manner of man is this, that even the winds and the sea obey him!" (v.27).

Despite the rain reducing the visibility we could still spy out the cliffs of the Golon Heights rising majestically on the east side of the Lake. They tower above the waters and are easily seen. Here as we ride north on the west bank of the Lake's southern half, we ride along the shore line with our wheels not far from the water. Mountains are to our left—outside of the

Golan Heights and the Geography Of Palestine • 123

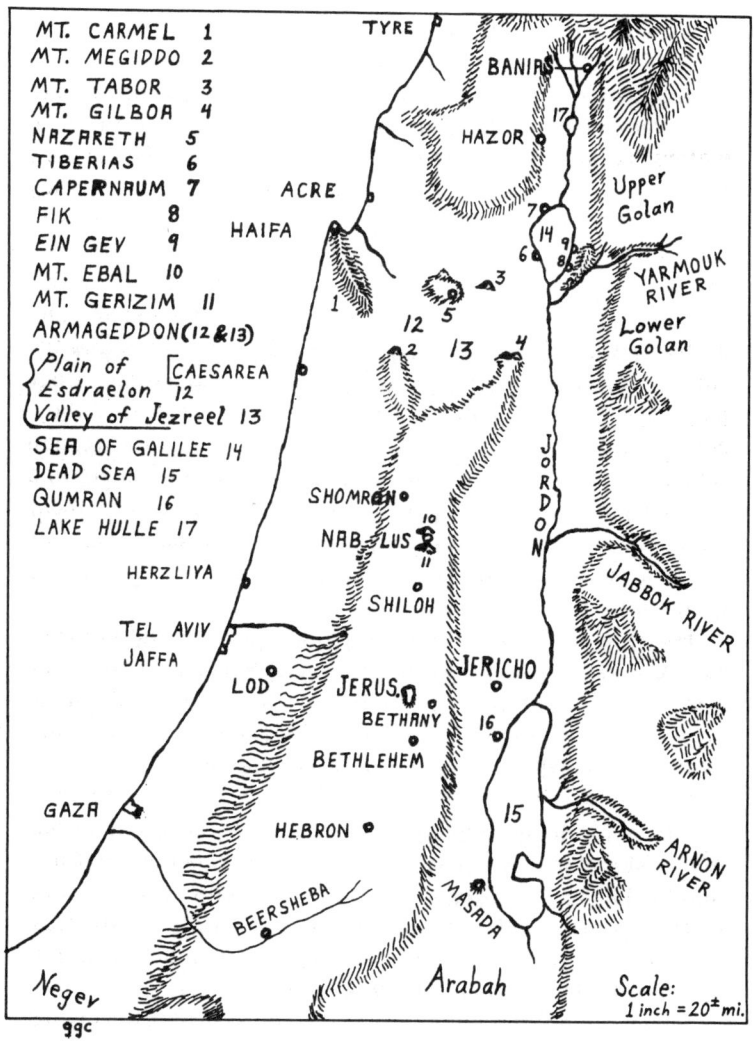

road. Palm trees line the water, and the scene reminds one of Florida. From here the viewer sees the unbroken ring of the Lake.

Upon entrance into Tiberias people are let off at the various hotels. The tour time was 9 to 4:40; the distance traveled was about 110 miles; and the route was from Tiberias around Lake Kinneret clockwise going as far north as Hermon's southern foot and crossing Golan Heights to the east of the Lake.

* * * * * *

THE GEOGRAPHY OF PALESTINE

On reaching the hotel I pointed out for our group on a sketched map the basic geographic layout of Palestine. Now that we had traversed much of the land, this study was more meaningful and quickly absorbed.

First, we observe the shape of the coast and the positions of the Dead Sea (1300 feet below sea level) and of Lake Galilee (600 feet below sea level) with the Jordan River flowing south connecting the two. Note that Haifa on Mt. Carmel is located on the coast about one-third down where it projects into the Mediterranean.

The three principal rivers that flow into the Jordan and Dead Sea are next to be positioned. These three are to the east of the Jordan, with the Yarmouk pouring into it just south of Lake Galilee. The Jabbok enters it between the Lake and the Dead Sea, and then the Arnon roughly bisects the Dead Sea itself.

The chief geographical regions of this area must be imagined as lanes running north and south (see map). These lanes will be easily observed once the two north-south lanes of mountains are emplaced. Between the Mediterranean coast and the Jordan runs the *"Central Mountain Range."* Next the *"Eastern Plateau" Mountain Range* running also north-south just east (right side) of the Jordan and Dead Sea is to be noted.

Now observe each of the north-south lanes into which Palestine falls:

On the far west along the coast we have (1) the *Maritime Plain* with the northern section called the "Plain of Sharon"

A Bedouin child living in the Sinai desert.

Remains of an old olive press that was typical of that used in the days of the Bible. Olive oil was not only a prime article of food, but it was used for cooking, for anointing, and as the fuel for oil lamps to give light. Anointing the head of a guest with oil was a mark of high courtesy (Luke 7:46). The large stone roller was usually turned by ox or donkey-power.

A rainbow over the Sea of Galilee.

128 • ISRAEL Land of Promise, Land of Prophecy

Even today you can witness this scene in the Holy Land. An Arab couple going to market...the husband riding on a donkey, the wife walking alongside.

Worshipping in Jerusalem.

Israeli farmers gather in the Jordan Valley to celebrate Shabuoth. This festival commemorates God's giving of the Ten Commandments to Moses. It is held at the time of the first wheat harvest, and thus it is also known as the Wheat Festival.

130 • ISRAEL Land of Promise, Land of Prophecy

Mt. Hermon, 9,101 feet above sea level, is by far the highest mountain in or near Palestine. Its Baal sanctuaries were well known before the Exodus.

In May 1970, guerrillas attacked this school bus in Moshav Avivim. The result of the blast is pictured.

A lonely sandel is a grim reminder of this bus tragedy where about 13 children lost their lives.

Masada from the air, a view that shows how difficult it would be to storm this fortress.

and the southerly sector the "Plain of Philistia" *or* the "Plain of Ashkelon."

(2) Beside the Maritime Plain, in the lower half of Palestine, there is the *"Shephelah"* or lowlands area, with rising and rolling hills forming a transition between the coastal plain to the west and the mountains to the east.

(3) Then comes the *Central Mountain Range* which is a continuation of the Lebanon mountain chain to the north. This Central Range is broken only in Galilee for the strategic *Armageddon*-Jezreel Valley to provide the east-west pass which leads down to the northern gates of Jerusalem.[1]

(4) Next comes the deep geological rift called the *Jordan Valley.* Notice the steep north-south descent: Starting at the peak of Mt. Hermon to the north at 9100 feet elevation, we reach Hermon's foot at Banias where the elevation is 1700 feet. From this 1700 feet we descend with the Upper Jordan (above Lake Galilee) until we reach the Lake which is 600 feet *below* sea level. Then we travel down the meandering brown Jordan about seventy miles to the Dead Sea, and we have now descended to 1300 feet *below* sea level. Thus nearby Jericho is the lowest city on the earth (except for perhaps other Dead Sea towns).

(5) Finally, to the east of the Jordan is the high *Eastern Plateau* mountain range. It meets the Jordan Valley with its sheer dropping cliffs. The region which we have toured today east of Lake Galilee is called "Golan Heights" and these mounts are part of this plateau. Upper Golani, north of the Yarmouk ranges, is from 6500 to 1800 feet above sea level and Lower Golani varies from 2100 to 900.

Add the location of the important cities and the geography of this region is well nigh mapped out. Also let us note the names of some of the other more renowned sectors. "Trans-Jordan" is that region east of the Jordan; "Galilee" is the land north, west, and south of the Lake; "Judea" is the Jerusalem region west of the Dead Sea; the "Negev" means

---

[1] Going from northwest to southeast this pass-plain through the mountains consists of the Plain of Esdraelon with its twenty battlefields, the Jezreel Valley, and then the north-south lowland pass which reaches down to Jerusalem.

the "Southland" southwest from the Dead Sea; and the "Arabah" is that vicinity between the Dead Sea and Eilat on the Gulf of Akabah. Here the desiccated and arid condition of the land, before the modern irrigation thrust utilizing the sweet waters of Lake Tiberias, earned the region the title of the "Arabah" or "Desert."

* * * * * *

The tour over, the lay of the land absorbed, we retired to prepare ourselves for the night's supper which is traditionally served later in the evening than customary in America. Each person in our party had the evening free. Since it was Sunday, however, it was fitting to devote at least part of the evening to Bible reading and prayer. It was the Lord's Day in the Lord's Land (Isa. 8:8). All was serenity in Tiberias. That evening Professor Dunzweiler and I had a fine opportunity to talk at length with three men staying at the Molan Ginton. Two were Australians visiting Israel and one was an Israeli from the Tel Aviv area here for the mineral baths. They listened eagerly when we told them that we believed Jesus to have fulfilled the predictions surrounding the coming of the Messiah to die as an atonement for sin (Isa. 53:6). They had not realized that the Hebrew prophets had prophesied that the Messiah was to have been born in Bethlehem. We had a fine talk on many subjects.

CHAPTER XI

THE LAKE, BETHSHAN, AND NAZARETH

Wet and dripping were our hands on this Monday morning of *January 15th*. Our group had just driven slightly below Tiberias after breakfast and we had now plunged our hands into the water of Lake Galilee. The water is crystal clear and the pebbles below the water are multicolored. Here on the west side there is a flat shore before the outer circle of nearby peaks begins. We beheld the Lake ringed with mountains.

VIGIL OF MOURNING

Facing away from the Lake, across the street, is a cemetery which the map marks as containing "Rabbi Meir's tomb." Such wailing and weeping I had scarcely ever heard before. Had they lost a loved one? Perhaps. Yet, since they wailed while walking from tomb to tomb it seemed to be a vigil. I could not help but recall 1 Thessalonians 4:13-18:

> "But I would not have you to be ignorant, brethren, concerning them which are asleep, that ye sorrow not, even as others which have no hope. For if we believe that Jesus died and rose again, even so them also which sleep in Jesus will God bring with him. For this we say unto you by the word of the Lord, that we which are alive and remain unto the coming of the Lord shall not precede them which are asleep. For the Lord himself shall descend from heaven with a shout, with the

voice of the archangel, and with the trump of God: and the dead in Christ shall rise first: Then we which are alive and remain shall be caught up together with them in the clouds, to meet the Lord in the air: and so shall we ever be with the Lord. Wherefore comfort one another with these words."

Riding south ten miles we came to the Lake Galilee-Jordan River Intercept where the Lake waters poured southward forming the source of the Jordan. Then our procession moved another twenty miles southward on a fast road. While moving south we constantly peered to our left observing the Jordan River and its valley east of our highway. The river paralleled us for the entire twenty-mile trip from Lake Galilee to Beit Shean and its distance from us was generally a half mile away. The river's bright green color at its source gradually suffered from the dye of the valley muds, and its hue became a light orange-brown as it wriggled southward to lower elevation.

BEIT SHEAN AND GILBOA

At Beit Shean each person was charged 1.50 Israeli pounds (lire) to enter the historic area. My ticket was number 23331 and the proprietorship was attributed to the "Society for Landscaping and the Preservation of Historic Sites." The Arab man who sold us the tickets was most polite. We were the only ones there at the time.

The green sloping flat-topped *tel* of the Biblical Bethshan looked the same as all of the other *tels*, but its excitement was not in the shape of the *tel* but rather in the history that it held. After King Saul and Jonathan were slain on Mt. Gilboa in the Armageddon-Jezreel Valley, here upon this very hill the Philistines hung their bodies upon the wall in Bethshan's Philistine temple. This occurred in 931 B.C. Further, 1 Samuel 31:12 tells us that the men of Jabesh-gilead arose in the night and risked their lives to rescue the bodies of Saul and Jonathan from these walls of Bethshan. Why did they do it? Answer: Because they were grateful to Saul for having saved them years before from Nahash the Ammonite who purposed to gouge out the eyes of all of the men of Jabesh (1 Samuel 11). Saul had risked his life and kingdom to save Jabesh; thus the men of Jabesh made a forced march through the night to reclaim the body of their former protector. They and Bethshan are a reminder to all of us to be loyal to those who have helped us in the past.

This *tel* of *Bethshan* is known as Tel el-Husn, and the Arab village of *Beisan* is nearby. From the name "Beisan" one can see the general permanence of names, with slight changes through centuries, in this part of the world. This *tel* was first excavated by the University of Pennsylvania in 1921-1933, and at present eighteen occupational levels have been identified extending back in time to about 3500 B.C.[1]

From Bethshan or Beit Shean, as pronounced today, we drove westerly some 36 kilometers to Nazareth. As we drove west we picked up an Israeli soldier. When we were only six miles out of Bethshan we began to drive by a mountain which was to our immediate south and which ran east and west for the next eight miles. I said to the trooper in our car, *Mah Harim aleh?* ("What mountains are these?") He responded, *Har Gilboa* ("Mt. Gilboa")! As Professor Dunzweiler drove we marveled and wondered at Gilboa's peaks, 1696 feet, where Saul and Jonathan had met their end. We could see in our mind's eye as we drove by that Philistine-Israelite struggle which claimed Saul three millennia ago.

AN ARAB RUNS TOWARD US

Our vehicles pulled into Nazareth. *Natzarot* means "seedling" or "branch" as in Isaiah 11:1 where it refers to the Messiah who shall grow up as a seedling from the nation of Israel.

We drove into the city and saw a parking area behind a large church. Pulling up, at once a middle-aged and fairly heavy Arab gentleman, well dressed in a suit, ran toward us. "Oh, oh, we must not be allowed to park here," moaned Professor Dunzweiler. Soon it was all clear. This gentleman explained that we had driven into the parking lot of the Church of the Annunciation and he was in charge of providing tours! An Arab young man in his early twenties was then promptly

---

[1] See *Archaeology and Bible History* by Joseph P. Free, 5th ed., Scripture Press, 1956, pp. 6-8, etc., on this mound.

introduced to us as our guide for the next hour and a half. He spoke flawless English and one would have taken this well dressed fellow to be a graduate student in some nearby university.

WONDROUS NAZARETH

He told us of Nazareth, this town in the midst of Israel which lies between the Mediterranean and the southern tip of Lake Galilee. The Boy Jesus grew up here on this elevated hillside village which rests in the midst of a basin of nearby surrounding hills. From these hills He could behold Mt. Carmel's heights to the west, Hermon's white peaks to the north, and Mt. Tabor's round summit to the east. To the south He could gaze across a gorge to the score of battlefields below lying in the great Esdraelon-Armageddon plain. Via the Damascus-Egypt trade caravans which skirted these hills, news would reach His ears telling of the decree of the emperor, the illness of the king-Pharaoh, and whispering of the words of the Jerusalem rabbis. This was the hidden but exciting Nazareth of Christ's youth. It had only one spring of water, yet it was a village washed by the history of the Israel which surrounded it on every side. Here the Boy Jesus grew up beholding the history of the Bible in every direction that He could peer.

We soon learned that Nazareth was the city in Israel with the greatest percentage of Christians, and that they were Arab Christians, Catholic, Greek Orthodox, and Protestant. The guide told us that in the recent June, 1967, War the Nazareth Christian Arabs did not fight against Israelis. In fact, later we learned of a slogan of some of the Moslems in that war, viz., "After Saturday comes Sunday." This meant that after they had wiped out the Jews who hold Saturday to be their Sabbath, they would next slay the Christians (Arabic included) who venerated Sunday. The Moslems, of course, celebrate Friday as their holy day.

It began to snow and the guide told us that we were experiencing weather which came only once in fifteen years. We were then shown the Basilica of the Annunciation still under construction, which had within it the Grotto of the

Annunciation. Here stood the most striking eight-pointed, star-shaped basilica with its great dome of white stone above. Inside of this million-dollar church, with all of its modern vaults and arches, there was a ground floor surrounded by a raised balcony octagonal in shape. Then at the very center, on the ground floor amid all that spoke of the newness of our day, was the approximately twelve-foot cubicle of ancient rock which had within it the traditional Grotto of the Annunciation. Around this rock cube were the remains of the pillars and walls of a Byzantine Crusaders' church. Can you see this picture? The outer ring is composed of the 1968 basilica; within that the next ring is formed from a Byzantine period (A.D. 330-640) church now seen only from its pillars and ruins; and within that at the center is the Grotto of the Annunciation made sacred some two thousand years ago, c. 4 B.C. Thus those who sit in this modern ediface look from their brand new seats and see the two-thousand-year-old Grotto before them.

We entered the Grotto itself. It was believed to have been part of Mary's home here in Nazareth. The stone and wood houses here were built in front of a cave on the hillside, the cave serving as our underground cellars do today. Upon the altar of the Grotto were inscribed words, *Verbum caro hic factum est* ("Here the Word became flesh").

Next we were taken to the adjacent St. Joseph's Church. Here was the site identified by the brilliant and careful Eusebius and Constantine's mother, Helena, c. 325 A.D., as the house where Joseph and Mary and the young Jesus lived and where the carpenter shop was. Under the home's level was a storage room grotto (the shop?) which had below it an immense water cistern in the rock. The cistern struck me to be the size of an average room, but we could only peer down into it through a floor hole in the rock. It must have been originally a natural air space within the rock. We saw the fifth century square and deep baptistry which one had to descend into by its stone steps.

After this we walked to Gabriel's Greek Orthodox Church which also claims to be the site of the Annunciation. Beside this church is the authentic "Mary's Well," so named because the women of this vicinity, which would have certainly included Mary, used to come here for their water. Here, as in almost all of the Greek Orthodox churches, it was what Americans would consider as overly-decorated. Pictures were everywhere, as were icons, and hanging sacred metal balls. I accepted the offer to drink some water from Mary's well; Professor Dunzweiler declined questioning its sanitation. He did not, of course, tell the monk at the church his reason. The others also were split on whether or not to drink.

SMALL SYNAGOGUE

Next we visited the small synagogue, restored, which Christ regularly attended "as his custom was" (Luke 4:16) as a youth. It was small; what an example! We then visited the "Shook" or old market place of the city, and inspected with delight the wares of the poor but very polite Arab merchants. Farewelling and tipping our guide, giving him a tract also, we drove north to leave this city. As we motored away we saw the northern section, New Nazarot, which is the modern Jewish section. The Israeli government has encouraged this section's growth and here are the modern apartment houses. The government, apparently, does not wish to see any one town or city become a ghetto for any one religion, race, or clan; thus they have encouraged Israelis to live in "Nazarot."

Just as we had seen on our entrance into the city from the south, now also as we left it going north, we spied its high escarpments. Perhaps when Christ said, "A city that is set on an hill cannot be hid" (Matt. 5:14), He was thinking of His boyhood and young manhood years when He would be returning home to Nazareth, and as always from a great distance He and those with him would spy their city. The candle and lamp lights would be seen for miles away; it could not be hidden.

As we drove, Mr. Dunzweiler pointed to the city's cliffs and called our attention to Luke 4:16-30:

> "And He came to Nazareth, where He had been brought up; and as was His custom, He entered the synagogue on the Sabbath, and stood up to read . . . the book of the prophet Isaiah . . . The Spirit of the Lord is upon Me. Because He anointed ("Messiahed") Me to preach the gospel to the poor. He has sent Me to proclaim release to the captives, And

recovery of sight to the blind, To set free those who are downtrodden, To proclaim the favorable year of the Lord" *(vv. 16-19, New American Standard Bible).*

Then Luke says, "He closed the book, and gave it back to the attendant, and sat down; and the eyes of all in the synagogue were fixed upon Him." After this some became infuriated with Christ's rebuking their unbelief by telling them that the Prophet Elijah did not stay with any of the many widows in Israel, but with a Gentile widow; and God did not cleanse in the days of the Prophet Elisha any of the many lepers of Israel, but only Naaman who was a leper from Syria, a Gentile. This so enraged the people that they sought to cast Him off of "the brow of the hill on which their city had been built, in order to throw Him down the cliff." We could well understand this as we looked with amazement at the sheer drops from Nazareth's heights. Such unbelief was not merely an intellectual position; it was a sinful rebellion against God and His Christ whose coming was self-authenticating. Unbelief then and now has a fury that when once aroused knows no bounds.

As we darted away our minds went to Luke 1:26-38, Gabriel's Annunciation to Mary in Nazareth telling this young Jewess that she was to have the supreme honor of bearing the Messiah, the Christ Child. This passage is one of the most beautiful in all the world.

Why did it happen here in Nazareth, a city that had a bad reputation? Nathaniel, when told by Philip that he had found the Messiah who was "Jesus of Nazareth," responded with the question, "Can any good thing come out of Nazareth?" (John 1:46.) Philip answered him with a classic reply, "Come and see," which has ever been the challenge of the born-again Christian to the non-Christian. Living in a town with a poor reputation, attending only a small synagogue, in youth left as the elder brother to help support His widowed mother and family—thus in every way the Son of God's taking upon His divine-eternally-existing-person a body of flesh in this sin-cursed world was a humiliation. Here in Nazareth "the Word became flesh." Christ is the Word, the outward manifestation of the unseen God, just as an oral "word" is an outward manifestation of what is inside of our hearts. This is the Hebrew concept of the "Word," of the *logos* (*mamre* in the Hebrew), and it is different from the Platonic-Greek concept of the *logos* which stood for a pre-existent *idea* state. Philippians 2:5-11 gives the classic passage on the humiliation of Christ, and this was in our minds long after Nazareth passed out of our sight. Yes, in Nazareth in Galilee of the Gentiles, "the people that walked in darkness have seen a great light" (Isa. 9:1,2).

* * * * * *

We then drove the twenty miles northeastward back to Tiberias from Nazarot. That evening for supper we were served St. Peter's Fish, the delicacy of the Lake. Professor Dunzweiler was not feeling too well and missed this supper. At this the subject of illness and suffering came up, and some of us sitting at the same table discussed it at no small length. We did this by considering the words of Christ in John 9:1-3:

> "And as Jesus passed by, he saw a man which was blind from his birth. And his disciples asked him, saying, Master, who did sin, this man, or his parents, that he was born blind? Jesus answered, Neither hath this man sinned, nor his parents: but that the works of God should be made manifest in him."

After having considered this subject, our conversation became chatter on topics of local interest. Dessert was consumed, while we scheduled our next seminar hour for the evening of the following day. It would be held right before the customary "Dinner at Seven" of the area, and it would leave the evening free.

Upon retiring from the hotel's dining area we talk with some of the other guests. It is evening and raining again. Storms seem to enter the scene suddenly in this Lake Kinneret Basin.

CHAPTER XII

CROSSING THE LAKE; EIN GEV; AND THE LIFE OF CHRIST

When the engines of the boat began to hum Professor Robert J. Dunzweiler's watch read 10:30 on this warm but windy Tuesday morning of *January 16th*. All of our party were aboard, along with others, as we were weighing anchor from Tiberias bound for Ein Gev which lay about seven miles across Lake Galilee to the east. The boat slowly pulled out with thirty total passengers upon its lower and upper decks. Its capacity looked to be about twenty above and twenty below.

This was one of the three trips run by this boat line, *Hevrat Shait Kinnereth, Ltd.*, of Tiberias, and the only one departing on this particular Tuesday morning. As the boat motored deeper out to sea I inquired of the Captain as to the dimensions of the Lake. His figures were 22.5 by 12.5 kilometers which would be 13.6 miles north-south and 7.6 miles east-west. The maps, encyclopedias, and almanacs, however, all offer slightly varying figures for these distances. These discrepancies, I like to think, result not from over-all sloppiness and inaccuracy on the part of so many who should have expertise in this field, but rather because—I hope—each encyclopedia independently measured the lake at different times when the varying water levels would cause varying length-width statistics. In any case, the figures differ.

The depth of the sea is "about 160 feet," said the Captain. This figure was also a disappointment for I had expected a seafaring man to respond with, "26.6 fathoms, mate." Besides this, a travel book said that it was 195 feet deep. The elevation was 686 feet below sea level, I knew, according to the Merriam-Webster *Gazetteer*; and not being confident that the Captain had adequate equipment for confirming this, I returned to watching the waves.

It is exhilarating to be upon these waters fished by Peter and Andrew, and James and John. Here Christ performed the miracle of stilling the storm (Matt. 8:23-27), and here upon these waters Jesus walked (John 6:16-21). The two miraculous draughts of fish were pulled forth at the Master's word from out of these waves (Luke 5:1-11; John 21:4-12); and many was the time when the multitudes of the listeners forced Christ to teach from a boat a little way from the land (Luke 5:1-3). And it was from these waters that Christ issued His challenge to Peter, Andrew, James, and John, viz., "Come ye after me, and I will make you to become fishers of men" (Mark 1:17).

SIGHTS UPON THE WATERS

Upon reaching the middle of the Lake, from the upper deck I cast my eyes about in a full 360 degree revolution. The Golan Heights to the northeast stood fast as one huge cliff. Mountains could be seen in every direction. There was only one low spot on the ring, where in the southern point the sea flows into the Jordan. Yet even here one could see the peaks farther to the south beyond. We are nestled in a mountain-basin Lake. What a joy it is to see, hear, and feel the waves of this hallowed ancient Lake. The spray blows in our faces, as we cling to the railings with delight as the waves heave us upward.

It was a clear day and from our position on the center of this sea we easily saw *Har Meiron*, Mount Meiron, which was the tallest peak entirely within Israel. It was about eighteen miles to the northwest of us, towering white, and its elevation of 3962 feet above sea level meant that it was 4648 feet above our below sea level Lake (-686 ft.). At an azimuth of twenty degrees east of north our eyes met Mount Hermon lunging above the Golan Heights and piercing the sky with its 9,232-feet height. Its southern foot now within Israel's borders, was forty miles distant from us and its northern foot another forty. A range in itself, dividing Lebanon from Syria, dressed in its frosty white ermine, it commanded the northern view in its silent and stable regal stance.

Our vessel churned through the now wave-covered, clear, blue water as spume, froth, and foam sprayed our faces as each new breaker crashed and splashed against us as it dashed itself upon our bow and beam. The wind, I suppose, rated now a number 5 on Beaufort's scale with the label of, "Fresh breeze, 19 to 24 mph." The boat swayed to and fro slightly as we sailed on. Because of the mountain ring and its illusory effect, at every moment it appeared to us that we were only a hundred yards from our destined shore. Yet, like the mythical Tantalus, the boat seemed never to reach the other side. [1]

At sighting with our own eyes within these sacred waves a school of fish, someone gave a cry which would vie in gusto with that much coveted first "white whale ho" under Ahab's flag. When near the east bank, we saw hundreds of minnows in the water. The previous evening we had dined on St. Peter's Fish, the specialty and treat of this sea, yet its most abundant crop is sardine. One on board told us that the Lake yielded many fish in quantity including the catfish which was not *kosher* or "clean" because it had no scales. Thus the orthodox Jewish people never eat it. (Compare with Peter himself in Acts 10:14 when the apostle declared, ". . . for I have never eaten any thing that is common or unclean." To this the Lord rejoined, "What God hath cleansed, that call not thou common" (v. 15), teaching Peter and all of the apostles that, with the sacrifice of the Messiah, God had opened up a fountain of cleansing for the Gentiles as well as for the Jews.)

---

[1] Tantalus, though he was a son of Zeus, was supposedly punished by being put in the nether world in water up to his chin with fruit laden branches floating on the waters. Each time he lowered his head to drink or went to eat the fruit the waters would lower and the fruit branches would sail away on a wave. He never could reach his goal. He was constantly *tantalized*.

EIN GEV

As we neared our shore line destination, Professor pointed our group's eyes to two fishermen engaged in cleaning and repairing their nets. When Christ gave His call to James and John to leave their fishing occupation and to follow Him as disciples, these two brothers were "in a ship with Zebedee their father, mending their nets" (Matt. 4:21).

We put ashore at last at Kibbutz Ein Gev, and walked the planked piers to the land some forty yards beyond. A gray-haired resident of this community was presented as our guide for a half hour's tour of this village on the east bank of this Lake. This guide looked to be sixty-five or seventy in age; he walked with a quick gait, and his speech was enthusiastic yet sage. His English was flawless and quick, though it had more of an American sound than the usual Israeli-British ring.

Someone: "And what does Ein Gev mean?"
Steve Reed: "Does it have to mean anything? It just means Ein Gev—it's a name."
Arlene: "Oh, Steven, don't always have a comment."
Guide: "Why don't I supply the answer? Ein Gev is Hebrew with *ein* representing 'spring' or 'eye' and *gev* translated as 'fountain.' Thus our name "Ein Gev" is 'Spring of a Fountain.'

"As we walk around be careful not to fall into one of these seven-foot trenches. These provided a network for our four hundred people to flee to shelter whenever Syrian shelling started before and during the June, 1967 War. Since then our fighting forces have taken us off of the border and put a ten-mile buffer zone between us and any enemy's potential artillery fire."
Dr. Schatz: "I thought that this entire eastern shore of the Lake was in Syrian hands before the Six Day War of June, 1967? So how were you here before the war?"
Guide: "Sir, we have been here for thirty years. At the end of the 1948 War for Independence Israel owned the entire western shore and the southern half of the eastern shore. Syria had the northern half of the east shore. But this kibbutz was here a decade even before 1948."

Crossing The Lake; Ein Gev; And The Life Of Christ • 147

From here we were taken to see fig trees and many other types of arboreal vegetation. Next, we stood before an auditorium which was immense for a kibbutz of four hundred souls. It was explained that it had a capacity of three thousand and it was used for concerts which drew music lovers from all of the north country. Upon someone's inquiring on how it came to be constructed, it being so large and financial resources of the Kibbutz appearing to be only moderate, it was explained that American Allied-Jewish Appeal funds and other funds had made it possible.

The entire settlement was most clean, the people dressed nicely, and there were many private dwellings. Initiated three decades ago from nothing, it was now a well ordered and fairly prosperous community with many children who looked to be well cared for and happy.

Guide: "My son was an Israeli frogman in the June, 1967 War. He was one of ten captured by the Egyptians, and now tomorrow we expect him to be released and to come home. That is why you see some of these flags up; they are in anticipation of his soon arrival.

"This bronze statue on the waterfront before us shows a woman holding up her baby toward the sky. She represents an Israeli widow who has lost her husband in our fighting for survival. She is holding up her child to heaven symbolic of our belief that the children are Israel's hope for the future."

Barbara Miller: "And these Hebrew words on this metal plaque upon the stone wall?"

Guide: "*Vehabonim esh charbo ahsoorim al-matnayi oovonim*, 'And the builders, each man having his sword girded upon his side, were building. Nehemiah 4:12.'

"It is 4:12 in the Hebrew verse numbering; in your English Bible the same verse in the same place may have a different numbering. I think that it is 4:18."

Barbara: "But there is no difference between the English and the Hebrew, is there?"

Prof. Dunzweiler: "No, you see the English is a translation of the Hebrew. Whatever is in the Hebrew is translated into

English; what is not in the Hebrew, of course, is not in the English. The verse numbering varies a bit in places, but the text is identical."

Arnold Escourt: "Is that a *tel* over there immediately behind the kibbutz? It looks extremely similar to those that we have already seen."

Guide: "You are quite right, that is Tel Hippos, one of the mounds of the ten ancient Hellenistic decapolis cities. Tourists have not been permitted there for over half a year now because of danger of Syrian shelling."

Lunch at the Molon Ginton awaited us upon our return. Various members of our party did sundry things. Professor Dunzweiler drove quietly off to Safad, a city twenty miles north of Tiberias. From there he jaunted the short distance to Mt. Meiron, Israel's highest peak. There he saw children from the local kibbutzim who were brought to the mount so as to see and touch their first snow. A lady told him that it had not snowed in Safad since 1950. The children were in ecstacy as they smelled, tasted, felt, and hurled the charming white frosty crystals.

At six o'clock, our group was dressed for dinner and assembled in one of the rooms of the Ginton.

ORIENTATION TO LIFE OF CHRIST

Prof. Dunzweiler: "While here in Galilee where Christ spent so much of His life, we thought that it would be profitable to devote an hour at this point to orient everyone on some of the basic aspects of the ministry of Jesus Christ. At this point I am going to give out mimeographed charts."

Casting nets in Galilee.

Where the Jordan River meets the Sea of Galilee.

A typical food market in Israel reveals the abundance of fresh produce in this land due to irrigation.

The Dead Sea with its familiar salt towers. The Dead Sea is 1286 feet below sea level, 46 miles long. Its greatest breadth is 10 miles, and its greatest depth is 1400 feet. As a consequence of the extraordinary evaporation, the liquid remaining in the immense basin contains approximately 25% mineral substances, 7% of which is salt.

THE LIFE OF CHRIST

	Matthew	Mark	Luke	John
The Years of Preparation				
Dec. 5 B.C.–Dec. 26 A.D.	1–2		1–2; 3:23–38	1:1–18
I. The Year of Inauguration				
a. Beginnings				
Dec. 26–Apr. 27	3:1–4:11	1:1–13	3:1–22; 4:1–14	1:15–2:12
b. Judea				
Apr. 27–Dec. 27				2:13–4:42
II. The Year of Popularity				
Galilee				
Dec. 27–Dec. 28	4:12	1:14	4:14	4:43
III. The Year of Opposition	to	to	to	to
a. Galilee				
Dec. 28–Apr. 29	15:20	7:23	9:17	6:71
b. Galilee and Golan Heights Apr. 29–Oct. 29 (Much time alone with the disciples)	15:21–18:35	7:24–9:50	9:18–50	
c. Judea				
Oct. 29–Dec. 29			9:51–13:21	7:1–10:39
The Last Months				
Judea and Perea				
Dec. 29–Apr. 30	19–20	10	13:22–19:27	10:40–12:11
The Last Week and After				
Apr. 30–May 30				
(1) The Passion Week	21–27	11–15	19:28–23:56	12:12–19
(2) The Olivet Discourse: Christ tells of his coming again in power and glory	24–25	13	21	
(3) The Resurrection and Ascension	28	16	24	20–21

For the next thirty minutes Professor Dunzweiler discussed the chart, attempting in his characteristic manner carefully and graciously to answer any questions that arose.

At the start of the second half of the seminar period Mr. Dunzweiler explained the Christian belief that Christ had died to make an atonement for our sins—not *merely* as a "good example." Upon his being certain that all understood this crucial point, he next distributed a second mimeographed page which had the following Scripture passage (1 Peter 2:21-25) on it:

> "21 For even hereunto were ye called: because Christ also suffered for us, leaving us an example, that ye should follow his steps:
> 22 Who did no sin, neither was guile found in his mouth:
> 23 Who, when he was reviled, reviled not again; when he suffered, he threatened not; but committed himself to him that judgeth righteously:
> 24 Who his own self bare our sins in his own body on the tree, that we, being dead to sins, should live unto righteousness: by whose stripes ye were healed.
> 25 For ye were as sheep going astray; but are now returned unto the Shepherd and Bishop of your souls."

On the lower half of the handout were the following words from page 291 of Arthur T. Pierson's *Knowing the Scriptures (Gospel Publishing House, N.Y., 1910)*. These comments referred to 1 Peter 2:21-25, above. They are as follows:

> "The Life of Christ which is held up as a "writing copy" for our close imitation (v. 21) is presented:
> First, in its practical sinlessness—"who did no sin" (v. 22).
> Second, in its faultless speech—"neither was guile found in his mouth" (v. 22).
> Third, its perfect self-control—"When he was reviled, reviled not again" (v. 23).
> Fourth, its faultless temper—"when he suffered, he threatened not" (v. 23).
> Fifth, its absolute committal to the Father—". . . but committed himself to him that judgeth righteously" (v. 23).
> Sixth, its self-sacrifice for human salvation—"who his own self bare our sins in his own body on the tree" (v. 24).
> What is further to be desired in an example for imitation?
> Disciples may here see a pattern of faultless conduct, speech, disposition, and even manners; with a will full of energy in all self-government, yet in all things surrendered to the will of God, and, to crown all the rest, sublime self-oblivion for the sake of others."

Minutes later we entered the Ginton's dining quarters. The lake, Ein Gev, and Safad with its Har Meiron were glorious today. Climaxing this, however, was our consideration of that perfect life which was lived upon this soil two millennia ago.

CHAPTER XIII

ROSH PINA; MAGDALA; AND CAPERNAUM

The morning and afternoon were unscheduled and free on this Wednesday, *January 17th*, the fourteenth day of our trek. As crows scattering, our small tribe dispersed into the various directions of the compass rose. To my lot fell the use of the rented French-made miniature vehicle signed out to "Bob Dunzweiler."

SHORT OF CASH

My aim was the north and with this path in mind I fled Tiberias at 9 a.m. driving toward Tel Hatzor (the *tel* of Hatzor or Hazor) which was twenty miles northward. Upon making contact with the mount I parked, and walked up the path. My desire was to explore the *tel*. Three days before while on the bus tour we had been at this site, but then time did not enable us actually to visit the summit of the mound itself. To my utter shock and dismay the man at the tiny booth said that the entrance fee here was twenty Israeli pounds which at one American dollar for three and a half Israeli pounds came to $5.72. This amount was far out of line with the price of entrance to the Megiddo and Bethshan *tels*, but perhaps this higher charge is made because Tel Hazor lies immediately beside a road in Galilee which seemed to be more traveled than the paths near the others. In any case, coming here so rarely it would be penny-wise and pound-foolish, considering the air travel cost, etc., not to see the *tel* while here.

Thus, after deciding to pay and enter, my eyes were almost beclouded with tears at my gaze into my wallet. In changing this money for this person and that for that person, I had only nineteen pounds and my travelers checks were at the hotel! Purposing to return later, I set my course for due south and the home base.

I stopped a mile from the Hazor *tel* and left the car to stare and appreciate Mt. Hermon whose south foot was twenty miles to the north northeast. It was a majestic white, and as it stood so much higher than the Golan Heights peaks to its right, east, it turned them into shallow hills.

It is most warm and I stand in shirt sleeves.

STRANDED IN GALILEE

I climb into the cockpit and again take off. After only one additional minute of movement under my motor's power, without warning the engine in an instant cuts off, and I glide in for a smooth emergency landing on the shoulder of the road. Harumph! No one at all is in sight; there are no houses or buildings of any type in view; no cars are passing; there are only tall green trees lining this lonely road in upper Galilee. A survey of the map indicates my position to be about midway between Tel Hazor which is a mile to the north and the town of Rosh Pina a mile to the south.

An inspection of the engine displays nothing of significance visually, but when I turn the key to start the auto there is only a slight noise. The lights work. It must be that the gas gauge is inaccurate—and it did read 'low'—and that I have run out of gas. How foolish of me this was. Now I must get the red gas can, put up the emergency reflector triangle which comes with the car, and make a land journey in payment for my lack of alertness.

As I walk southward toward Rosh Pina I hold my hand out for a ride at the lone car which would pass every now and then. Since hitchhiking in Israel is a necessity and much safer than in America, it was not long before someone stopped. It was an Israeli auto supply salesman who had a dozen years before emigrated from Australia. He first took me back to my car so that he might examine it.

When success in attempting to start the engine proved elusive, he told me to put the required emergency reflector triangle inside of the car and to set it up in the rear window. The directions on the triangle, I explained, called for the warning triangle to be a hundred feet to the rear of the car. He smiled and said, "That would be very nice, chum, but people are people, and if you leave it a hundred feet behind your auto it will soon be spirited away and then it will be many thousands of feet from the auto and do you small service." "Do you mean that someone might steal it?" quizzed I incredulously. He replied, "Not 'might steal it,' friend, but some rover will positively steal it. In fact, since it has been left out already for fifteen minutes, it is a blooming marvel that you still have it."

As he drove me to Rosh Pina he told me of the snows that had fallen earlier this week in Jerusalem. "It is the first snow there in fifteen years, as I recall," he said, "and some of the tropical type trees like the eucalyptus cannot hold the snow's weight so their branches have broken off everywhere." "Cars have been damaged; it is a shame. They are not prepared to handle snow in Jerusalem—but it is almost gone now and it probably will not come back for a decade."

This fellow was certainly kind. I talked to him more about other matters as he drove me back to the car with the benzine. This did not change anything, so he returned me again to Rosh Pina and bade me adieu. I handed him a "How to Recognize the Messiah" tract and he thanked me for it as he vanished.

RAGE AT ROSH PINA

Fortunately, there was an Avis car rental office at this small town of Rosh Pina! That was a providential blessing, for I had feared the necessity of wiring Haifa or Tel Aviv, and then being possibly delayed for days. The Avis quarters were a tiny wood frame roadside building—though the word "building" is too pretentious a way to describe the place. Just as one labels star magnitudes by comparing the star to be described in relation to two known objects, i.e., brighter than such and such 5th magnitude star but dimmer than such and such 4th magnitude star, I must say that the Avis edifice was below a "building" but greater than a "hut."

It was lunchtime, I was informed at the nearby luncheonette. The manager said that I might as well eat while I waited. She also mentioned that the Avis agent was her son (perhaps in the back room eating?), and that he would take care of me after I had eaten lunch at her counter. I obligingly ordered a corned beef sandwich and an orange soda.

The name of this town is quite interesting. Rosh Pina occurs in the Hebrew Bible in Psalm 118:22. There it says, "The stone which the builders refused has become the *rosh pina*" (the "head-of-the-corner," i.e., the "cornerstone"). In Luke 20:17,18 Christ quotes this verse in the light of the unbelief of the Jewish religious authorities in His Messiahship. He is that stone which they as the builders, the religious authorities, had rejected. Yet God has made Jesus the keystone of true religion, the "cornerstone" from which all else is laid out. Rosh Pina, the name of this small city of Galilee, reminds us of this Old Testament prophecy and of God's fulfillment of it in Christ.

The Avis manager was most cordial despite his youth. He called the mechanic who at once was prepared to depart for the car. "If it can't be fixed, I'll give you another vehicle," promised the manager and I was most pleased with such service. As we started to go, the mechanic asked me, "Is it a French or a Japanese car? We rent both in Israel and I want to know which set of tools to take." Recalling perfectly Professor Dunzweiler's firm words to me, viz., "It's a French built car," without hesitation I so informed the craftsman.

Upon driving out to my nonfunctioning conveyance, the mechanic jumped out of his side of the truck, looked at my car, threw his tools down in a rage, and shouted, "It's Japanese." (Later Professor Dunzweiler explained, "I'm so sorry; the paper I signed said French and when I looked at the car it had 'that foreign look' so I took it uncritically to be French.") Beyond this, the mechanic was cordial, and he soon discovered that it was an electrical short circuit; I had not run out of gas. With thanks I soon was rolling toward Tiberias once more.

Here in Galilee from the car window one sees miles and miles of desolate rock-covered land. Here it surpasses even what I have seen in the southwest of America—miles of nowhere with no man in sight; only rock-covered fields and rock-covered hills and mounts. Boulders, boulders, boulders; all gray, round, and about a foot in diameter! Sheep and cattle came into sight every few miles. This was a land devoid of people.

MAGDALA AND CAPERNAUM

At Tiberias Professor Dunzweiler leaps into the car and we are off again toward Hazor. It is a clear "spring" day in January. Three miles north of Tiberias on the road beside the Lake we halt the car at a yellow sign which reads, "Magdala." Once long ago this place had been called, *Migdal-Nunia*, or "Tower of Fishermen," and today there still stands here a stone tower not too far from the sea. The tower stands out of the ground about fifteen feet and its base is below the road level so that one has to walk down off of the road to get to the tower's door. Perhaps it extends down into the mud and so was higher years before. The sea may also have been adjacent to it then. In any case, once inside with only tiny window openings, it makes the ideal retreat for a few fishermen who wish to eat in seclusion during a storm.

In Matthew 15:39 we see that after Christ had fed four thousand He took a boat and sailed upon Lake Galilee to Magdala, called *Magadan* in the Greek. A famed woman who came to know and to love Jesus as her Saviour came from Magdala; she was "Mary of Magdala," better known as "Mary Magdalene" (Matt. 27:56; Mark 16:1).

Orienting the Lake with twelve o'clock to the north, Tiberias is at the nine position, Magdala is at the ten, and Capernaum is at the eleven. Arriving at Capernaum, we paid a fee and then were treated to walk amid the ruins of the stone synagogue which had been constructed at about the year 200 A.D. It in turn had been built upon and out of the ruins of the Capernaum synagogue in which Christ Himself had taught. As we entered we were confronted by a huge stone wall of the synagogue still standing and in front of this there stood fast four ancient white pillars all joined by a common bridge across their capitals made of huge stone beams. The four pillars had Corinthian style capitals and one had on its face some now much eroded Greek uncial writing. All over this site in an orderly fashion there were the rectangular stones that once made up the walls and other portions of this ornate and good-sized synagogue.

OLIVE PRESS AND MILLSTONE

Nearby was a dark grey basalt olive press assuredly from another millennium. It was composed of a circular base stone which was about two feet high and six feet in diameter. It looked like a huge solid stone stump of a sawed-off giant redwood tree now ossified. Its outer edge had a raised edge all around and the center section was also likewise raised, leaving a circular gouge in the stone the width of which was about a foot and a half. In other words, it would look like your coffee saucer with the outer edge raised and with the center section raised up instead of being depressed. This saucer, however, was six feet in diameter.

Upon the groove or gouge which was one and a half feet wide and which ran in a circle upon the top of the base stone, there stood a one and a half-feet-wide stone wheel which was about two and a half feet in diameter and which had a hole for a wooden axle through its center. The device worked thus: Men or animals on each side would walk in a circle pushing the wooden axle which would in turn push the stone wheel. The stone wheel would then follow the one and a half-feet wide circular groove in a never-ending path around the top of the base. Olives, after pitting, would be placed in the groove on the base and the enormously heavy stone wheel would crush the oil out of them as it made its rounds. Thus was the need supplied for the obedience to such commandments as Exodus 27:20,

> "And thou shalt command the children of Israel, that they bring thee pure oil olive beaten for the light, to cause the lamp to burn always."

We then beheld a millstone. It was about three feet high and also made of the dark grey spotted basalt stone. This, like the olive press, operated by men or beasts turning an upper stone by means of two wooden poles, and the upper stone turning upon a base stone. In the case of this millstone, however, the upper stone was in the shape of a sand-filled egg timer with its top and bottom open. The grain would be placed in the opening at the top and as the hour-glass-shaped upper stone would be rotated the grain would be crushed into flour as it escaped out of the bottom funnel. The bottom of such an upper stone was usually shaped so as to force the grain to move in an outward direction so that it would come under the rotating stone's weight and be crushed into flour.

The upper stone, known as the "millstone," with its height of three feet and widest diameter about two and a half feet, despite the vertical bore which runs through it, must weigh about three hundred pounds. From this we can see the point made by Jesus in Matthew 18:5,6:

> "And whoso shall receive one such little child in my name receiveth me. But whoso shall offend one of these little ones which believe in me, it were better for him that a millstone were hanged about his neck, and that he were drowned in the depth of the sea."

Among other interesting Biblical passages which have light shed upon them by a knowledge of the ancient millstone assembly are: Deuteronomy 24:6; Judges 9:53; 2 Samuel 11:21; Matthew 24:41; Revelation 18:21-22. He or she who has the time to examine them will be rewarded.

Before departing from Capernaum we were handed a small paper which told a great deal of the Biblical history of this place, and which touched us anew as we stood here. This paper said:

Kefar-nahum (City of Nahum)

Position: On the sea road, country of Zebulon and Naphtali (Mt. 4:13-16; Isa. 9:1).

Importance: It was the city of Jesus (Mt. 9:1)—i.e., his headquarters for a season. Levi (Matthew) worked in the custom-house there (Mt. 9:9; Mk. 2:14; Lk. 5:27-29).
Residence of Peter and Andrew (Mk. 1:29).
Synagogue where Jesus taught (Mk. 1:21-29).
In this synagogue was given the "promise of the bread of life" (John 6:24-60).
This city was the scene of numerous miracles, cures, teachings, etc., of Jesus. The most important are given below:—

Miracles:
Jesus walks on the water (Mt. 14:25-33; Mk. 6:48-51).
Jesus stills the tempest (Mt. 8:23-27; Mk. 4:37-40).
The tax and the fish (Mt. 17:23-26).
The daughter of Jairus raised from the dead (Mk. 5:22-43).

Cures:
Man sick of the palsy (Mk. 2:1-12); Leper (Mk. 1:40-25); Man possessed by the unclean spirit (Mk. 1:23-28); Man with withered hand (Mk. 3:1-5); The Centurion's Servant (Mt. 8:5-13; Lk. 7:1-10); Peter's Mother-in-Law (Mk. 1:30-31; Mt. 8:14-15); The woman with an issue of blood (Mk. 5:25-34); Others sick and possessed (Mt. 8:16; Mk. 1:32-34).

Teachings: See Matthew chapters 5,8; etc.

Curses:

"13 Woe unto thee, Chorazin! woe unto thee, Bethsaida! for if the mighty works had been done in Tyre and Sidon, which have been done in you, they had a great while ago repented, sitting in sackcloth and ashes.

14 But it shall be more tolerable for Tyre and Sidon at the judgment, than for you.

15 And thou, Capernaum, which art exalted to heaven, shalt be thrust down to hell.

16 He that heareth you heareth me; and he that despiseth you despiseth me; and he that despiseth me despiseth him that sent me." (Luke 10)

* * * * * *

We walked away from the site as we read the above paper on this now all-but-forgotten city. Luke 10:15 tells us of Christ's prophecy concerning this city. It had been exalted to heaven by His performing so many of His miracles there. The Sermon on the Mount of Matthew, chapters 5-7, was given on a nearby hill. Yet despite this exaltation and privilege, though the people of Capernaum knew in their heads much Scripture and went through the ceremonies of worship dedicated to the true God, yet they rejected *God's* Messiah, and they and their city were from hence destined to judgment. We do know the location of the synagogue, but, nevertheless, archaeologists and historians still have spent many an hour in weary debate to locate the heart and extent of the once thriving city. It is gone.

On leaving these ruins while yet on the lakeshore drive, we are stopped by a herd of black goats on the road. These are led by two Arabic children dressed poorly. Our heart goes out to the poor children of this area who need both the bread of this earth and the Bread of Life. I hand the boy and his sister money. They smile, motion, and speak their thanks. All Americans are financially rich when compared to these little ones.

From here next we journey by our car to Kibbutz Ayelet Hashahar which is about eleven miles to the north. We intend to visit the Tel Hazor Museum there and then the mound. As we drive every now and then we see the "British pill boxes" as they are called. These are small concrete towers, tiny capsule sized fortresses, built by the British in their former Palestinian Mandate days. It is still daylight and well before the supper hour. Mr. Dunzweiler and I pick up two Israeli young girl hitchhikers. I ask them if they think it safe to journey so. They reply that there is at present really no other choice for them, cars being incredibly expensive here and buses on this road a rarity.

JOSHUA BURNED HAZOR

After spending some time at the Hazor Museum, which is again a very small one by American standards—yet extremely well done and informative—we drive south to the mound. Hermon is to the north and still glistening in its glory.

Alas, the hour has passed; Tel Hazor is closed! Everyone has disappeared and we stand at the tel alone. We pause as we note the approach of twilight. I decide that there appears to be no harm for me to walk by the now abandoned toll gate. The entrance fee of 20 pounds ($5.72) is saved because there is no one present to collect it! Here Paul and Barnabas have their difference and separate, though in this case there is no "contention." I enter precincts of the *tel* while Professor Dunzweiler elects to remain in the car. Here as the light begins to fade, for twenty minutes I tread upon the historic city hill. The signs, white letters on blue as at Tel Megiddo, are yet visible and I examine the remains of Solomon's Palace and that which has been unearthed from the plethora of buildings which had stood once on these acres through its twenty-one levels of habitation. Here 3500 years ago Joshua burned Hazor which was the chief city of the Canaanite Northern Confederacy (Josh. 11:1-13).

That evening at supper I noted that the members of our party were making some acquaintances with the Israeli hotel guests. Professor Dunzweiler and I thought that it was a better practice to occupy what might be called a base camp in each region. Then, using the base camp as the hub of the wheel, we spied out the surrounding territory in every direction. In this way we did not have the unpleasant chore of packing afresh each morning and unpacking anew each night. We were able to meet some of the local people and get to know them well enough to converse beyond the mere one-day-tourist "hello" stage. We also could thus become better acquainted with each area as we did not have to revise our bearings daily.

After supper we again spoke to the three Hebrew men (the Israeli and his two Australian friends), and I marveled anew how here they even drew us out in their desire to hear about the Bible events and the Christian faith. In America, for one reason or another, my impression is that there is a greater barrier facing a Christian who wishes to tell a Jewish person of Christ. Of course, Professor Dunzweiler and I did not speak to every Israeli, but we did speak to a good many from all walks, and never once did anyone say something like, "I don't want to discuss religion." I wonder why? As I wonder I go upstairs to pack, for tomorrow we head for Jerusalem.

CHAPTER XIV

THE JOURNEY SOUTH (CANA, SAMARIA, SHECHEM, SHILOH)

An early breakfast marked the dawning of Thursday, *January 18th,* for our caravan shared that universal desire to hasten to Jerusalem. An air journey would have involved a flight of minutes over the approximately seventy-five air miles between Tiberias and the Sacred City, but by a scenic land route winding amid the mountains and hills we would need the entire day.

WINE AT CANA

After migrating eleven miles west we reached the now quiet and old city of Kafr Cana where Jesus performed his first miracle. The New Testament account relates it thus in John 2:1-11:

> "And the third day there was a marriage in Cana of Galilee; and the mother of Jesus was there: and both Jesus was called, and his disciples, to the marriage. And when they wanted wine, the mother of Jesus saith unto him, They have no wine. Jesus saith unto her, Woman, what have I to do with thee? [Madam, what is this to me and to you?] mine hour is not yet come. His mother saith unto the servants, Whatsoever he saith unto you, do it. And there were set there six waterpots of stone, after the manner of the purifying of the Jews, containing two or three firkins apiece. Jesus saith unto them, Fill the waterpots with water. And they filled them up to the brim. And he saith unto them, Draw out now, and bear unto the governor of the feast. And they bare it. When the ruler of

the feast had tasted the water that was made wine, and knew not whence it was: (but the servants which drew the water knew;) the governor of the feast called the bridegroom, and saith unto him, Every man at the beginning doth set forth good wine; and when men have well drunk, then that which is worse: but thou hast kept the good wine until now. This beginning of miracles did Jesus in Cana of Galilee, and manifested forth his glory; and his disciples believed on him."

A helpful young Arab lad led us to a not large church reported to be built on the spot where this miracle of Christ was accomplished. Here we saw in a glass case an old handmade ceramic waterpot about two feet tall from the time of Christ. On the case were the words from John 2:6 in Latin, *Secundum Purificationem Judaeorum,* "According to the purifying of the Jews."

Christ's remark, "Mine hour is not yet come," indicates that He saw in Mary his mother a desire for him to take advantage of this lack of wine to initiate His active ministry by a wondrous supernatural feat and thus display to all his Messiahship. His reply, "Mine hour is not yet come," signifies that His special time to reveal the supreme token of His Messiahship had not yet arrived. From Christ's own words it is plain that "His hour" to demonstrate to the world that He was the Messiah was His crucifixion as the sacrificial Lamb of God for the sins of the world and His subsequent resurrection from the dead (Matt. 26:45).

Nevertheless, here Christ first manifested His glory at a wedding celebration, and He thus showed Himself approving and blessing entirely the divinely ordained state of marriage. The clarity of the Biblical account in declaring that this was His "beginning of miracles" (John 2:11) gives the lie forever to those non-Biblical wives' tales which convey magical stories of the Boy Jesus doing miracles while at play.

After purchasing some mementoes at the Cana Church souvenir shop, and a few of our party taking advantage of the sip of Cana wine offered to all, we sped away. Our bearing was now southwest, and traveling eighteen land miles through Nazareth, Afula, and the Jezreel Valley, we arrived once again at Tel Megiddo. From the heights of Nazareth, Christ for three decades, could behold ten miles to the southwest

Armageddon where some day the Messiah was prophesied to come to destroy the gathered armies of the Antichrist, to end this present age, and to establish His Kingdom (Joel 3; Rev. 16:13-16).

APPREHENSIVE

Having lunched at Megiddo, we motor marched twelve miles toward the southwest to Jenin (Beit Hagan). At the four-mile mark from Tel Megiddo we left that land which belonged to Israel before the June, 1967 War, and now for the final eight-mile stretch to Jenin our caravan has been treading upon soil recently conquered from Jordan. Some of our troup were outwardly apprehensive concerning this portion of our journey, and feared to get out of the cars when we called for a halt at the Arab town of Jenin.

The populace of Jenin, as it turned out, were most cordial in every way. We took photos, and then, to be gracious, we purchased oranges and talked to the local children and to the merchants. How to describe the town? It appeared like a western frontier town with wooden houses dominating a central main street. Instead of cowboys with rattling spurs walking out of the stores and houses, Arabs with flowing robes dotted the scene.

PROUD SAMARIA

Moving eighteen miles to the south we came to the region of Shomron-Sebastiya. Here our cars were stopped by huge ruts in the road at the base of the three-hundred-foot-high hill which once was the proud city of Samaria, the capital of the Northern Kingdom.

Here we explained to our group, as we stood beside our autos at the foot of the hill, that after the death of Solomon in 931 B.C. the nation of Israel was divided into two. Rehoboam, Solomon's son, had proclaimed that he was going to increase the austere building program of his father which had become by this time a great burden to the people. The idolatrous Jeroboam then led the northern ten tribes in a revolt away from the son of Solomon and his southern tribe of Judah (I

Samaritans celebrating the Passover. Leader holds the famed ancient "Samaritan Pentateuch," their copy of the first 5 books of the Old Testament.

Bethpage. This is the area where quite possibly Jesus began his triumphal entry into Jerusalem on a colt. See Matthew 21:1-11.

Hikers rest atop Mount Sinai.

Jews at Wailing Wall. Men and women are separated by a fence.

One of the rare occasions when there is snow in Jerusalem. Here Hasidic Jews worship at the wailing wall in ankle deep snow.

The Samaritans offering Passover prayers.

A Rabbi discusses the Bible with army pupils.

The handkerchief dance highlights the wedding night celebrations.

A little Arab boy cautiously holds his father's coat in the Sinai as two Israeli soldiers stand guard.

The Journey South (Cana, Samaria, Shechem, Shiloh) • 177

Kings 12). Fifty years later, Omri, king of the northern ten tribes, at about 880 B.C. moved the capital of the Northern Kingdom from Tirzah to Samaria. It remained at Samaria from this time until the fall of Samaria and the Northern Kingdom to Assyria in 722 B.C. With this fall of Samaria half of the nation was captured. "Israel," as the northern half of Israel was called, was now gone. Next the southern half, called "Judah," with its line of David, would soon fall prey to the rising power of the Neo-Babylonians who would take Judah captive for seventy years (c. 605-535 B.C.) and destroy Jerusalem and its Solomonic temple. (586 B.C.).

The policy of the cruel Assyrian conquerors of Israel in 722 B.C. was to induce a forced population migration into all conquered lands. This policy led them to deport most of the Jews of the northern ten tribes into foreign countries. This brought about what is known today as the *diaspora*, which is the Greek word meaning "scattered." From that day unto this, Jews of the Northern Kingdom have been scattered over Europe and Asia because of this initial population manipulation by the Assyrians. The scattered *diaspora*, because of persecution and a common religious heritage, never entirely lost their identity. They especially never fell off the end of the world and became "the lost ten tribes of the house of Israel" which turned up fifteen hundred years later in Britain as the advocates of the British-Israelite theory suggest.

At the same time the Assyrians imported other foreign peoples into the city of Samaria, and the northern land of Israel thus developed into that group known in Christ's time as "Samaritans." This latter group with their half-Jewish religion followed *only* the Pentateuch and *not* the Prophets, and centered their worship on Mt. Gerizim, about 7 miles south of Samaria. These Samaritans were constantly at great odds with the Jews during Christ's day. This was so much so that both the Samaritan woman of John 4 and also the disciples of Jesus marveled that Christ, a Jew, would be willing to be seen in broad daylight conversing with a Samaritan woman (v. 9,27). He, coming as the "light to give light to the Gentiles," was not only willing to talk to a Samaritan, but He led many of the Samaritans to a personal trust in Him as the

Messiah (John 4).

BEDS OF IVORY

Archaeological discoveries here have brought to the light of day the foundations of King Omri's palace (c. 880 B.C.) and of the palace of his son, Ahab, which was even larger. Both of these structures were on the summit of Samaria. From these palaces on the top of the high hill these wicked kings could look through an east-west valley and see the Mediterranean at what is now called the coastal city of Netanya which lies twenty miles to the west.

Archaeological excavations have uncovered *thousands of pieces of ivory* at Samaria, many mortised and tenoned so as to be part of the construction of beds and couches. This confirms the literalness of Amos the Prophet's denunciation of the evil-doers in this capital. His thundering words were pronounced,

> "Woe to them that are at ease in Zion, and trust in the mountain of Samaria... That lie upon beds of ivory, and stretch themselves upon their couches...the houses of ivory shall perish, and the great houses shall have an end, saith the Lord" *(Amos 6:1,4; 3:15).*

Since we could see the classic blue and white signs on the ruins of the palaces up on the hill, before leaving we attempted again to gain the summit, but the now eroded roads forbade. After almost having our own vehicle go into a pit, I rejoiced at being able to evacuate the site without having had a mishap. Today one can yet see the remains of a dual-towered fortification upon the hilltop.

We continued on our way to Jerusalem. First south and then east, seven more miles brought us next to the ancient city of Shechem, known in the modern era as Nablus.

MTS. EBAL AND GERIZIM

As we were driving east through this completely Arab city we stopped at its center on the road. To our immediate north there stood Mt. Ebal and next to us to the south was Mt. Gerizim. We were in the central valley between these two parallel and adjacent peaks. Ebal stood 940 meters high and

Gerizim rose 881 meters—related Professer Dunzweiler from his guidebook. This made Ebal 3,080 feet high, and Gerizim its twin was therefore 2,890 feet in elevation.

Moses had at about 1400 B.C. commanded that when Israel entered the land the tribes of Simeon, Levi, Judah, Issachar, Joseph, and Benjamin would stand on the summit and slopes of Mt. Gerizim and repeat aloud the blessings promised to Israel if she would obey the commandments of Jehovah (Deut. 27 and 28). Then, standing upon Mt. Ebal, the tribes of Reuben, Gad, Asher, Zebulun, Dan, and Naphtali would repeat the curses prophesied to befall Israel if they would not harken to God's commandments (Deut. 27 and 28). All of this was accomplished soon afterward under Joshua (Josh. 8). On this day we were standing in that natural amphitheater between these two mountains of witness. Our ears could hear the thousands and thousands of Israelites reciting these words which would echo and reverberate between these two almost-touching mountains.

As we drove away, these peaks testified to us of the prophecies spoken upon them that Israel would be eventually scattered from her good land for disobedience. And as we looked around our eyes testified that it was so.

Yet before the mounts disappeared behind us one could only think of Deuteronomy 30 which contains God's admonition to Israel to recall these things when they are scattered throughout the earth, for He will yet someday bring them back to this land and cause them to return to Him. When the car stopped I read these verses. And now before the mountains fade away from us, dear reader, I invite you to stop and read from your Bible the words of Deuteronomy 30:1-14. Let everyone next note how Paul uses Deuteronomy 30:1-14 in support of his argument in Romans 10:5-9. He uses it to show how close the Lord is to each one of us if we but desire from our hearts to put our faith in Him.

Before leaving the town, we stopped to acquaint our company with the fact that here between the mountains of testimony, at Shechem (Nablus), the Lord first appeared in Palestine unto Abraham. God said here, "Unto thy seed will I give this land" (Gen. 12:7). This is the reason that the mounts of Gerizim and Ebal were so fitting for that ceremony wherein

God challenged Israel from the Mount of Blessing and the Mount of Cursing to obey Him and *thus be allowed to keep the land*—for here between these two mountains did God first promise to Abraham and the Hebrew nation this land.

Here, too, Jacob and his family came and erected an alter (Gen. 33:18-20); and here was Joseph finally buried after his body was carried from Egypt. Why here? Answer: Joseph prophesied of Israel's exodus from Egypt back into the promise land. Where better could this prophet of the promised land be buried than in Shechem, the original site of the promise of the land! (Gen. 50:24-26; Exod. 13:19; Josh. 24:32).

DRINKING AT JACOB'S WELL

Upon our seeking to visit Jacob's well a host of young Arab girls and little boys, giggling, pointed us to the eastern side of Shechem, a spot known in the New Testament days as "Sychar" (John 4:5). Girls with metal cans were congregating at the bubbling water source from every direction. Twenty or thirty of them were here and all seemed to be in the seven-to-thirteen age bracket. Instead of the ancient style pottery water jugs, each carried a two to five gallon metal gasoline can. To our " *Zeh beer Yakov* ?" ("Is this well-of Jacob?") came the negative, " *Lo, lo, lo.* " Now they were as one pointing. One who could speak some English said, "Speak English? I speak little English. This is not Well of Jacob; that is over this way hundred meters. Come, I show you." Our guide was a lone little boy about nine and we followed with our female retinue harem following behind with obvious delight.

Arriving at what was an old white walled church, we were taken by the adult in charge to Jacob's Well. We could not force a coin on the little Arab boy who had led us although we tried with all sincerity. The adult explained that the place where we had seen the village girls getting their water as in days of old was fed by the same underground stream as that which feeds Jacob's Well.

He took us to the well and upon it was a stone cap about a foot and a half thick and over a yard in length and width. Through this was a hole approximately a foot and a half in

The Journey South (Cana, Samaria, Shechem, Shiloh) • 181

diameter. As we one by one stared down into the well's shaft we were overwhelmed by its depth. We poured some water down by a cup and it seemed to take three seconds to fall before we heard the splash from below. A guidebook said that the well was today 125 feet deep. Visually it appeared that the top of the well's water was about 80 feet below. If this was so, then the water this day would have attained to a level of 45 feet above the bottom of the shaft. This well, no doubt, was enlarged and deepened through the centuries in times of drought until it attained to its present depth.

The custodian then offered us a drink from the well. The water was raised via a long rope with a bucket at the end. Most of our group partook of the water as did I, but some followed Mr. Dunzweiler's more cautious example and declined, causing the custodian to look at them quizzically. As the water was swallowed by us I said, "We are drinking of the well where at Christ told the Samaritan woman of the Water of Life." With great emotion we recalled the account of this found in the Gospel of John, chapter 4, verses 5-15:

> "Then cometh he to a city of Samaria, which is called Sychar, near to the parcel of ground that Jacob gave to his son Joseph. Now Jacob's well was there. Jesus therefore, being wearied with his journey, sat thus on the well: and it was about the sixth hour. There cometh a woman of Samaria to draw water: Jesus saith unto her, Give me to drink. (For his disciples were gone away unto the city to buy meat.) Then saith the woman of Samaria unto him, How is it that thou, being a Jew, askest drink of me, which am a woman of Samaria? for the Jews have no dealings with the Samaritans. Jesus answered and said unto her, If thou knewest the gift of God, and who it is that saith to thee, Give me to drink; thou wouldest have asked of him, and he would have given thee living water. The woman saith unto him, Sir, thou hast nothing to draw with, and the well is deep: from whence then hast thou that living water? Art thou greater than our father Jacob, which gave us the well, and drank thereof himself, and his children, and his cattle? Jesus answered and said unto her, Whosoever drinketh of this water shall thirst again: but whosoever drinketh of the water that I shall give him shall never thirst; but the water that I shall give him shall be in him a well of water springing up into everlasting life. The woman saith unto him, Sir, give me this water, that I thirst not, neither come hither to draw."

THE LESSON OF SHILOH

Once again our caravan took off for the south land. Outside of Nablus two camels passed us by. As we progressed through more of this formerly Islamic-owned land, Moslem prayer towers lined the road, one to each small village, almost as mile markers. By the time we had accomplished crossing thirteen to fifteen miles of highway southward from Nablus it was becoming twilight and the unlit roads were darkening by the minute. After some twisting on the road we came all of a sudden to a sign along the road which had only two words inscribed on its face with an arrow pointing to the left. The sign said, " *Ancient Shiloh.* "

Using a great deal of my energy to cajole all into at least a minimum willingness, our cars inched along the side road which we were now turning upon. The map showed Shiloh to be three kilometers off of the main road, so in we went. We agreed that since Jerusalem still lay twenty miles to the south and since no one had eaten supper, we would not remain long at this spot after we had once briefly inspected it. By the road we see tents and fires. Road workers, perhaps? We realized that for many reasons the Israeli government was hiring Jordanians to improve the second class roads in this area. The workers seemed happy, for the opportunity now was afforded to some of them to bring home regular pay. Thus at the same time local people were made content and roads were improved both for humane and strategic reasons.

It is dark now. There are no street lights on the main road upon which we have today traveled, let alone this third class outcropping. Soon the road comes to a vast field and two old stone buildings are to our right. Ruins stand silently, but not imposingly, to our foreground and to the left. A small sign read by our flashlight declares, "Shiloh." We are here. The stars are above, and all is quiet. No sign of life is anywhere. Our only company is each other, some rock remains, and two antique buildings—and both of these are small and very old. A bat flies out of one of them. It seems very flat here. Perhaps it is the darkness, but I see no mountains. This is Shiloh now deserted by man and beast. We are at a dead end to nowhere and a place where only bats dwell. Everyone feels frightened.

Could this barren desolate dreary wasteland, unlit by so much as one candle, be ancient Shiloh? Alas, is this the Shiloh where the ark and tabernacle were set up...where the thousands and thousands of Israel's host once gathered (Josh. 18:1; 1 Sam. 1:3; Jud. 21:19)? Yes, this is Shiloh, Israel's worship city during the time of the Judges—and now behold its utter emptiness.

Now in the lonely darkness of this place we can at last understand the force of Jeremiah's words to Judah and Jerusalem, telling them that if they would not repent,

> "Then will I make this house like Shiloh, and will make this city a curse to all the nations of the earth." (Jer. 26:6)

CHAPTER XV

WALKING THROUGH BIBLICAL JERUSALEM

Friday, January 19th. A sense of anticipation greeted us when we found ourselves arising this dawn in our rooms in the *Melech David* ("King David") Hotel. Professor Dunzweiler and I were in Room 440, and the others were yards away.

As we ate breakfast composed of orange juice, sour cream, smoked fish, rolls, and coffee (Prof. Dunzweiler having scrambled eggs), we discussed the pre-dawn wail of the first of the five daily Moslem prayer calls. They were in these modern times recorded and played out of a loud-speaker system high atop the nearby towers of the Old Walled City of Jerusalem which was a scant three-tenths of mile to our east. As we finished our coffee, in walked a man whom we had telephoned late last might.

Mr. Howard Carlson was a splendid young man in his twenties. Tall, lean, dark hair, glasses, and a look of kindness composed his appearance. Upon introducing him to our companions, we explained that he and his wife Bonnie with their three children were serving with the Independent Board for Presbyterian Foreign Missions as missionaries to the Arabs in nearby Bethlehem. Howard, a Highland College and Faith Seminary graduate, had volunteered to be our local guide while we were in the area.

As we were leaving the hotel I mentioned to the attractive blonde cashier that since the lights had gone out part of the previous night our bills would probably be reduced for that night because of the inconvenience. Perhaps she thought that I was a hotel auditor, for she almost went into a legal tirade over the question. Regret on having initiated the conversation was written all over my face, and I tried to withdraw graciously, assuring her that she had convinced me. No sooner had I backed away, when a couple in a huff came to the desk (which in this large hotel had about five persons behind it), and said that they were leaving. When I heard them mention the matter of the lights going out, after some other matter concerning the plumbing, I departed. Actually, however, the hotel, its facilities, stores, restaurants, and services were all excellent. The rates, even with all of the lavishness of this place, were incredibly low for such a "Class A" hotel. It was just that alterations were under way during this month on the fourth floor and there were bound to be some who were inconvenienced.

As we went out into the yet cool morning air we were approached by two Chasidic students or teachers (they were about twenty years old and so it was difficult to say which). These both wore their traditional *large* brimmed, black hats and they had a lock of hair coming down in a curl at each sideburn. One said,"You American? Give five dollar bill for poor children." Perhaps they were sincere and in charge of some orphanage, but this type of approach without credentials makes one wary. Certainly we all wish to give to charitable causes, but we have the concurrent responsibility as stewards before God to see exactly where our gifts go and how they are used.

Before climbing into our engines, Howard explained to all that Jerusalem is located fifteen miles west of the northern extremity of the Dead Sea, and it is five miles northeast of Bethlehem. It is a high city built upon a plateau with deep valleys U-shaping around its southern half. In population it has about 185,000 souls.

Since June 6-11, 1967, the Six-Day War, Israel is in possession of the "Old City" of Jerusalem formerly held by Jordan. Mr. Carlson went on to explain that before that, he himself had been unable to see the newer western section of Jerusalem. Bethlehem had been his region, and travel between the Jewish and Jordanian sectors was not previously permitted.

TODAY'S JERUSALEM: A CLOCK

I suggested to our people that they might best get the lay of the land by imagining Jerusalem as the face of a clock with the twelve to the north.

At the center would be the still walled *Old City* of Jerusalem wherein the kings of Judah, the prophets, and Jesus once walked. Today the walled city is roughly a square three-quarters of a mile to a side. The walled city in 66 A.D. was about two miles north to south and a mile and a quarter at its longest east-west width.

At the *one o'clock*, position is Mount Scopus. From its summit pilgrims from the north would first spy Jerusalem's walls a mile to the south. Here Titus and the Roman legions camped in 70 A.D. when they besieged the city. Today on this site stands the Hebrew University and the Hasassa Medical Center.

At *two and three o'clock,* a half mile from the walls of the Old City, is the raised summit of the Mount of Olives. From here looking west one can see over all Jerusalem. To the east is seen the Dead Sea and the mountains of Moab including Mt. Nebo from which peak Moses beheld the Promised Land. From this mountain, the Mount of Olives, Jesus ascended into Heaven forty days following His resurrection from the dead.

The area from *seven to twelve o'clock* is the built-up, more modern section of New Jerusalem. At the *twelve* one finds the tombs of the Sanhedrin. At the *nine*, not far from the center, is the Israeli Parliament Building, the Knesset; and farther from the center is the hilltop park overlooking the city with Herzl's tomb upon it.

Two interesting items are at the *eight*, viz., a bit over a mile from the central Old City walls stands the white-capped round top of the Shrine of the Book, the Israeli Dead Sea Scrolls Museum; and then at the extremity of the eight position, about three miles from the center stands the Holy Land Hotel which houses the model of the Second Temple which we will soon visit.

"THE MOST AMAZING MODEL"

Arms now at my sides, the pointing to the clock positions being over, we mounted our autos parked in the adjacent lot, and under Mr. Carlson's navigational guidance we zoomed to the Holy Land Hotel which lies at the eight o'clock angle of the city. Here beside the hotel was the most amazing model that I had ever seen. At the grand scale of 1 to 50, accurate in every detail as far as today's knowledge permits, we saw stretched before us an outdoor stone and wood model of the City of Jerusalem.

It was as it stood in its outward glory in 66 A.D. at the start of the first revolt against Rome. Known as the Model of the Second Temple, it was a reproduction built by skilled technicians and archaeologists of the Jerusalem of that day, right before the Roman destruction of 70 A.D. Its size, 1 to 50, almost a quarter inch to an actual foot made the model immense, approaching two hundred feet by one hundred feet. The northwest tower, Psephinus, for example, has its 115-foot height represented by a not small two-foot, three-and-a-half inch stone tower. This model is beyond doubt, for those interested in Bible history, one of the great spectacles of all Israel. Only the World's Fair miniature cities can hope to compare, but even they fall short of this in historical significance.

The entrance fee was very small. I offered to pay the way in for two small girls, but the gate attendant refused my money and waved the waifs in for free. The guidebook alone was worth the price of this visit, and that was handed to each of us upon entrance. Before we had left I climbed up a wall and to the proximate roof of the gift shop so that I could capture a picture of the entire model.

Before we started to walk around the model of the ancient city for about ten minutes Mr. Howard Carlson presented an historical introduction:

He began by stating that in John 2:19 Jesus had stood in front of the Temple sanctuary building and said, 'Destroy this temple, and in three days I will raise it up.' Jesus thus at the beginning of His ministry made a remarkable and indelible remark which those crowds assembled at the Temple would not easily forget. He did this in order that, when He was crucified and then later raised on the third day, they might understand that He had prophesied of His own resurrection from the dead, the raising of *the temple of his body*—and that on the third day. To the mobs and even to His own disciples it seemed as if He were speaking of His somehow miraculously reconstructing the Temple buildings. This was the very point of His making this declaration while standing in front of the actual Temple; this made the saying so vivid, so astounding, and so indelible."

"Yet historically, the reply to His assertion by the people in the audience that day is enlightening. They countered, 'Forty and six years was this temple in building, and wilt thou rear it up in three days?' (John 2:20.) Since Jesus was about thirty when this was said, the reply of the crowd showed that the Temple construction had begun forty-six years before, or, since Christ was born at about 4 B.C. (right before Herod died—and we now know that he died at 4 B.C.), it was begun at about 20 B.C."

"This accords with what we know from Flavius Josephus' writings, and from the Talmud, that Herod the Great launched his construction program of the Temple Mount at about 20 B.C. It was 46 years in progress when Christ began his ministry, and building was still going on at the close of Christ's ministry, three and a half years later (Matt. 24:1). The whole remaking of Jerusalem with the completion of the Third North Wall, was not culminated until A.D. 66 when the Jewish-Roman War erupted.

"Herod reconstructed the sactuary building, the Second Temple from Nehemiah's and Ezra's time, in less than two years and this was completed at least a dozen years before the birth of Christ. But the entire Temple Mount— with its many porticoes and columns and courts—and the new city with its new northernmost third wall was not completed until 66 A.D., some eighty-five years after the program had begun.

"When it was all completed in 66 A.D., in its glory who would have thought that Christ's prophecy of Matthew 24:1 and 2 would so soon find its fulfillment? The Romans came in 69 and the city was destroyed in 70 A.D., forty years after Christ predicted this:

" 'And Jesus went out, and departed from the temple: and his disciples came to him for to shew him the buildings of the temple. And Jesus said unto them, See ye not all these things? verily I say unto you, There shall not be left here one stone upon another, that shall not be thrown down.' "

COME; JERUSALEM CALLS

This explanation over, we signalled the guide that he could begin to show us the view from A.D. 66. He began to talk, and we opened our eyes and beheld the city.
Come with us now and slowly view the chief city of the Bible. Let us together visit the ancient places. Bring your Bible along so that you can refer to it now and then. You can come with us by traveling upon the grid map of the Old City which will be found on the next page. Them item by item on the *list* of the next pages, locate for yourself the building or pool or valley described. After all, this is what we had to do as we walked. Read each explanation, look up the verses, and see how each piece stands in relation to the others and to history. Best of all, go slowly and meditate often. Think of the Bible events which occurred at each place and those who stood and spoke there, who walked on this or that spot in the days when great events happened.

Take an hour or two; don't rush. Perhaps your Sunday school class can travel with you. By the end of the trip you will know Jerusalem better than many a visitor who has stepped upon that soil itself. Go with a friend if there is one near; find the locations together. Come ahead, the voice of the guide has

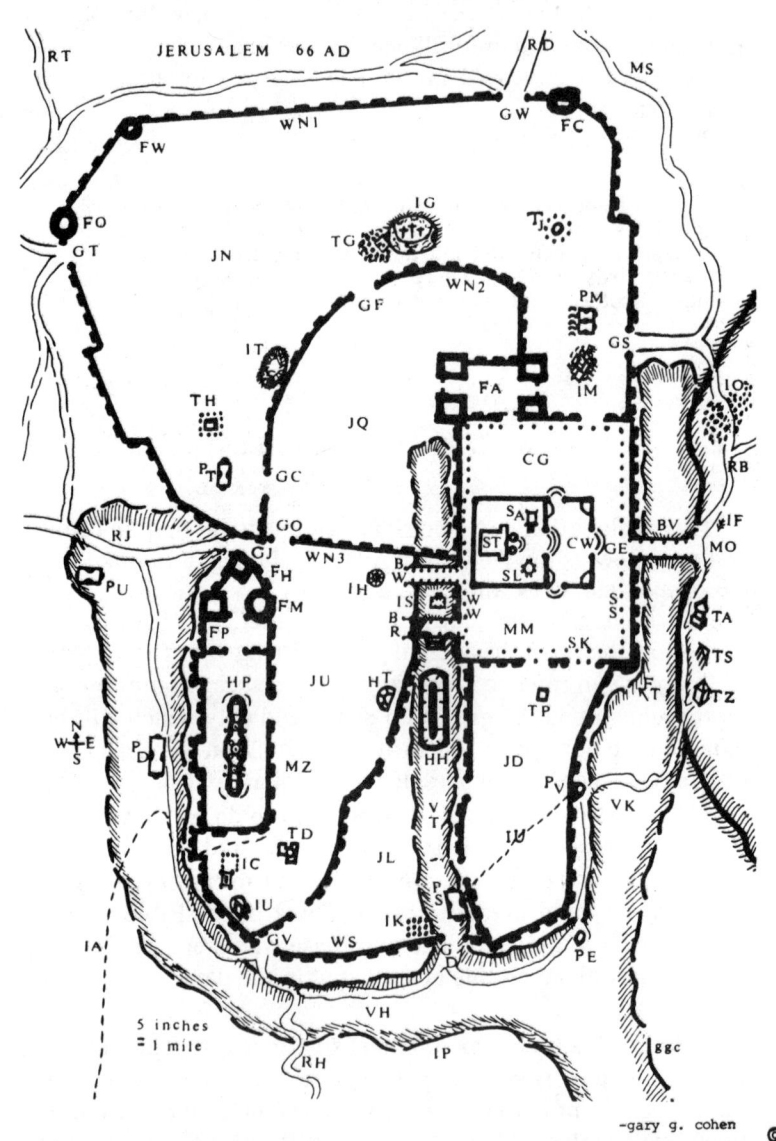

JERUSALEM 66AD

J - Jerusalem

JD	David's city
JL	Lower city
JU	Upper city
JQ	Quarter, second
JN	New city

V - Valleys

VK	Kidron
VH	Hinnon
VT	Tyropoean

G - Gates

GT	Tower
GW	Women's
GS	Stephen's
GE	East
GD	Dung
GV	Valley
GJ	Jaffe
GO	Old
GC	Corner
GF	Fish

R - Roads

RT	Tyre
RD	Damascus
RB	Bethany
RH	Hebron
RJ	Jaffe

T - Tombs

TH	Hyrcanus
TJ	Jannaeus
TG	Garden
TA	Absalom
TS	Seir's sons
TZ	Zechariah
TP	Prophetess
TD	David

W - Walls

WN1	North 1st
WN2	North 2nd
WN3	North 3rd
WS	South
WW	Wailing

B - Bridges

BV	Valley
BW	Wilson's
BR	Robinson's

H - Herod's

HP	Palace
HT	Theater
HH	Hypodrome

S - Sacred

ST	Temple
SA	Altar
SL	Laver
SS	Solomon's porch
SK	King's porch

C - Courts

CG	Gentiles'
CW	Women's

M - Mounts

MS	Scopus
MO	Olivet
MM	Moriah
MZ	Zion

P - Pools

PT	Tower
PM	Market, sheep
PV	Virgin's
PE	En-rogel
PS	Siloam
PD	Dragon's
PU	Upper

F - Fortification towers

FO	Octagonal (persiphanus)
FW	Women's
FC	Corner
FA	Antonia (praetorium)
FT	Temple (the pterugion)
FP	Phaesel
FH	Hippicus
FM	Mariame

I - Interest points

IG	Gordon's calvary
IT	Traditional calvary
IM	Market, sheep
IO	Olive-press garden(Gethsemane)
IS	Sanhedrin (between bridges)
IU	Underground water tunnel
IU	Upper room (traditional site)
IC	Caiaphas' palace
IK	King's garden
IH	Hasmonean palace
IP	Potter's field area
IF	Fig tree site, the cursed

-gary g. cohen ©

started. Look at the map, look at the list, and let's begin our tour. If you should find that you cannot locate some of the places, don't be discouraged—for all travelers have this problem from time to time. Some of the locations may be difficult; but these are the very ones which offer to you the joy of discovery. Of course, as on all side trips, those who don't feel up to it need not go. They may omit this walk and wait for the next chapter to continue with the main group. If you, however, feel up to it, you will, I promise, learn a great deal and reap a benefit from the exercise.

Here we go—

Jerusalem A.D. 66—The tour starts here! First find each main area, then by the use of the descriptions below and the grid letters, locate and identify each item.

TEMPLE MOUNT (Mt. Moriah—Where Abraham was to offer Isaac)—MM.

Court of the Gentiles—CG—large open area surrounding the Temple Square; colonnaded: Gentiles could not enter beyond here (Acts 21:28).

East Gate (Golden Gate)—GE. Eastern wall gate into Temple Mount (Ezek. 44:3).

Court of the Women—CW. Cross-shaped court in Temple Square; women could go no farther.

Beautiful Gate—East entrance into Court of the Women (Acts 3:2-10).

Nicanor Gate—Gate between Women's Court and Temple Area. Note the 15 steps (semi-circular) on the E of this gate in the Court of the Women upon which the choir sings the Psalms on feast days.

Temple—ST. This building is the *naos* or Temple proper. See the columns in the porticoes surrounding its court. In the lower right of this area you can see the Altar with its ramp (SA). The main Temple lies in the Court of the Priests. Each court is named so as to denote the farthest area towards the Temple which the named group could go. (Contrast Psalm 65:4; Hebrews 10:19.)

Court of Women's Four Corners—CW. Lepers, upper left; Wood, upper right; Oil, lower left; Nazarietes, lower right.

An orthodox Hasidic Jew looks back at an Armenian priest in Jerusalem.

Reminiscent of David and Goliath, a judo exhibition is given at a Maccabees celebration. The Maccabees defeated the Syrians under Antiochus IV and rededicated the Temple in Jerusalem about 165 B.C.

• 195

A Bar Mitzvah celebration in Jerusalem. This is a solemn ceremony held for admitting a Jewish boy (usually at 13) as an adult member of the Jewish community, after having completed a study of Judaism.

A Hasidic boy on his way home with some "goodies" confronts the hopeful gaze of some children who want to share in his good fortune.

Solomon's Porch—SS. This is the colonnaded east porch which runs the length of the Temple Mount. Surviving from *Solomon's* day, it was supported by a high wall which went into the Kidron Valley beneath. (John 10:23; Acts 3:11.)

Pinnacle of Temple—FT. Top of tower at SE corner of Temple Mount. This "Ophel Corner" marked the high spot of the wall, being 211 feet. From here, it was said, one below looked "like a worm." (Matthew 4:5)

Wailing Wall—WW. Containing Solomonic stones unmoved through the centuries. It is a N-S running portion of the lower Western wall surrounding the Temple Mount.

VALLEYS

Valley of Hinnom (Gehenna)—The VH here denotes this extremely deep valley just S of the City. Its fires burning the refuse of the city at night pictures hell. (Matt. 5:22.)

Aceldama (Field of Blood)—IP. Where Judas hanged himself.

Gate of Essenes—GD. One of the S gates. Also called, Dung Gate as people came here to toss garbage into the Hinnon Valley.

Gate of the Valley—GV. This is also called the Zion Gate.

Valley of the Kidron—The VK denotes the N-S valley whose great depth guards the southwest of the city.

Gihon Spring—PV. (also known as Pool of the Virgin). These waters feed the Pool of Siloam (PS) through an underground water tunnel (IU) dug in Hezekiah's day.

Pool—PE. This is actually *En-Rogel* Spring.

Pool—PD. called the "Dragon's Pool."

EAST OF THE CITY

Mount of Olives—MO. This mount overlooks the city. It is just E of the city. It runs N-S, and its elevation is 2680 feet.

Garden of Gethsemane ("Oil Press" literally)—IO. Where Christ prayed.

Pillar of Absalom—TA. Built for David's son.

Tomb of the Prophets—TS. One of the many tombs of prophets and rabbis.

Tomb of Zacharias—TZ. See Matthew 23:35.

DAVID'S CITY (JD)

This city is the ancient Jerusalem and Jebus, the Jebusite Fortress which David captured. It is shaped much like Tel Hazor. (2 Samuel 5:6-9).

Monument and Tomb of the Prophetess Hulda—TP (c. 650 B.C.). 2 Kings 22:14, 2 Chronicles 24:22.

Huldah Gates—Can you see these two gates North of the Hulda monument between the Temple Mount and David's City?

Ophel—This is the N high quarter of David's City. "The High Place" (2 Chron 23:3, 33:14; Neh. 3:26-27).

LOWER CITY (JL)

Pool of Siloam—PS. This pool is 20 by 30 feet and is fed by the Gihon Spring, 150 feet higher (PV.) The two are connected by Hezekiah's 1800-foot long, underground tunnel described in the Siloam Inscription. See John 9:7; 2 Chronicles 32:30.

Rose Garden—IK Also known as the "King's Garden" (2 Kings 25:4; Jer. 39:4). This is to the left of the Pool of Siloam.

Hippodrome—HH A small version of the Circus Maximus of Rome. Herod built this for horse and chariot races.

Robinson's Bridge—BR. Called "Robinson's Arch" for the large arch of this E-W running bridge discovered by Robinson. It enters the *Tyropoeon Valley* (the "Cheese Makers' Valley") which valley runs N-S through the lower two-thirds of Jerusalem. This valley runs from the "Second Quarter" (JQ) to the S end of the Lower City where it goes into the meeting of the Kidron and Hinnom Valleys. It has been greatly filled in modern times. Wilson's Bridge (BW) crosses the valley.

Sanhedrin Meeting Place (Council Chamber) and City Archives—IS This is immediately N of Robinson's Bridge, and left of the SW portion of the Temple Mount.

Industrial Quarter—The SW corner of the Lower City (JL).

The Two Walls—At the SE tip of the Lower City. (See Isa. 22:11; 2 Kings 25:4, Jer. 39:4.)

UPPER CITY (JU)

Herod's Palace—HP. This is surrounded with walls and towers.

The Three Towers—Herod built these between 37 to 4 B.C. The northernmost one is *Hippicus* (FH). It housed a water reservoir. It was 132 feet high. Its name is for an unknown friend of Herod.

The westernmost tower is *Phasael*—FP—(today's Tower of David). It was named for Herod's brother; and it is 148 feet high.

The southernmost tower is *Marianne*—FM—74 feet high, and it is named for Herod's queen whom, though he loved her, he put to death.

These three towers form an impregnable W guard.

Joppa Gate—GJ. Through this gate merchants and travellers came from Joppa.

Herod's Theatre—HT. A Hellenistic semicolosseum. The Jewish traditionalists deplored its obvious Gentile design. Compare Acts 19:29, 31 in Ephesus.

Palace of the High Priest Caiaphas—IC. S of Herod's Palace.

The Upper Room—IU (traditional site), S of Caiaphas' Palace.

David's Tomb—TD. Some, however, think that David is buried at the S end of David's City (JD).

Hasmonean Palace—IH. See the two towers on the NE portion of this palace. Between these, on a roof, men addressed people in the courts below. Beside the palace courts, to the right of the two towers, is the large court and market called the "Xystus Court" (Hasmonean-Maccabean).

Fullers (Dyers) Quarter—The SW portion of the Upper City.

Wall of the Upper City—Wall between Upper and Lower Cities. Planned before the Maccabean struggle, the Upper City's streets are right angled and the large houses Greek in style.

NORTH WALLS

Old—NW3. Separated Upper City from Second Quarter.

Second—NW2. Surrounds the W and N of the Second Quarter.

Outer—NW1. The outermost N wall, it goes around the W, N, and E of the New City. King Herod Agrippa I, ruled 41-44 A.D., began this wall. He felt it necessary to provide added security for the N of the city which was always in the direction of attack against the city. This was so because the Southern valleys were (and are) of such depth that an attack on the S half of Jerusalem was almost impossible. The Romans in A.D. 69,70 attacked the city and then destroyed it only after piercing one by one the 3 N walls. This Outer N wall enclosed much undeveloped land to allow for later expansion. The wall was completed in 66 A.D. only to be destroyed by the Romans in A.D. 70.

Sheep Gate—GS. Near the Sheep Market (PM). John 5:2.

Women's Gate—GW. One of the many gates of the city.

Stephen's Gate—GS. Presently so named as it is believed that Stephen, the first Christian martyr, was stoned outside of this gate. This is also called the Lion Gate.

SECOND QUARTER (JQ)

Antonia Fortress—FA. Herod's four-towered castle occupied by the Roman authorities in Christ's time gave immense protection to those within, and to the Temple Mount. An underground huge water tunnel could be emptied in minutes to permit Roman cavalry to ride into the Temple Mount to quell an uprising or disturbance. The SE tower was slightly higher than the others rising to 115 feet. The Antonia's court is known as the "Lithostratus" because of its large "pavement" stones (John 19:13). Upon these Christ stood when Pilate condemned Him. They can be seen today under the Church of the Sisters of Zion. They stand 1.5 meters below the modern street level. Note the ramp on the W edge which permits or bars entrance to troops and cavalry. Normally this housed the "Praetorium," the assembly hall of the Roman imperial bodyguard. Some, however, prefer to locate it in Herod's Palace (HP) or in the Barracks of the soldiers just North of this palace.

Corner Gate—GC. This gate permits E and W passage at the S end of the Second N Wall.

Old Gate—GO.

Tyropoeon Valley—VT. As stated above, this valley runs N-S through the Second Quarter of the City as well as through the Lower City to its S. Tyropoeon is Greek for "Cheesemaker." Basically, the E side of this valley is Mt. Moriah (MM) and W of it is Mt. Zion (MZ)!

NEW CITY (JN)

Pool of the Market—PM. This large pool is also named Bethesda because this is the Bethesda Quarter of the City. It was a twin pool, named also "Bezetha" and "Sheep Pool," as it was located near the Sheep Gate in the Sheep Market Square (John 5:2)-IM. It has five porches, and was 360 by 120 feet and 80 feet deep, being a large reservoir and bathing pool.

Alexander Jannaeus Tomb—TJ. Constructed for the famed ruler of B.C. 103-76. He fought with the Pharisees.

Calvary, the Traditional—IT. Now covered by the Church of the Holy Sepulchre.

Calvary, Gordon's—IG. This is the hill also called on its Eastern side "Jeremiah's Grotto." Today one can still discern the face of a *"skull"* (*Calvary* in Latin; and *Golgotha* in the Hebrew-Aramaic) here beyond the bus station outside the Damascus Gate (Luke 23:33).

Garden Tomb—TG. The nearby tomb in which Christ's body was laid Friday afternoon just before sundown marked the coming of the Sabbath. Christ then rose early on the first day of the week (Sunday; Luke 23:53-24:3).

Tomb of John Hyrcanus— TH. High Priest 133-106 B.C. He was the second son of Simon Maccabeus. In 109 B.C. he destroyed the temple on Mt. Gerizim. He conquered land E of the Jordan. He had a fortification constructed at the NW corner of the Temple Mount. It was called "Baris." Herod the Great a century later rebuilt it into the Antonia (FA), naming it for his friend, Mark Antony.

Pool of the Towers—PT. Also called the "Amygdalon Pool" and the "Hezekiah Pool."

* * * * * *

A SECOND TOUR: CHRIST'S LAST WEEK

Friend, if the above Tour of Jerusalem has not wearied you, now that you know the city, take some time to follow Christ through the movements and events of His last week. Follow Him back and forth over Jerusalem as they kept Him up all through the final night to try somehow to condemn Him "legally." Is the journey long? If so, think of that One who walked it those years ago so that all who would believe in Him might not perish, but have everlasting life. Come, the crowds are yelling, "Hosanna," at the Sheep (Stephen's) Gate.

I. *From the Triumphal Entry to the Olivet Discourse*

Christ's triumphal procession into Jerusalem on *Palm Sunday* from Bethany and the Mount of Olives enters the city at the Sheep Gate (GS) as the people cry, "Hosanna," and lay palms in His path. Luke 19:29-44.

He passes through the Gate and teaches in the Temple courts (CG and CW). Mark 1:11.

Leaving the Temple and city by the East Gate (GE), He returns for the night to the house of Lazarus, Mary, and Martha in Bethany (RB).

On *Monday* morning the barren fig tree is cursed (IF). Mark 11:12-14.

The Second Cleansing of the Temple (CW). Mark 11:15-18.

On *Tuesday* morning the barren fig tree is seen withered (IF). Mark 11:19-25.

Controversy in the Temple courts (CG and CW) with the Sanhedrin Religious Rulers. Matthew 21:23-22:14.

The Pharisees, Herodians, and Sadducees attempt to entrap Jesus with clever questions while He teaches in the Temple courts (CG and CW). Matthew 22:15-46. He denounces the Scribes and Pharisees. Matthew 23:1-36. He likens them to the nearby Tombs of the Prophets (TS) and the Tomb of Zechariah (TZ).

Christ from the Mt. of Olives (MO) weeps over Jerusalem. Matthew 23:37-39.

Re-entering the Temple, Christ observes the widow casting her two mites into one of the 13 chests of the "Treasury" which was in the Court of the Women (CW). Mark 12:41-44.

Leaving the Temple by the East Gate (GE), Christ and the disciples observe the latest building additions and climb to Olivet (MO). From here Christ gives the great eschatological "Olivet Discourse." Matthew 24 and 25; Mark 13; and Luke 21.

Luke 22:66-71. Perhaps this took place at the Sanhedrin's meeting place (IS), or perhaps still at Caiaphas' Palace (IC) John 18:28.

Judas in remorse returns the thirty pieces of silver to the chief priests by the treasury in the Court of the Women (CW), and he hangs himself in the *Aceldama* ("Field of Blood"—IP). Matthew 27:3-10.

Early Friday morning Christ is brought from Caiaphas' Palace (IC) to the Praetorium (FA) to stand before Pilate the first time. John 18:28-38. The Roman Governor had to confirm the death sentence pronounced by the ecclesiastical rulers; he alone had the power over life.

Pilate sends Jesus to stand before Herod at the Herodian Palace (HP). Luke 23:6-12.

Near sunrise (John 19:14) Christ is returned to appear again before Pilate at the Lithostratus Court of the Antonia Fortress (FA). John 18:39-19:16. The crowd chooses to release Barabbas the robber instead of Christ.

The soldiers mock Christ in the Praetorium (FA). Matthew 27:27-30. This takes place Friday, between 6 and 9 a.m.

Christ walks the *Via Dolorosa* ("the Road of Sadness") *Friday yet before* 9 a.m. Luke 23:26-33. This goes from the Praetorium and Lithostratus (FA), through the Second Quarter sector of the city (JQ), through the Fish Gate (GF) which is today called the "Damascus Gate," and from there outside the city to "Calvary" (IG), a skull-faced hill, upon which Christ died for sinners. If the "Traditional Calvary," whereupon today rests the Church of the Holy Sepulchre, is the correct location (at IT), then the route is slightly different.

IV. *From the Cross to the Ascension*

Christ's hours upon the cross, 9 a.m. to 3 p.m. and His death are recorded in John 19:18-30; etc. Here the prophecies were fulfilled amazingly and minutely. See Psalm 22, especially verses 13-18.

He is hurriedly buried in a "rich man's tomb" in a nearby Garden (So said the prophet in Isaiah 53:9, 700 B.C.!) *located at TG*. This is done so as to have his body disposed of before the imminent beginning of the Sabbath—for He died on Friday afternoon and if His body was carried after Friday

6 p.m., the start of the Sabbath, a riot could ensue. Luke 23:50-56.

Christ is risen! (TG) The empty tomb stands forever as a witness to Christ's victory over death. John 20. He arose on the third day just as He had said (John 2:19; Matt. 16:21).

Christ appears to His disciples again and again over a forty-day period in Jerusalem's Upper Room (IU), and also in Galilee, in Tiberias, by the Lake. John 20 and 21. Over 500 saw Him (1 Cor. 15:16).

Christ ascends into Heaven from the summit of the Mount of Olives (MO) in plain view of many disciples. Acts 1:3-12. It is to here some day soon that He shall return, says the Prophet Zechariah (14:4)!

* * * * * *

Thus we visited Old Jerusalem via the model; and it was thrilling. We then returned to the King David for lunch.

CHAPTER XVI

JERUSALEM TODAY

January 19th, Friday, now 1 p.m. Howard Carlson has returned to Bethlehem. After eating the noon repast, we hastened out of the hotel doors to the small bus depot north of our King David Hotel. There down the street as we look east is the Old City of Jerusalem. Our hotel is within a quarter of a mile of it. It is now time for us to mount the bus for United Tour Number 8, 1 to 3:30 p.m. This trip usually is taken from 8:30 to 11 a.m., but we are partaking of it in the post meridian hours by special arrangement.

UNITED TOUR No. 8, COMBINATION OF SELECTED HISTORICAL SITES. Through the Valley of Hinnom—MT. ZION, visit traditional Tomb of King David and Cellar of Holocaust—enter the OLD CITY through Zion's Gate—JEWISH QUARTER—visit WAILING WALL—DUNG GATE—Emek Yehoshafat, visit ABSALOM'S PILLAR, TOMB OF THE HIGH PRIESTS (Cohanim), TOMB OF ZACHARIA and SPRING OF GIHON—drive via MT. SCOPUS, explanation of historic Jerusalem, on the ancient Cemetery and Tomb of Hulda—return to town.

Our guide in this transit was a handsome star-type who was about forty years of age, spoke excellently and even passionately, and one who seemed to be an ideal man in many ways. As we drove he explained the various details concerning each place, weaving the Biblical and historical together with cross-threads of the modern and commonplace.

GEHENNA

Guide: "... Below you is the Valley of Hinnom, or in Hebrew, *Ge* ('valley') *Hinna*, or *Gehenna*. They burned trash and refuse of the city here, since the days of King Josiah. He ordered this in order to bring the Molech worship held in this valley—with its sacrificing of infants—to an end. Because of the stench, the fires were kept going night and day. Thus Christ used it to illustrate the unending fires of hell (Matt. 5:29-30)."

Barbara: "Look, did you ever see a deeper valley in your life? Its depth is simply incredible. No wonder the city never gets attacked from the south."

Guide: "... We are now on the Mount Zion southern section of the city. You should realize that the walls today are not the same as those of 66 A.D.'s Jerusalem. Those walls were demolished almost entirely by the Romans—at least as far as that which stand above the ground. The present-day walled Old City forms roughly a square with three-quarters of a mile to a side. These walls were erected by Soliman the Magnificent, a Turkish Ottoman sultan, in 1537-1541 A.D. He put them up on Roman and Byzantine Medieval foundations."

Harold Fisher: "How does their configuration compare with those of A.D. 66—like those that some of us saw earlier today at the Second Temple Model?"

Guide: "On the west and east they essentially run along the same lines. However, the line of the northernmost third wall of A.D. 66 has today been moved to the south about a quarter of a mile and the south wall has likewise come north a quarter of a mile. Therefore today the southern portion of 'Mt. Zion' is outside of the present walls. And the original 'City of David' is entirely south to today's walls.

"... We are on Mt. Zion and the wall is to our north; but in 66 A.D. or before, we would still be standing within the walls. Do you understand? . . . There are eight gates to the present city. They are: Damascus, Herod's, Stephen's, Golden, Dung, Zion, Jaffa, and New . . ."

MLK DVD

We entered a cave-like affair which was explained to us as the traditional Tomb of David. A great tomb was before us covered by an extremely sizable blue velvet covering. Royal embroidery was upon it with the Hebrew *MLK DVD* (*Melech David*—"King David") at its center. Silver torah cases, or Biblical scroll cases were placed above on the ledge, as were silver crowns.

The guide asked if anyone wished to have the rabbi, one of the two there, bless him? One lady nodded, and the rabbi gave a blessing which at first stunned my ears. He was not speaking in Hebrew, the language of the Old Testament and of the nation Israel! He was blessing her in *Yiddish*—which is basically German with some Hebrew vocabulary. However, it is written solely in Hebrew characters. The guide, when I asked, explained that the very orthodox Jews, the *Chasadim*, who inhabit the *Mea Shearim* sector of the new city (the close-to-the-center 10 o'clock section) believe that Hebrew is too holy a language for anything but prayer and Bible reading. Thus they speak in Yiddish amid a Hebrew ocean. Since 1948 Israel's language is Hebrew, and the children born in 1948 and after know no other native tongue. It is the speech of newspapers and street signs, yet some of the older generation and the Chasadic families cling to the Yiddish.

Prof. Dunzweiler: "David's tomb; I'm almost speechless . . ."
Prof. Cohen: "And the height and thickness of those city walls! I never had realized that they were so immense. 'Immense,' that is the word. The heights of these walls and the depths of the cavernous valleys around the southern half of the city cannot be imagined unless one sees them."

Soon we had walked over to the Cellar of the Holocaust. Here is a memorial on Mt. Zion to the memory of the six million Jews who died in Hitler's Europe. A 24 by 12 by 1 inch marble plaque is bolted to the wall for each European town that had Jews in it taken off and murdered. There are 3600 of them here! We gasped, but it was so; there were here tunnels filled with them in this eerie catacomb which mutely gives the lie to that error of humanism that affirms that mankind has not fallen in sin.

Outside in the light was the Monument to the Children. It was a solid gray stone of about seven feet in height. Certain carvings represented items that one associates with children. The water which ran steadily down its side represented the tears of the 200,000 (!) children murdered by the Nazi maniacal genocide dream. Our guide began to sob as he read to us the verse etched below into the stone, "A voice was heard in Ramah, lamentation, and bitter weeping; Rachel weeping for her children refused to be comforted for her children, because they were not" (Jer. 31:15; so, too, Matthew 2:18).

As we entered the walls of the Old City our guide explained that inside the area of this Dung Gate was the Jewish Quarter of the city—at the south portion. Here in the June 6-11, 1967 War there was bitter fighting and much destruction from mortar fire. He pointed out where various companies of Israeli arms did this or that in the struggle, and he showed us stone piles where bodies were yet entombed. Seven months after the war and there is still body-hunting here. (Compare Ezek. 39:14 which tells of a similar circumstance in a yet future day.)

Someone: "We have heard stories of Israelis not permitting Arab bodies to be buried. Are they true?"
Guide: "They are ridiculous. It is not so; never. Of course, I am speaking on the whole, and from what I know. Who can deny that we too have some soldiers who might . . . but let me tell you what I know that some on the other side did. They . . ."

THE WALL

Before us now was the Wailing Wall. It was a portion of the wall running north-south on the western side of the Temple Mount. Its lower seven courses of "enormous drafted ashlars" (and more courses underground below these) stand from the Second Temple of Herod. In fact, of the seven lower layers of giant stones which make up this fitted and unmortared wall, the bottom three as well as those yet underground rows are thought to be Solomonic. Thus because of this standing antiquity which has weathered so much of Jewish history, this 48-meter-long passage of wall is the "principal Jewish holy site" in the Old City, that is, in the "Walled City."

There were not too many here at the wall at this time. When later that night some of us on our own returned here, the scene was unbelievable. You see, at dark, it now being Friday, the *Shabat* or "Sabbath" comes. Then we saw the Chasidim here in multitudes, all with their huge brimmed black hats, many rimmed with fur, and their side curls. They must have been fifteen thick at the wall, and the chanting was so loud it was as if a thousand bees were buzzing in a cherry tree in full blossom. Some were beating their breasts, others swaying back and forth, and some from side to side. A huge sign was in place which read, *"Forbidden to take Photos on Shabat."* I thought of Stephen and earnestly believed that not only would it be disrespectful to take a picture here on the Sabbath, but it very well could mean jeopardizing one's life.

As we walked through the Dung Gate our guide was telling us how the plan of the Israeli army in June of 1967 was to recapture the Old City by first seizing the Dung Gate. The soldiers complained that this would sound degrading as the place where so momentous a victory was won. Amid the growing dissatisfaction over this ill-sounding prospect, some soldier recited Judges 20:18, the Lord's commandment in the case of the Anti-Benjaminite Civil War. That is, "And the Lord said, Judah first." Since the St. Stephen's Gate was also known as the "Lion Gate" or the "Judah Gate"— the Lion being the symbol of Sultan Beybars, who had two lions carved inside the gate, as well as being the emblem of the tribe of Judah, Genesis 49:9; Revelation 5:5—the soldiers asked if the Judah or Lion Gate could be the place where they first would attack and seize an entrance into the sacred plateau. This was soon granted by the commanders, and it was thus that here Judah went first into the battle as of old. When the gate was seized there lifted a volley of cheer on high here; and at home did our own minds not lift in remembering, "... Jerusalem shall be trodden down of the Gentiles, until the times of the Gentiles be fulfilled..." "When ye see these things come to pass, know ye that the kingdom of God is nigh at hand" (Luke 21:24-31).

We marveled in the Kidron Valley at the Tomb of Zacharia (Map: T Z) and at Absalom's Pillar (TA), both of which were extremely tall. Absalom's Pillar (2 Sam. 18:18) is 47 feet high and a monument to a long chain of sinful acts, revenges, and half forgivenesses which all started when Amnon lusted for his half-sister Tamar (2 Sam. 13 to 19).

There was a hole in a twenty-foot rock cubicle which invaded the seemingly authentic 3000-year-old base of Absalom's Pillar. Our guide said that Turks had made this to empty the monument of its contents, but upon making their frontal entrance they discovered a rear channel dug perhaps centuries before by earlier tomb robbers!

On seeing the Golden Gate's propylaeum entrance the guide informed us that this gate has been sealed shut for centuries in line with Ezekiel 44:1-3, "... the gate of the outward sanctuary which looketh toward the east; and it was shut ... This gate shall be shut, it shall not be opened, and no man shall enter in by it; because the Lord, the God of Israel, hath entered in by it ... It is for the prince; the prince, he shall sit in it to eat bread before the Lord ..." The guide explained that the orthodox expected the Prince, the Messiah, to enter next through that gate. Would Jesus not be the One who has already entered in by it, and for whom it now prophetically awaits?

The Mount of Olives was breath-taking. Here we beheld the city just as did Christ. Here Christ ascended; and from here we can look eastward and see Moab and the Salt Sea. Today from here one peers to the west to see the Islamic Golden Dome of the Rock Mosque in the center of the Temple area. On the south also in the same Temple region is the silvered domed Mosque of El Aksa—also sacred to the Moslems.

Before the tour was completed we had been in that

charming Garden of the "Olive Press," *Gethsemane* in Hebrew, where Christ prayed. We had also walked down into the cavern of Hezekiah's tunnel dug from Gihon to the Pool of Siloam (map: PV to PS).

Our bus returned us for supper at the Kind David. Our heads and hearts had already tasted far more than a person could hold. What a privilege to be here; how much there is to learn; and how much there is to realize and to pray. This is truly the "City of the King."

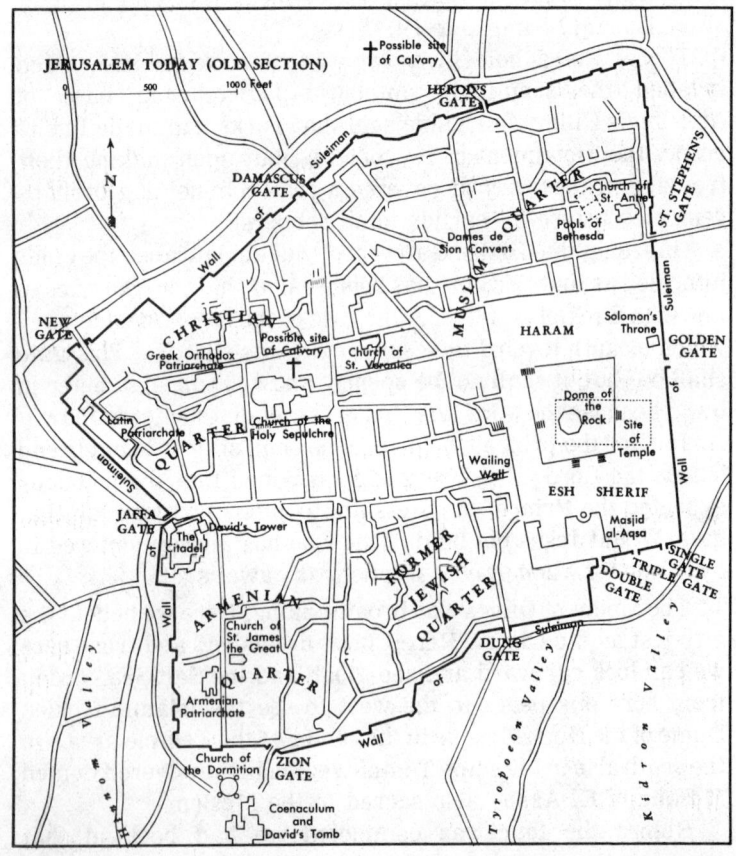

Looking at the Golden Gate from **inside** the wall. Few tourists take time to see this scene. What a glorious day that will be when suddenly the Gate is opened and the Messiah at last walks through in triumph!

214 • ISRAEL Land of Promise, Land of Prophecy

The Knesset, or Assembly Building, is in Jerusalem. The congressional assembly of Israel is named after Haknesseet Hagdola ("The-Assembly, the-Great"), the 120-man lawgiving body of Jews during the Persian rule of Israel which started in 550 B.C. In the foreground is the Shrine of the Book where the Dead Sea Scrolls are housed.

Garden of Gethsemane where Christ prayed before going to the cross. Look closely at this photograph. Look at the olive tree. You will see in its gnarled branch the formation of a face as though it were praying. There may not be any special significance to this... but it appears most remarkable. How many people have walked through Gethsemane and failed to see this face? And, more important, how many people walk on God's earth, see His handiwork, read His Word and yet fail to grasp His message of eternal life for those who believe!

216 • ISRAEL Land of Promise, Land of Prophecy

Planes soar over Jerusalem in the 25th Anniversary celebration.

Sign in Jerusalem admonishes visitors to dress properly.

218 • ISRAEL Land of Promise, Land of Prophecy

Nuns praying at Wailing Wall. This portion of the western wall of Herod's temple was preserved by the Romans when they destroyed the city in 70 A.D. Here the Jews gather to wail the loss of their Temple.

Senior citizens of Jerusalem voicing their opinion to the Inspector-General of Israel police.

The new Israeli Diamond building on the outskirts of Tel Aviv. It has 28 stories of which 3 are underground and designed with strict security arrangements.

CHAPTER XVII
INSIDE THE WALLS

It was still Friday, *January 19th,* and as supper concluded we turned our faces again toward Jerusalem. We had eaten earlier than usual and it was still light as we walked that quarter-mile jaunt from the Molon Melech David to the Old City. The *Shabat* (sabbath) would be upon us within the hour.

We entered the city through the portal of the Jaffa Gate, which, since it was on the west side of the city, was closest to our hotel. Coming from America and being unfamiliar with seeing actual fortresses, palaces, and walled cities, I stood aghast and gaping at the size of the stone walls and the gate before me. It was built in 1540 A.D. and it replaces the ancient Biblical Gate that was located in this position. It is the main gate of the city today, and nearby, to its south-west, on the wall is the mighty base of the Tower of David. The top of this tower, called Phasael was constructed by Herod to the grand height of 148 feet, but it is now gone. Instead there is a smaller (but no mean thing) Moslem prayer tower cylindrical in shape which now looms as the upper portion of David's Tower.

THE HOLY SEPULCHRE

A well-spoken, bespectacled, English-looking gentleman of about 55 with an umbrella offered to guide us and we nodded in assent. He took us to the Church of the Holy Sepulchre which stood over the traditional Calvary. There the Greek Orthodox

Church owns the primary place over the hill thought by many to be Calvary—and perhaps it is. The hill is now underneath the floor of the church. Because of souvenir hunters chipping away rocks it had to be encased in marble. One may, however, bend down and place his hand through a slot and touch for himself that sacred hill. The Roman Catholic Church owns the spot to the right of the Greek Orthodox Church's Calvary altar, as you face it, and they have the right at certain times to enact their own rites at the main altar. It is overly ornate by any standard, with silver spheres hanging from the ceiling in multiplied numbers as is the Greek Orthodox custom with this type of icon.

Across the hall is this huge church is the room of the Empty Tomb. How I praised the Lord to myself that the tomb is empty. Here the tomb is a small rectangular shaped room everywhere marble covered, with a shelf in the right as you enter the door where the body had lain. All of this, however, is not that which is thought to be the real tomb; that is below this one. Because of rock chippers and wear and tear, and because of what was considered the holiness of the site, it has been preserved just below the tomb all enter today. In the upper tomb that we entered, two at a time because of its size, a Greek Orthodox priest always remains in prayer vigil. One was here as we entered, bearded and dressed in black. It was a sacred moment standing in the place where Christ may well have been raised out of the dead as the "firstfruits" of many brethren.

THE LITHOSTRATUS

This church, built with its great giant dome by the Crusaders, is a marvel. The guide pointed to the dome and said, "Sixty-five feet in diameter." Repairs were taking place and a general first class restoration was in process. The work, however, was not now being done because of the near approach of the sabbath. As we walked we saw on the walls the many hundreds of carefully chipped squaretype crosses, each about one and a half inches high and wide. Each Crusader tried to leave one of these here.

At the site of the Antonia Fortress, along the crowded narrow streets with stone houses and cutaway areas like caves for stores, we came to the church-convent of the Roman Catholic Sisters of Zion. One sister, a young and silent girl from Canada, took us on the tour of their domain. Outside over the street, she explained, was the "Ecce Homo Arch" (*ecce homo* being Latin for Pilate's words to the crowd. "Behold the man"—John 19:5). The Sisters of Zion bought this property years ago to obtain this arch, but when obtained they discovered that it had apparently been built by the Roman Emperor Hadrian at about 130 A.D., and hence it was not the Ecce Homo Arch, unless it was the original rebuilt. Disappointed, the Sisters decided to build their church here anyway, and when they had dug one and a half meters below the modern street level an important find was exhumed. The diggers had uncovered in perfect preservation the large stones (about 2 by 3 feet) which paved the "Lithostratus." John 19:13 reads:

> "When Pilate therefore heard these words, he brought Jesus out, and sat down on the judgment-seat at a place called The Pavement (Greek: *Lithostrotos*), but in Hebrew, Gabbatha" (A.S.V.).

From the account of John we know that here Pilate condemned Christ to be crucified so as to please the screaming crowd who had been stirred against Christ by the religious authorities of the nation.

The nun said that this Lithostratus pavement, which composed the western half of the Antonia, was excavated only forty years ago just as she had described. She pointed out upon one of the large stones of the court a carving denoting the Greek dice game called, *Basileus* or "King." The Roman soldiers may well have played this right here as they mocked Christ for being a king. The letters in Greek (which the Roman soldiers would speak) of the word "king" could be easily made out, although they were made centuries before and in rough style, obviously not the straight lined lettering of a professional stone carver.

She showed us the water tunnel below through which the Romans, after emptying the water in it, could send soldiers on horses to the Temple's outer court when disturbances arose.

The tunnel was longer, she continued, but her group and the adjacent Greek Orthodox could not agree, and a wall had to be erected to separate the portion of this large tunnel which pertained to each. I would estimate it to have been about fifteen feet wide and high. She told us that the water here was used for the bathing of the nuns. I asked, letting the words escape before thinking, "Do you mean that you take baths by sort of swimming around in the water in this tunnel?" She turned red, gave a smile, and said, "Oh, no, we don't swim here; the water is pumped up to the bath tubs." She then thought of something or other upstairs that we should at once go to see. We left this cistern-tunnel, and went up the stairs to the church again.

She gave a touching talk in the chapel about living for Christ. She called it, "My little sermon that I give everyone whom I take around." After hearing this, in a most cordial manner, I asked her if she were truly trusting Christ and His finished work for her salvation; and not in ceremonies of her church. She said that she was trusting in Christ Himself. May it be so! She was certainly charming and filled with kindness, devotion, and love as far as one can look into another's heart.

A COSMOPOLITAN DUO

After this we were seized by two sixteen-year-old Arab boys who wished to be our guides. One either took guides, giving them some slight sum at the end of the tour, or one spent all of his time fighting off would-be guides. The two Arab boys, one a Moslem and the other a Christian, were most polite and eager. These boys spoke perfect English, this being the foreign language taught first in the Arab schools (though in other regions many of the Arab children do not get to attend school).

The boys said that they hoped to be official guides someday soon. They lamented the June 1967 War because "it has scared all of the tourists away." Their overt kindness to us betrayed no anti-American sentiment in the least; nor were they anti-Jewish. They were a cosmopolitan and tolerant duo. The Moslem Arab boy said that money was harder for him to come by and prices higher since the war. Both wished to live in America someday.

The Moslem boy did most of the talking. He pointed to the site of Antonia and its Praetorium, and then he guided us out through Stephen's Gate, across the Kidron, and to the Garden of Gethsemane. (As we walked he explained that because it was Friday, the Moslem holiday, the Dome of the Rock was not open to visitors today. This Dome Mosque was now standing on the Temple area.) Upon reaching Gethsemane, we stood with quiet joy and delight amid the interwined trees and the gnarled and twisted olive trunks. Had it changed much in two millennia? The trees looked very old here. Looking upward to the east we beheld across the valley the scaled Golden Gate waiting for its Messiah to come.

He explained that after the city's destruction in A.D. 70 by the Romans at the end of the first revolt in the years c. 130-133, the Emperor Hadrian desired to rebuild the city as a Roman city. He outlawed, because of the two revolts, all Jewish people from coming within ten miles of the city under pain of death. Then he rebuilt the city leaving outside of the walls the southern portion of the city, viz. Mount Zion's Upper City, the Lower City, and the City of David. These three, going left to right when looking north, are now south of the south wall. Later in the 1537-41 restoration by the Turk, Solomon the Magnificent, the walls of today were built on this same Hadrianic foundation and pattern.

Next we saw the Wailing Wall with its crowds chanting on this *Shabat* Friday evening. The lowest three exposed layers of stones, now blocked from view by the devout, were Solomonic; the next four rows on top of these were also large Herodian blocks; above these were squared boulders from the 16th century—Suleiman's accomplishment—and these were of a smaller size than those below; and finally, there were rows of small cinder-block-size brick work built in recent times because of sniper fire or some other exigency of the war. Since in the previous chapter I have discussed the chantings, the swayings, and the posted sign, *"Forbidden To Take Photos On Shabat,"* I will not repeat them here, except to reiterate that here I saw a religious zeal and, shall I say, a fanaticism unparalleled in my days. Scenes like this must have prompted Paul to write the words of Romans 10:2.

We then returned to the hotel, but by cab. Our guide was

most anxious to obtain business for some of his Arab driver friends, and we for goodwill complied. Because of certain regulations the Arab drivers moaned to us that they were not permitted to drive us to the King David. I am not certain of the details, whether it involves payment of license fees or district cab regulations or what. The driver, however, told us that it was most unfair. We simply could not comment.

It was now fully dark and thus *Shabat*. All stores almost everywhere were closed and as we discovered on the next day, Saturday—still *Shabat*, all gasoline stations were closed. Money was not exchanged in many places. Everything but walking and talking had come to a grinding halt. Even the nonreligious observed the sabbath if for no other reasons than to keep the goodwill of the orthodox and to be spared the insults and at times even the spitting of the zealous sabbatarians.

As Christians, for those who are such, we believe that the worship day has been transferred to the first day of the week. This was done to hallow the new rest day—the day the redemption work was finished! For, on the first day of the week, Christ came from the tomb alive (John 20:1). Thus the apostles and the early church met not on the sabbath any longer but upon the first day of the week (Acts 20:7; 1 Cor. 16:2). Their instructions to do so may well have come during the post-resurrection period from Christ Himself. In any case, the apostles were given the authority to bind regulations upon us as they declared the mind of Christ (Matt. 18:18), and since they clearly met for worship and fellowship on the first day of the weeks, so followed the church.

So, too, Paul the Apostle said, "Let no one act as your judge in regard to ... a Sabbath day" (Col. 2:16).

It was now evening, and we were back again at our hotel. What exultation we had felt as we walked inside the walls!

CHAPTER XVIII

THE ISRAEL MUSEUM AND AFTER

January 20th, Saturday. Prompt as usual, before breakfast we heard Howard Carlson's knock upon our door. Not more than eighty minutes later, breakfast having been handily accomplished, we found ourselves motoring upon the now lonely streets of Jerusalem. It was *Shabat,* "Sabbath," and few cars were seen driving. The benzine stations were uniformly closed either because of sabbath observance, lack of sufficient business, a desire to show respect to the national religion, and/or a wish to keep the peace with the Chasidim who were outspoken enemies of sabbath violators. To our surprise even many of the street lights were now not operating; but rather they were standing in quiet sabbath observance and reminding all others of this by their mute speech.

Professor Dunzweiler and I were in Howard Carlson's car, for ours was low on gas, and we feared running out of fuel in this area on the sabbath. This would mean that the car would have to be abandoned where it halted, and we preferred to avoid such an exigency. One could not fail here to begin to grasp the significance of Christ's words concerning the prophesied flight of the Jerusalemites after the Abomination of Desolation has been committed (Matt. 24:15-31). Jesus said, "But pray that your flight may be not in the winter, or on a Sabbath" (v. 20). With traffic lights out, gas stations closed, few policemen on duty—no heavy traffic could move. It would only take one auto per road to run out of gasoline and that avenue would be in a hopeless tie-up.

As we drove, here and there other cars appeared. Our small caravan soon landed in the western portion of the New City. Here before us was the Israel Museum which was open on *Shabat* to those who had purchased their tickets earlier in the week. No tickets were sold on this day, of course, it being *Shabat* .

Our first enterprise was a stroll through the open-air Billy Rose Sculpture Museum. As we strode around the various and sometimes perplexing items of statuary, Miss Barbara Miller, who knew somewhat of such craft, attempted to give us something of permanence to take with us.

OLIVE OIL LAMPS

The second portion of the museum was the three-building Museum of History and Archaeology. Here we saw glimpses of ancient and modern Israel in textiles, urns, tombs, and sundry other interesting and fascinating fragments made usually of stone or pottery. As we admired a four-inch-long, three-inch-wide, and one-inch-high-oil lamp from the Hellenistic Period (330 to 63 B.C.), Mr. Carlson explained to our group that he often used one of these. When the lights in his Bethlehem house are unfortunately extinguished because of a frequent power failure, he and his wife fill this small pottery handmade lamp with olive oil. They insert a piece of rope, string or cloth for a wick, and, once lit, it burns brighter than most candles for about three hours. This provided an ideal night light for a room when the power is off and the electric lights are not functioning. It also provides the atmosphere of antiquity for an "Oil Lamp Supper."

Christ told the famed parable of the ten young girls with their oil lamps:

> "Then shall the kingdom of heaven be likened unto ten virgins, which took their lamps, and went forth to meet the bridegroom. And five of them were wise, and five were foolish. They that were foolish took their lamps, and took no oil with them: but the wise took oil in their vessels with their lamps. While the bridegroom tarried, they all slumbered and slept. And at midnight there was a cry made, Behold, the

bridegroom cometh; go ye out to meet him. Then all those virgins arose, and trimmed their lamps. And the foolish said unto the wise, Give us of your oil; for our lamps are gone out. But the wise answered, saying, Not so; lest there be not enough for us and you: but go ye rather to them that sell, and buy for yourselves. And while they went to buy, the bridegroom came; and they that were ready went in with him to the marriage: and the door was shut. Afterward came also the other virgins, saying, Lord, Lord, open to us. But he answered and said, Verily I say unto you, I know you not. Watch therefore, for ye know neither the day nor the hour wherein the Son of man cometh" (Matt. 25:1-13).

THE ISAIAH MANUSCRIPT

From the museum buildings we walked to the Shrine of the Book. Here was the museum of the Dead Sea Scrolls. When we previously had driven here we could see this shrine while we were yet a great distance away. It had a great black slab which jutted into the air and near this was a large white flying saucer shaped structure.

This latter white cap of the shrine building seemed to represent the lid of one of the urns within which the Dead Sea Scrolls were found at Qumran in 1950. We entered the white-capped edifice and descended the stairs.

Here a most attractively presented cave exhibit gave us an atmosphere of discovering the old parchments in a cave. Howard Carlson marveled at the beauty and lack of crowding of this museum, and declared that the same type of finds were never in other places displayed in such a startling and overpowering fashion as was here done.

Inside there were the various exhibitions of the variations in the formation of the Hebrew letters through the various centuries. Thus one could generally date a manuscript find at least within an identifiable period by observing the manner that the penman used in making his letters.

At the center of the Shrine Hall in a circular case was a portion of one of the Isaiah manuscripts. As we looked at it breathlessly Mr. Arnold Escourt broke our awesome silence.

Arnold: "Well, can you read? It is shockingly readable. I would have never dreamed that it would be so legible."

Prof. Dunzweiler: "Yes, it is indeed quite legible. One can read it clearly after he has oriented himself to the style of Hebrew lettering, the orthography used here ....Look here. Here is a correction. It appears that the copyist skipped a few words, discovered this fact, and then inserted them by using a caret-shaped arrow and writing the omitted words above the line. Remarkable."

Prof. Cohen: "I had thought that at least this portion of the scroll would have had to have been entirely recopied. Perhaps this scroll during certain periods would have been unacceptable for official usage because of such a correction?"

Prof. Dunzweiler: "Yes, perhaps. But it looks official enough, and it would have been a relatively easy task, in comparison with the job of copying all sixty-six chapters of Isaiah, to have replaced this portion of the scroll?"

Florence Escourt : When did books with pages come in? And how old is this scroll?

Prof. Cohen : "Paged books, or 'codices'—singular, 'codex—originated at about 250 A.D. What we have here, however, is a scroll which was rolled upon a stick at each end. It is composed of sheep or other skins sewed together."

Florence : "And what is the significance of the Dead Sea Scrolls?"

Arnold : "Does the main significance of these scrolls have to do with the Essene Community at Qumran by the Dead Sea where these were unearthed?"

Prof. Dunzweiler: "What you have mentioned is significant indeed, but for the Biblical scholar and the Bible believer there is something much more significant."

Arnold: "Which is ?"

Prof. Dunzweiler : "Which is this. Prior to the finding of the Dead Sea Scrolls at about 1950, our oldest Hebrew Bible text dated from about the year 1000 A.D. This is often called the 'Massoretic Text' because the Massoretic Scribes, 6th to 10th centuries A.D., passed it on to us. They added certain tiny dots and dashes under the various letters to enable later readers to retain the traditional pronunciation. Hebrew, as you know, is made up of letters which are nearly all consonants. The vowels are understood. However, the Massoretes rightly feared the gradual forgetting of the vowel sounds so they added them. For example, *RD* could be *ReaD* or *ReD*, but the native Hebrew reader would know from the context. 'He *RD* the book' or 'The barn is *RD*.' To save the later reader from this problem, and to preserve the traditional pronunciations (Qere's) which at times favored one possibility against another of the same consonantal lettering, the Massoretes added their own synthetic system of vowel points, and hence their text is called 'The Pointed Text.' This is the text from which your English Old Testament has been translated.

"The problem was that this text was copied on scrolls in the Middle Ages. So when our English Bible was translated we had to use texts copied no earlier than the medieval times. We did not possess copies earlier than from this age when the pointing was added."

Florence : "You don't mean that these Massoretes changed the wording of the Hebrew Bible?"

Prof. Dunzweiler : "Oh, no. Their added vowel pointings were placed below the letters of the text, or on the left sides of the letters. The text itself was sacred to them; they made no changes whatsoever."

Florence : "Then what is the problem?"

Prof. Dunzweiler : "The problem is this—Isaiah was written seven hundred years before Christ, and the oldest Hebrew Bible we had was from about 1000 A.D.; that is, seventeen centuries after Isaiah wrote! Some therefore said that during those intervening centuries there had been so much miscopying that if we were ever to exhume a text from centuries earlier we would have to throw out our present copies. In other words, the problem was the accusation that during the centuries the copying was perhaps not always done carefully enough so as to give us today a really reliable Old Testament.

"Therefore can you imagine the excitement a few years ago when the Dead Sea Scrolls were uncovered and dated as having been copied c. 200 *B.C.?* Would they contain in the Isaiah manuscript a manuscript essentially identical in the Hebrew with our tenth century *A.D.* text, or would they be so different as to render our present copies void? This was a manuscript find that marched us twelve hundred years further into the past!"

Florence: "And the result? Tell us."

Prof. Dunzweiler : "The result was that the Dead Sea Scrolls' major significance was to substantiate and corroborate the accuracy of the Massoretic Text from which our present-day Bible has been translated. In every essential the Dead Sea Isaiah manuscripts of c. 200 B.C. are the same as our c. 1000 A.D. manuscripts....The Bible has been copied carefully and accurately through the ages, that is the significance. God has providentially preserved His Word.

"The Hebrew text that Christ used is the Hebrew text that Bible-believing pastors and seminarians study today. We use the same Old Testament, and the Qumran finds prove that its appearance before Christ's time, at Christ's time, and in our present day is one and the same. The *canon,* or the roll of books, of the Old Testament was completed and closed about 400 B.C. with Malachi's promise of the Messiah and His forerunner's soon coming (Mal. 3:1-3; 4:5,6). From Josephus' remarks on the canon and from Christ's own words we know that it consisted of what was then enumerated as twenty-two books, precisely the same as the number of letters in the Hebrew alphabet (Josephus flourished 70 A.D.), and that it was divided into three sections; viz, the law of Moses (Genesis, Exodus, Leviticus, Numbers, Deuteronomy) called the *Torah;* the Prophets *(Navim);* and the Psalms or Writings *(Cathuvim).* These books, though then arranged in a different order, are the same—no more and no less—as the thirty-nine books of the Old Testament which Protestants today possess (so Christ in Luke 24:27,44). We count 39 and they 22 because we separate many books which they counted together. For example, we count Jeremiah and Lamentations as two books; they as one, since Jeremiah wrote also the Lamentations. Christ's Old Testament is our Old Testament, and this is not only an historical confirmation and a religious nicety; it is our evidence from our Guide, the Son of God

Himself (so Luke 24:27,44, etc.) that our Old Testament is the inerrant Word of God, for He so used it and so considered it (Matt. 5:17,18; Luke 24:25-27, 44-48)."

Arnold :   "So the scroll before us tells us that our Bible has been copied accurately through the centuries."

Prof.Dunzweiler :   "Yes. That is the message."

Steve Reed :   "But didn't some say that alphabetical writing was not in existence during Moses' time?"

Arlene: "Oh, Steven, please don't show your ignorance. It has been proved and everywhere accepted years ago that alphabetical writing was in existence in Mesopotamia centuries before Moses. Why......"

Arnold :   "Yes, she's right. Writing is pre-Abrahamic (he lived at about 2000 B.C.), and therefore pre-Mosaic (c. 1500-1400)."

Soon we were about one mile west of the western walls of the Old City. We were beholding Jerusalem from atop Mt. Herzl. We beheld the black marble sectioned stone rectangle which marked Herzl's tomb. A taxi driver explained that we were on Jerusalem's highest point. He pointed to Herzl's tomb and stated that the black marble came from Eilat. Inscribed on this huge stone marking the founder of the modern-day movement to establish a homeland for the Jews on the land of Israel were the four Hebrew characters which made up his last name—HRZL.

The cab driver—he had driven some of our touring squad here—pointed out the high tower of the YMCA, the highest Jerusalem building. When he discovered that we had not yet gone to visit this building he expressed his overt astonishment. He could not understand how any Christians could come to Jerusalem and not at once visit their own building...He pointed out the square for ceremonies and memorials, and it was quite large and spacious, and it made one realize that the summit of Mt. Herzl was quite sizeable.

THE MERCHANTS REJOICE

We returned to the hotel for lunch, and spent the afternoon walking within the confines of the Old City walls. After sundown, just before returning to supper, Professor Dunzweiler walked into our room and slumped down in his chair looking like a whipped tiger. He sighed and I inquired what had so beaten and burdened him. He then went on to explain the source of his miff.

Prof. Dunzweiler :   "I am really miffed. You know that I purchased this wooden camel in Tiberias for ten American dollars. (He pointed to an attractive hand-carved wooden camel about eight to ten inches high.) Let me open my suitcase and show you what I purchased in Bethlehem yesterday when I took a short side trip to a store there." (Unlatching the case, he produced a camel not unlike the former Tiberian model, except that the one from Bethlehem was varnished and more attractive.) This one which is better than that beast from up North cost $4. Don't moan. There's more to this miff. Look here. (He produced a third of essentially the same vintage as the prior two. He scowled.) This cost $2.50. Thus my net loss is $1.50 on the Bethlehem camel, and $7.50 on the Tiberian camel."

At supper Dr. Schatz hee-hawed over this and had all of our companions laughing. Poor Professor Dunzweiler! Then Dr. Schatz laid on the cruelest blow by saying, "Once as a boy when I made an exceptionally poor purchase my father quoted to me this proverb (he gave the Hebrew)...In the English it means, 'When the merchants saw you coming they rejoiced!'"

THE RABBI'S BOAST

After supper in the lobby of the King David Hotel, we met two interesting personages. The one was an attractive young lady medical doctor who had just completed her studies and internship in her native South Africa. She told us that she was considering taking a posistion on the staff at the Jefferson Hospital in Philadelphia. She had been on the Jerusalem tour with us on the prior morning. After recovering from the shock that so young a girl was a full physician, and quite an intelligent one judging from her conversation, we chatted for a time, profitably listening to her tales of Africa.

Next we happened to speak to a rabbi who was reared in the Germantown section of Philadelphia. Professor Dunzweiler and I soon were discussing the Bible with him. He announced to us, upon learning of our faith, that he himself could boast of never having read one word of the New Testament. At this we took the liberty to tell him about this wondrous book, and he listened with obvious interest and intent. Every now and again he would bring up some old wives' tale type of objection to Jesus—"But I have been told that Jesus was...." Each time we were able providentially to supply him with an answer.

Finally, the rabbi said that we had interested him greatly, but that before he could read the New Testament he felt an obligation to reread the entire Old Testament and then the entire Talmud. We smiled. The obvious end of such a pious reading schedule would be for him never to get to the New Testament—for the Talmud is a long collection of many, many books that few if any have ever read through in a lifetime. It is as if you asked a man to read today's stock market reports, and he replied that he would do it as soon as has completed his reading of the current *Encyclopedia Britannica* which he would begin reading tomorrow after breakfast.

As the devout rabbi told us of his effort to keep the Jewish ceremonial laws, of his desire to please God more than anything, our hearts were moved with love for him just as was Christ's heart for a man in somewhat similar situation some two thousand years earlier. I told the rabbi of this, and then quoted Christ's words to the man who wished to have eternal life. When Christ reminded the man of the commandments which bring to the attention of every mortal his sinfulness, the man replied to Jesus, "Teacher, I have kept all these things from my youth up" (Mark 10:20). At this, Christ looked at this man with love, and said, "One thing thou lackest..." (v. 21). "So you see," continued I to this one who had aroused our compassion, " 'One thing you lack.' You have tried to fulfill all of the ceremonial laws, and all of these ceremonies, such as the sacrifice of the first-born blemishless lamb at Passover, speak of Jesus, the Messiah. Yet you are unwilling to read of Him in the New Testament. You say that you love God, He has promised to send His Messiah, and you will not even investigate this cry in the wilderness that the New Testament clearly reveals that Jesus is the Anointed One. 'One thing you lack.' You lack a personal trust in the Messiah, the One described as, 'A light to lighten the Gentiles, and the glory of thy people Israel' "—Luke 2:32.

He was obviously moved as we parted. We prayed that he might turn to the pages of the "New Covenant" as had many rabbis before him, to discover its proclamation that Messiah has already come. And, yes, He will come even again.

Professor Dunzweiler remarked to me after the young rabbi's exit that here our studies and training had come in handy. When he made suggestions concerning the texts of the Old Testament and the New we were able to supply him promptly with answers which could hold. Here even our knowledge of New Testament Greek had swept aside one odd objection against the New Testament which he had somewhere gathered.

SNOBS AND LAY-POPES

Prof. Cohen (responding): "An education in the Biblical field is not only an end in itself, it is also a means to a higher end—service to God and to one's neighbors. While some are not privileged to acquire such an education, some are too lazy to grasp for it. Still others have fallen into an even more pernicious error: that is, they have come to admire their own knowledge and have gone on to become intellectual snobs and lay-popes. They wish all to admire their erudition; and, if any should have the temerity to disagree with an opinion of theirs on some obscure text or on any subject of secondary importance, they put the ban on that foolish one. They speak ill of the great theologians of the past (Jude 8-10), they despise all who hold different views than their own (Romans 14:3), and thus they become the seat of all authority. Often they are the first to denounce popery, yet this is their very crime and they commit it with neither fact nor tradition. They have little love in their speech and so blatantly violate Corinthians 13; yet they

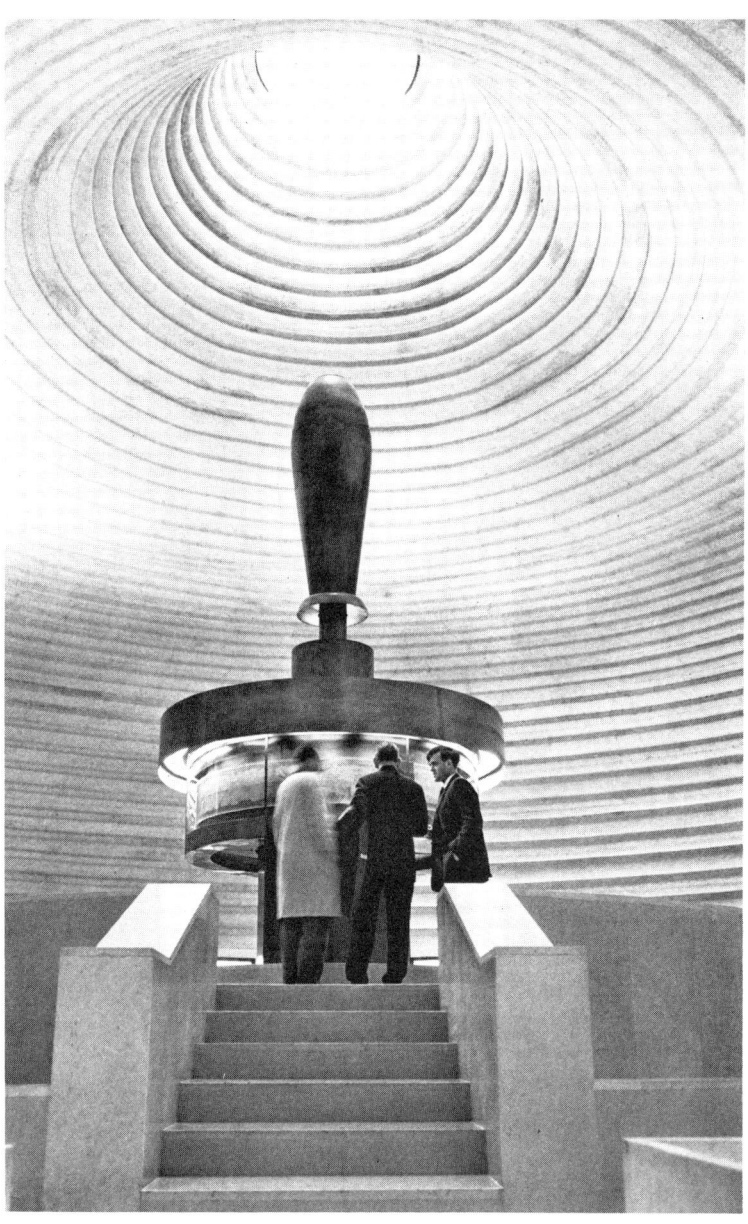

The Book Sanctuary in Jerusalem guards, among other things, the Dead Sea Manuscripts, famous from the day of their discovery. Among these finds were complete copies of Daniel and Isaiah dated at 200 years B.C.

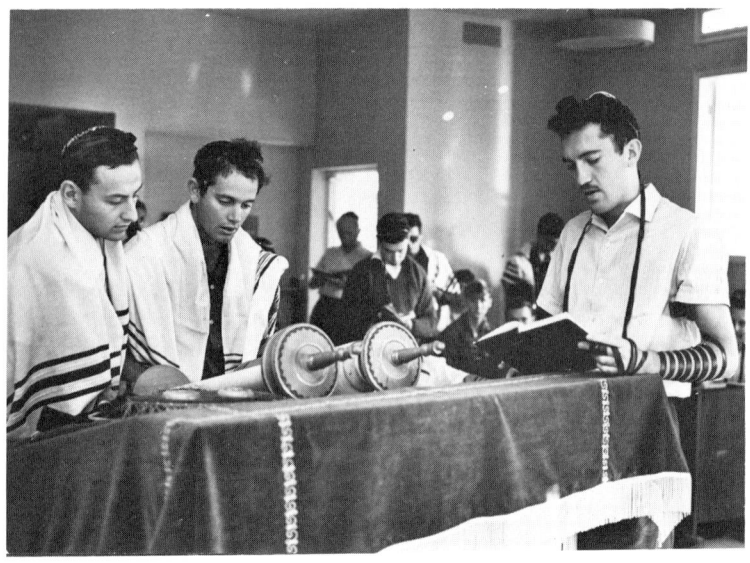
Students at the Bar-Ilan University synagogue reading the Torah.

Pilgrims carry palms down the Mount of Olives on Palm Sunday.

An orthodox Jew in Jerusalem looks over the city.

A porter in Jerusalem carries a very cumbersome and heavy load on his back. What a picture of doubters...who, heavy with burdens...fail to take God at his Word and continue to carry their burdens rather than leaving them at the Lord's feet. "Casting all your care upon Him; for he careth for you" (1 Peter 5:7).

pass this off as unimportant although Christ and the Bible make having love quite important. They have self-wisdom and pride as the giant log in their own eye, but yet in their spirtual hyperopia, far-sighted diseased condition, they, failing to see their own huge proximate sin, glare at the specks of theological minutiae wherein they believe the eyes of others err (Matt. 7:1-5). Thinking themselves to be the greatest in the kingdom, they become the very worst of its hypocrites (Matt. 7:5 and chapter 23)."

"Bravo," responded he in agreement, "and I know a couple who fit this perfectly." We acended in the elevator.

Once in our room Professor Dunzweiler showed me a chart which he had been developing. It was entitled, "Three Meanings of the Term 'Creation.'" He had composed an obviously well-thought-out theoretical map of the Creation account of Genesis. This chart appears on the next page and is worthy of careful consideration.

It was now eight o'clock at night and time for another of our sixty-minute seminars.

* * * * * *

THREE MEANINGS OF THE TERM "CREATION"

1. EX NIHLO CREATION—The bringing into being of that which did not (either in its substance or its form) previously exist.
2. IMMEDIATE CREATION—The bringing into being of that which did not (in its form) previously exist, employing previously existing substance.
3. MEDIATE CREATION—The bringing into being of that which did not (in its form) previously exist, employing both previously existing substance and secondary causes.

One Possible Structuring of the Creative Events of Genesis 1 and 2

Yom (Day)		Event	Reference
Pre-I	(1)	EX NIHILO CREATION of the matter-energy complex and of space (together with their properties)	1:1
	(2)	MEDIATE CREATION of the structured universe	1:1
	(3)	MEDIATE CREATION of our Milky Way Galaxy	1:1
Yom I	(4)	MEDIATE CREATION of our solar system (thus light, and thus day and night)	1:2-5
Yom II	(5)	MEDIATE CREATION of the atmosphere, and the subsequent separation of water above the surface of earth from water covering the surface of earth	1:6-8
Yom III	(6)	MEDIATE CREATION of dry land, by the structuring of earth's surface into lands and seas	1:9-10
	(7)	IMMEDIATE CREATION of land plants	1:11-13
Yom IV	(8)	MEDIATE CREATION of the appearance of sun, moon and stars in the sky (as viewed from earth's surface)	1:14-19
Yom V	(9)	IMMEDIATE CREATION of aquatic animals and of birds begins	1:20-23
Yom VI	(10)	IMMEDIATE CREATION of terrestrial animals begins; IMMEDIATE CREATION of aquatic animals and birds continues	1:24-25
	(11)	IMMEDIATE CREATION of man	1:26-31 2:7
	(12)	IMMEDIATE CREATION of the Garden of Eden	2:8
	(13)	IMMEDIATE CREATION of woman	1:27 2:19-23
Yom VII	(14)	Cessation of IMMEDIATE CREATION; MEDIATE CREATION continues	2:1-3

CHAPTER XIX

SACRED PLACES IN JERUSALEM, BETHLEHEM, AND HEBRON

Sunday, *January 21st*, was a free day for our group. Professor Dunzweiler and I spent it in worship as did some of the others. In the morning Mr. Carlson took us to the Barachah Church in Bethlehem where we worshiped with wonderful Arab Christians. I was asked to preach and I spoke on John 4, "Christ and the Samaritan Woman." A Mr. Victor Diab interpreted the message into Arabic. A chorus was sung by a group of blind Arab girls being educated nearby. At the end of the service I said "Hello" to each of the dozen or so of these smiling blind girls. I took each one's hand as I spoke, and each in turn giggled, and smiled. It was a great joy to be there.

The service was followed by dinner in Bethlehem at the Carlson's and Mr. Dunzweiler sat at the table eating between two gasoline fed heaters as he attempted to retain his normal body temperature on this chilly day. The Carlson's, Howard, Bonnie, and their three little ones, wore sweaters upon sweaters and thus stayed warm while keeping the fuel bill down.

Following a drive, we had next a service in Jericho where I discussed the falling of its walls. Since a visit here with our entire group was planned for the coming Tuesday we did not at this time do more than merely survey Tel Jericho.

Supper was had with Dr. and Mrs. Thomas Proctor who work at the Baraka Hospital which specializes in curing both the physical and spiritual ills of the Arabic people west of the Jordan in the Bethlehem region. The Proctors, like the Carlsons, had three sweet and playful children. It was a joy to hear from them how Dr. and Mrs. Thomas Lambie started the Baraka Hospital to treat those who had turberculosis and to tell them of the love of Christ. It was then our privilege to see the hospital.

When in the hospital, Howard Carlson introduced me to a patient, and he said, "Mr. . . . (I did not catch the Arabic name fully) is a patient here, and today he is very sad. He was told yesterday that his only son had been killed in an accident." How thankful we were all at such a tender moment for Christ's assurance in John 11:25 and 26 that death is not the end, for He said:

> "I am the resurrection, and the life; he who believes in Me shall live even if he dies, and everyone who lives and believes in Me shall never die" *(A.S.V.)*.

As we departed Howard told me of the great love of the Arabs for their eldest sons. Once a man has a son he is referred to as *Abu* (father of) and then the son's name. So "Abu John" is the name for the "Father of John." Only in the promises of God can one find solace for such a loss (1 Thess. 4:18).

In the evening service at Bethlehem the sermon text was Isaiah 11:1-12 which tells us of the age of millennial peace which will yet come to pass upon the earth.

That night as we retired our heads spun with joy at the thought of having been able to worship God at such places as Bethlehem and Jericho. We thought of the joy of those blind girls who had seen Christ. We thought of the chilling breezes through the Carlson's house warmed by their love for Christ. Our minds turned to the Proctors who, like the Carlsons are missionaries under the Independent Board for Presbyterian Foreign Missions. Here they were serving where the need was great though the practice was not a lucrative one as might be had back home. We laughed as recollections came of the Carlsons at dinner and the Proctors at supper rolling with laughter as joy filled their houses during our visit. Bonnie Carlson had giggled so much that the tears finally ran, and Mrs. Proctor did about the same. Bars were on the windows, but joy was within as the Spirit of Christ filled us with something more lasting than merely the ephemeral laughter of this world.

I packed away the four Jericho oranges given to me by our kind Arab hostess who entertained us there in that oasis city amid the dryness all around. Mmmmm, will the folks at home be thrilled when they bite into these—Jericho oranges!

FORBIDDEN TO ENTER

Monday, *January 22nd*, saw us as usual awakened by the Moslem prayer call at daybreak as its lingering, crying strains filtered into our hotel windows from the Davidic Tower of the Old City.

Following Meal One of the day, our party hastened to begin today's itinerary of the sacred places of Jerusalem, Bethlehem, and Hebron. This was a tour of our own composition and we pursued it with delight and avidity. On foot we marched the quarter mile to the Old City and then through the narrow streets of stone. With shops and churches on all sides we made our way again to the Wailing Wall. We prepared to enter the Temple Area itself, but we were abruptly stopped at the stone doorway by the warning words of the sign above it. We photographed it, and its message read thusly:

Hodah Veahzaharah

Asor lefe diyon torah licol adam lihacenes lishtach hor habayet mipeney kidoshto. — *Harabinot Haroshyet, Liyisroel*

Notice and Warning

Entrance to the area of the Temple Mount is forbidden to everyone by Jewish Law owing to the sacredness of the place. — *The Chief Rabbinate of Israel*

Avis *et* Avertissement

L'entree dans l'emplacement du mont du temple est interdite a tout le monde par la loi juive en vue de la sanctete du lieu. — *Le Grand Rabbinat D'Israel*

Here was a sign in three languages, exactly as was the sign which Pilate had placed upon the Cross (Luke 23:38). To our companions its ominous benediction mourned a dreadful dole of denial to one of their fondest wishes—a visit to the Temple Mount itself.

As some began to turn away we saw other people walking right through the arch with no hesitation. After a short consultation with those nearby who apparently were in the know and who were of no little authority, it was made clear to us that according to the civil law of Israel all who wished to enter could do so. The religious law, however, forbade such an entrance; yet the religious law was not civilly binding and Israelis as well as tourists went to and fro into the sacred precincts unmolested. At this time the religious authorities of Israel were somewhat akin to their counterparts of Christ's day. They had some authority, but all real civil authority rests in the Israel Knesset which does not forbid entrance into the Holy Mount.

We entered through this gate facing east which was just south of the Western or Wailing Wall. Passing by a laver with many faucets, which the Moslems use for washing before entering the holy places, we came to the Dome of the Rock which now stood on the site where the Temples of Solomon (B.C. 967-586), Zerubbabel (B.C. c. 516-16), and Herod (B.C. c. 16-70 A.D.) once stood. The latter two together are referred to as the Second Temple since Herod's construction was basically an enlargment and reconstruction of Zerubbabel's temple. Here some day, either on this exact spot or somewhere in this roomy but yet largely vacant Temple area, perhaps soon, the Temple shall be yet again rebuilt and the Antichrist shall enter it and commit what is known throughout the scriptures as the Abomination of Desolation (Dan. 9:27; Matt. 24:15; 2 Thess. 2:3,4). One Israeli told us that an announcer on the radio pleaded that now that Israel has its own Knesset (Parliament and Parliament building) and now that it has also recovered the Old City in the June, 1967 War, it ought to go ahead and reconstruct its supreme monument, the Temple of Adonai (Jehovah). Yet the strict Chasidim opposed any Temple building; they say it is unlawful until Messiah comes (Mal. 3:1).

Sacred Places In Jerusalem, Bethlehem, And Hebron • 247

We heard tales of rocks having already been quarried from Indiana for the new temple, but with the land of Israel having so much rock in it that it almost becomes a plague, it is difficult for me to imagine them using stones from Indiana with a "Made in U.S.A." aura hovering above. However, who knows? Strange things will happen in those final days. Perhaps stones from all over the world will be used in some sort of world-ecumenical endeavor? Perhaps...!

THE DOME OF THE ROCK

We paid the necessary fee and removed our shoes, as required, in preparation to entering the Dome of the Rock. It was constructed at A.D. 688-91 by Umaiyad Caliph Abd-el Melik over the large gray *rock* from which Moslems believe Mohammed ascended into heaven while astride El Buraque, his steed. It is of simple design and moderate size. Basically it is a simple building canopy over the sacred gray rock. Its eight walls join together to form a regular octagon and above this is a large gold overlaid dome which itself rests upon two rows of Roman columns. Within, the octagonal walls are covered by eight century mosaic work, below is a marble floor, and above is intricate Armenian faïence tile work which is a wonder to behold.

As we trod inward we saw that the entire center of the structure was occupied with the hallowed gray monolith at its center. A wooden fence about four feet high prevented anyone from touching this stone outcropping which I should *estimate* was something like thirty by twenty-five feet in length and breadth. It jutted out of the floor some three feet and it was basically flat on top with ripples here and there—yet clearly it was entirely one rock cap, the descent of which into the earth could only be speculated upon.

As we stood before this sacred gray slab I whispered to our band the following:

Prof. Cohen (speaking in very low tones): "As far as we can ascertain from historical and Biblical study we are now standing before one of the most sacred of all of the Bible sites. This stone is the cap of Mount Moriah and according to God's command 4000 years ago Abraham brought Issac here to offer him as a sacrifice to God (Gen. 22:2-4, 9). Here it was that the Angel of Jehovah called to Abraham and told him that it was not necessary for him to slay his only son, for God had provided a ram for the sacrifice whose horns were now caught in the adjacent thicket. It was here, says Hebrews 11:17, that:

'By faith Abraham, when he was tried, offered up Isaac: and he that had received the promises offered up his only begotten son, of whom it was said, That in Isaac shall thy seed be called: accounting that God was able to raise him up, even from the dead; from whence also he received him in a figure.'

"Here a thousand years after Abraham and the millenium before Christ, on the height of this then wind-swept rock was the threshing floor of Ornan the Jebusite. Here God appeared unto his servant David (2 Chron. 3:1). Jewish tradition tells us that upon this very gray crag Solomon built the Altar of Burnt Offering twenty cubits square (30 by 30 feet) and ten cubits high (15 feet; 2 Chron. 4:1). The altar that then stood here almost 3000 years ago was years later repaired by King Asa (2 Chron 15:8); cleansed by King Hezekiah (2 Chron. 29:18); repaired by King Manasseh (2 Chron. 33:16); and battered down by the Babylonians in their conquest of Jerusalem in 586 B.C.

"Later at c. 530 B.C. the Altar of the Second Temple was again constructed in this same location (Josephus, *Antiquities,* xi, 4, 1) even before the Temple itself was begun (Ezra 3:3-6). Here the Syrian Antiochus Epiphanes in c. 168 B.C. polluted the Temple and sacrificed an unclean sow, and thus this persecuting 'beast' (Cf. Rev. 17:11) became a type of the awful coming Antichrist who will, like his predecessor, commit an Abomination of Desolation (Dan. 9:27; Matt. 24:15; 2 Thes. 2:3,4). In 165 B.C. Judas the Maccabee cleansed the Temple and the altar which stood here over this rock.

"In 16 B.C. Herod refashioned it for his Temple and in 70

A.D. it was destroyed. Then in 688-91 A.D. it was surrounded by this present firm but slight and thin-walled structure, and thus we stand before it today. Here patriarchs, kings, fathers of dynasties, and prophets have stood. Here we are reminded, as we think of the destructions effected by man's sin which have occured at this site throughout the years, and of the multitudes of sacrifices offered here as commanded in the Torah, that the words of Hebrews 9:22 are true. They say 'Without shedding of blood there is no remission (of sin).' How thankful we must be that,'Christ (Messiah) was once (and-for-all) offered to bear the sins of many' (Heb. 9:28). Thus there is no longer the need for the perpetual daily and yearly sacrificing of offerings. Christ has done it all once in His shedding His blood for our sins. We need only trust in this all-sufficient sacrifice in order to be saved from God's wrath and judgement which rightly comes upon all sin and impenitent sinners (John 3:16,36)."

THE BELL

After standing in meditation for a time, I decided to attempt to photograph this sacred stone. As I snapped the shutter a loud bell rang throughout the place, and my heart sank. "I'll be happy to escape with only the loss of my camera," thought I. A man hurried toward me and I prepared myself for the worst. He came beside me and I tensed. . . . He ran right by me, and picked up the receiver of a telephone located at the wall. Was this call from an observer located above in some inaccessible balcony? As nothing happened, I decided that one photograph of the sacred stone was sufficient and did not hazard another attempt. Once outside, we discovered that 35mm. slides of the rock and the Mosque were available by the multitudes. In fact, one could hardly take five steps in the Temple Mount Area without being buttonholed by a peddler of slides of one type or another. The slides, however, were generally quite good and the price was usually most reasonable after the first minute of bartering.

We observed next the sealed Eastern Gate, and then we went to the larger, though not as hallowed, Mosque of El Aksa which was at the south end of the present Temple Mount Area. Caliph El-Walid built this huge Mosque in 709-15 A.D. He was the son of the builder of the Dome of the Rock. Caliph Omar had had a mosque here previously which the Knights Templar used for their own temple (1099-1187 A.D.). Saladin recaptured it, however, in 1187, and it remains today as an Islamic shrine. Below its level are the remains of the two southern Hulda Gates which in the Second Temple admitted those from David's City into the Temple Mount.

Recovering our shoes, we strolled upon the remains of Solomon's Porch, and then the half mile or so through the narrow streets to the northwestern gate of the Old City, the Damascus Gate. This gate was so named because it placed one upon the road which led to this famed Syrian city to the north. We saw above the Achad Bus Station the rock identified as "Gordon's Calvary" and the eyes and the nose bridge of the skull face stood out in large bold relief (IG on the map of Chapter XV).

We then visited the adjacent "Garden Tomb." What thoughts and prayers passed through our hearts as we looked upon Calvary and walked amid that little garden nearby with its precious restored and preserved rock tomb. Christ Jesus died for our sins on Calvary's cross and, rising out of the tomb on the third day, He became the firstfruits of them that sleep.

TO BETHLEHEM

Post-lunch we zoomed via auto into Bethlehem, the city of David, the city of Christ's birth. Here churches packed against churches, crowded together and sharing common ancient walls, took away from our anticipated manger and hillside scene of Bethlehem of yore.

Our band entered the Church of the Nativity, guided by the Rev. Mr. Carlson. Here Greek, Roman Catholic, and Armenian churches join together in a pressing squeeze to occupy the holy place. The Greek Church, however, here owns claim to the primary Church of the Nativity, the believed site of the manger and Christ's birth. Christ was born in Bethlehem as the Hebrew Prophet Micah foretold seven centuries before His advent in Micah 5:2 (numbered 5:1 in the Hebrew Bible):

> "But thou, Bethlehem Ephratah, though thou be little among the thousands of Judah, yet out of thee shall he come forth unto me that is to be ruler in Israel; whose goings forth have been from of old, from everlasting."

Here in this prophecy we see the Messiah's humanity (He comes forth out of a human city), His office (ruler of Israel), and His divinity (His goings have been from of old even from everlasting). Matthew 2 and Luke 2 tell the beautiful story of the Saviour's birth in great detail. How did this birth in Bethlehem come to pass so as to fulfill the prophecy? Did Jesus also plot this? No, it was of God; Jesus is truly the Christ, the promised Anointed One that was to come. Even wicked Herod's advisors knew that Bethlehem was to be the place of Messiah's birth (Matt. 2:3-6). So it was here in Bethlehem that that arch spirit called Satan, working through Herod, just as God often works His will through men, killed the infants in order to slay the new King who had been born. But thanks be to God, Joseph was warned in a dream, and the Christ Child was taken to Egypt until the death of Herod.

A monk showed our party around and explained that this Church of the Nativity was first constructed by the Christian Emperor of Rome, Constantine, at c. 330 A.D. Eusebius of Caesarea, the scholar, and Constantine's mother, Helena, researched the location of these Palestinian sites. In 521 A.D. the Samaritans tore down the church; but in 531 the Emperor of the Eastern Roman Empire, Justinian, the Law Codifier rebuilt it. By 638 the Arabs had desecrated it; and centuries later in 1163 the Crusaders refurbished it.

It was a hallowed and quiet moment as we stood in the Greek portion before the Grotto of the Nativity where Christ was born. We then were taken to the Latin sector and into the clean and whitish now well-lit cave wherein the great scholar and ascetic, *Saint* Jerome (A.D. c. 342-420) had lived. Having come to Syria to master Hebrew from the tongues of the rabbis themselves, he labored here and brought forth the Latin Vulgate. Here from 386 on he studied and slept. I recited my Hebrew paradigms as we started to leave. As we filed out the monk stated that from here Jerome ruled his monastery. A contemporary of the great Augustine, the fiery Eusebius Hieronymus Jerome was probably the greatest scholar of Christianity's first four centuries—eclipsed only by a Paul or Augustine.

We were shown the Grotto dedicated to the Innocents slain by Herod, and we saw inscribed in stone the prophecy of Micah 5:2 from the Latin Bible of Jerome. We departed filled in our hearts with that which was, which is, and which is yet to come.

We had already today visited the sacred spots of Jerusalem and Bethlehem, but now our autos were rolling southward. Bethlehem was about four miles south of Jerusalem, and now our goal, Hebron, was another fifteen miles south of Bethlehem. Mr. Howard Carlson was leading our pack and now with him was his house guest of the evening, a Mr. Young Yune. Mr. Yune was a Korean who was now studying his Hebrew at the Hebrew University. He had previously studied in Korea and America; he was now in Israel studying; and he hopes yet to study his Greek more in Greece itself. This was a well-studied theological student indeed, and one who had years for such an enterprise which few others have at their disposal.

Driving, we saw Solomon's Pools outside of Bethlehem; the Barachah Valley ("Valley of Blessing"); rock tombs; and the Halhul Maccabean Fortress site. As we rode Howard pointed out to those in our car the field where the twelve spies gathered the grapes of the land. This was the Valley of Eshcol, the *Ge Eshcol* or the Valley of the Cluster (Num. 13: 24). It is somewhat north of Hebron and even today its grapes are the supreme ones of Israel. Next he pointed westward and said that about ten miles hence was Shochoh and beyond that Gath from which Goliath came. There at Shochoh, somewhere in the valley west of us, David slew the tall giant Goliath (I Sam. 17: 1).Then we came to a natural fountain and Arab girls from all around were there to gather the water. All was breathtaking and thrilling in this land of the Bible.

IN ANCIENT HEBRON

We dismounted from our vehicles at Hebron and at last saw what a real Arab town looked like; that is, one from the ancient world (some of the Arab capitals are, of course, modern cities). Here the elevation was about three thousand feet and the population 36,000. Arab men and children were everywhere, in ancient trailing costumes with the trademark head scarfs and bands. Here and there a woman was to be seen, and Israeli soldiers with machine guns or rifles appeared every now and again. These seemed to be often conversing with the people and laughing, and tension was not in sight even if it lurked under cloaks.

We walked through the *shook*, "market," and came to the building front of the Mechpelah Cave. We saw an Israeli soldier at the door as the guard and also signs in Hebrew, English, and Arabic. As we entered I mentioned to our company that here Abraham settled by the Oaks of Mamre (c. 2000 B.C.) and here he built an alter to the Lord (Gen. 13:18). Here Sarah died, and was buried in this cave of Machpelah wherein we now stand (Gen. 23). Through here came the twelve spies (Num. 13:22); and some forty years later, c. 1400, Joshua fought against this city of Hebron and executed the Lord's decreed capital punishment against its wicked inhabitants (Josh. 10:36,37; Gen. 15:16). Caleb, one of the two good spies, was given this city which was previously known as "Kirjath-arba" (Josh. 14:14,15; 15:13). David ruled Judah for seven and a half years from Hebron (2 Sam. 2:1,11) at about 1000 B.C. Through the years people of Judah lived here even to Nehemiah's time, 450 B.C., and after (Neh. 11:25—Kirjath-arba being Hebron).

We entered softly and in a large chamber, well lit, we saw two tent-like structures, each *about* ten by fifteen feet and *about* nine feet high, with the top coming together into a point.

Apparently these were tomb monuments with the actual bodies interred just below in the cave itself. On the left tent Barbara read the lone Hebrew sign out loud, *Kavar Rabekah Ahmanu* and then gave the translation, "Grave-of Rebecca, Our-Mother." On the right tent she read, *Kavar Yitzchak Ahvenu* and pronounced, "Grave-of Isaac, Our-Father."

Then in the next chamber we saw on each side an opening in the wall, and on each side through the wire meshed large opening a high catafalque stood. Both had a large padlock upon their wire mesh door. To the left Barbara again read, *Kavar Avarham Ahvenu,* "Grave-of Abraham Our-Father" and then from the words written above the door on the right, *Kavar Sarah Ahmanu,* translated. "Grave-of Sarah Our-Mother." The scene was desperately touching and solemn with Moslems nearby seated on the floor and an armed Israeli in olive drab uniform before us.

After these we crossed an open walk to two more chambers. Here were two more tombs. The one said, *Kavar Yaachov Ahvenu,* "Grave-of Jacob Our-Father"; and the second, *Kavar Leah Ahmanu,* "Grave-of Leah Our-Mother." Harold Fisher asked concerning Rachel's resting place, and Dr. Schatz quietly responded, "Harold, Rachel is buried back in Bethlehem if I am not mistaken."

As we move out of the Machpelah Cave the patriarchal history of almost 4000 years ago no longer seems so far away. We walked again through the *shook* and saw many poorly dressed children, but yet some finely clad. People, we note, live in the second and third floors above the first floor market area. All of the wares are in the open; and shoe stores are composed of a man and one or two youngsters making shoes in the front half, and a gigantic pile of shoes, tied together in pairs but all unboxed, in the rear half. Sheep and goat skins are hanging everywhere and some of the garments made from them are most beautiful. Carved wooden work and metal work abound as do foodstuffs. The lean and youthful Mr. Carlson inquired as to the price of a sheepskin jacket, and as a true native (though he came from Tacoma, Washington) he began by asking the price of items far away from that which we were interested in. The exact price I can no longer remember, but I recall that it was high in my estimation even by American standards, and we passed up the goods.

We passed by the meat shops with their camel's heads hanging as a delicacy. Howard Carlson purchased some Arabic Chubuzz bread for us, and when we drove home we stopped at his house to devour it. First, his wife Bonnie recooked it in the oven as a sanitary precaution, and then we enjoyed it. It was passed from one to another in Arab fashion with each breaking off a piece of the Chubuzz and dipping it in the radish-mustard-like Hummuz sauce. As we ate and talked and laughed, it was a delight to all of us to recall the joy of the Arab merchants when we would walk in upon them and recite all of the Arabic at our command, viz, *Mir chabbah.* They like Americans who can at least give the Arabic "Hello."

What a day this had been with our visitation of the Jerusalem Temple Area, the Dome of the Rock, the Mosque El Aksa, Gordon's Calvary, the Garden Tomb, Bethlehem's site of the Nativity, Jerome's Cave, and Hebron with its Cave of the Patriarchs. This night the Bible seemed more real and alive than ever before. What thoughts to sleep upon we had!

CHAPTER XX

A DIP IN THE DEAD SEA AND AN INVASION OF JERICHO

Tuesday, *January 23rd*. All were on their own this morning, and Professor Dunzweiler took our car to purchase medicine at an apothecary shop which he was told was not far from the Old City. Dr. Proctor, the missionary doctor of Baraka Hospital, had been kind enough to issue him his needed prescription and so now he was off hunting for a refill of his necessary benign chemicals. Some in our group wandered again into the ever-drawing towers of Jerusalem, while others worked on their customs declarations. One may bring into the United States $100 worth of purchases from abroad duty free; but one must have a list of what he bought no matter how slight the amount.

CONVERSING WITH JERUSALEM ARABS

At about nine o'clock this morning a few of us were walking through the Damascus Gate at the northwest of the Old City. One kilometer west is the site of the Mandelbaum Gate which from 1948 to June, 1967, marked that rare and infrequent ambassadorial movement of this or that official between Israel and Jordan's possessions west of the Jordan. We walked again the Via Dolorosa. Stopping at a gift shop, an American-looking, attractive Arab girl in her early twenties conversed

Bedouin at market in Beersheba remind us of Joseph's coat of many colors.

Great stone tower at Jericho. Now standing at 20 feet, it was probably the main lookout of this ancient city. Jericho is the oldest known city to have been lived in, existing years before Abraham. Jericho's first mention in the Bible is when it was captured by Joshua and the invading Hebrews as the opening wedge of their campaign to take Canaan, 1400 years B.C. (Joshua 6).

Photo by Doreen Kirban

Would you believe that this picture was taken in the middle of a desert? Diane Kirban stands on a lush lawn resplendent with blossoming flowers in a kibbutz in Israel. Through modern methods of irrigation the desert is beginning to blossom as a rose.

Photo by Doreen Kirban

260 • ISRAEL   Land of Promise, Land of Prophecy

Sunset over the Mediterranean.

An old Bedouin, an Arab of the desert, uses a stick to keep his eye open.

An Israeli woman.

An Arab mother.

Two veiled Arab women in Hebron.

A Dip In The Dead Sea and An Invasion Of Jericho • 265

with us. She was a salesgirl in one of the countless gift shops. She revealed to us that she was a Christian, saying, "I am a Christian like you; I can see it in your face." She wanted to come to America for a greater opportunity, "For," she explained, "since the June, 1967 War many tourists are afraid to come, and work is no longer plentiful." She said that in her opinion Syria was the "warmonger" of the Middle East, as was Egypt. She wanted only peace, and stated that she favored those Arab states desiring peace, and was against those desiring war.

Later a nineteen-year-old Arab guide, a boy, began to take us around. He said that in one month he was going to travel to Pennsylvania to study. He was dumbstruck when none of us recognized the name of the town where he was headed, and a look of terror and alarm covered his face. Perhaps it was his pronunciation of the name? We tried to explain to him that Pennsylvania has so many towns that one cannot expect all Americans to be familiar with the smaller ones. He cheered and his color returned; but every now and then a new doubt gripped him and he awaited our reassurance that his dream-town goal which had been arranged for him by interested Stateside people was no doubt a real town in Pennsylvania.

He took us to the pinnacle of the Mount of Olives and we climbed to the top of the tower of the Church of the Ascension there. To the west was Jerusalem and the Mediterranean far beyond. To the northwest the Judean mountains; and to the east the Jordan Valley and the Dead Sea. Beyond this were the Trans-Jordanian mountains, and the guide pointed out that distant peak of Mt. Nebo from which Moses viewed the Promised Land. Nebo was among the mountains of Moab which rose east of the Dead Sea. From Jerusalem Nebo's Mount is forty miles straight to the east and a line between the two is tangent to the northern tip of the Dead Sea. Moses, therefore, only saw the land afar off (Deut. 32:49; 34:1) from that Moabite rock peak named for one of the evil Canaanite deities (Isa. 46:1).

We were then shown the traditional footprint of Jesus at the base of the church. After this, to keep the peace, I consented to have two photos taken (with my own camera) with a smiling Arab and his photogenic donkey—cost, two Israeli pounds.

After the meridian repast of blintzes and sour cream with coffee—Professor Dunzweiler alone sticking to scrambled eggs—we were loaded aboard a tour bus as the engines were warming up. The program of the trip specified the log as follows:

Tour No. 7   Depart 2:00 p.m.   (Half Day)

JERICHO—JORDAN RIVER—DEAD SEA

Depart Jerusalem—via BETHANY, explanation of the Tomb of Lazarus and the House of Mary and Martha—through the WILDERNESS OF JUDEA—Good Samaritan's Inn—JERICHO, visit excavations of the old Walls of Jericho, ruins of Ommayad Palace and 5th century Synagogue mosaics, view of MT. OF TEMPTATION—RIVER JORDAN, place of Baptism—to the DEAD SEA, lowest point on earth—return to Jerusalem.

Tour IL. 16.50   Entrance fees IL. 2.00   Total 18.50 IL.

We are now aboard the bus which is driving the twenty-five miles between Jerusalem and the northern end of the Dead Sea. Since Jerusalem is some 2200 feet above sea level and the Dead Sea is about 1300 feet below sea level we are making a 3500-foot descent. We are descending at a rate of 140 feet per mile eastward and the expressions, "Down to the Sea" and "Up to Jerusalem," are beginning to take on new significance. As we drive eastward along the road we periodically see signs, "Sea Level Point," "600 Feet Below Sea Level," et cetera. It is all most exciting.

Our guide is explaining aloud as we drive that we are now on the Jericho Road which is going through the brown and still barren Wilderness of Judea wherein Christ was tempted (Matt. 4:1; Mark 1:12; Luke 4:1). Upon the brow of the hill on the left side of the bus, the guide explains, one can see the Good Samaritan Inn. In Luke 10:30-37 Christ tells the parable of the man who fell among the thieves who hid in the multiplicity of

A Dip In The Dead Sea and An Invasion Of Jericho • 267

caves along this route upon which we are now riding.

The priest and the Levite walked by the wounded traveler, left for dead by the thieves. But a "Good Samaritan" came along and took him to a nearby inn and paid for the food and lodging of the wounded Jewish merchant. Our guide continued and told us that the inn which we just passed was built upon the site of another inn, and who knows whether or not that was the very inn which Christ had in mind? I thought that though we are not sure of the location of the inn, we are sure of the interpretation of the parable, and all who profess true faith should also manifest that true love which springs out of the true faith. In this parable of Luke 10:30-37 Christ admonishes us to follow the love of this Samaritan who was *slightly* off on his ecclesiology (where the church should worship, John 4:20-24); rather than the priest and Levite who were so right on their doctrinal *details* but who manifested no love or compassion for their neighbors—which was one of the great commandments of the Law.

As the Dead Sea drew into view our guide recited: "The Dead Sea is the name that the Romans gave to this body of water some 2000 years ago. Before that it was known by its Biblical name, the Sea of Salt. Its ancient Latin name is *Lacus Asphaltites*. It is forty miles long, running north to south; its surface is 370 square miles; and its level is 1286 feet below the sea level of the Mediterranean, with another 1200 or 1300 feet to its lowest depths. At its southern base, now covered by ebbing waters, archaeologists and Bible scholars believe are the twin cities of iniquity. Sodom and Gomorrah (literally, 'fields' and 'inundated'—probably due to periodic overflows of it by the Salt Sea). In Genesis 19:24 we read that the Lord destroyed these two cities of the plain with 'fire and brimstone from heaven.' Brimstone is a burning sulfur or sulfur salt compound, and in this region there is an abundance of this very chemical."

"Yes," thought I, "the Scriptural account will always fit the discoveries of science, once all of the data is in." I whispered to Professor Dunzweiler beside me, "The verse, Genesis 19:22, wherein the angel declares that he cannot destroy the city until Lot and his loved ones are outside of it, argues strongly in principle for a pre-tribulational rapture of the believers (1

Thess. 4:13-18). The Church may experience tribulation and persecution from the hands of sinful men, but the wrath *of God* will never fall upon the redeemed in this life (1 Thess. 5:9). Hence Lot had to be out of the city before the fire fell; and hence the church will have to be raptured out of this world before the fearful Tribulation judgments of God begin to fall upon the Sodom of this world at the end of the age.

THE SEA OF DEATH

We had at last arrived at Kal Ya, a small village at the northern extremity of the Dead Sea. We climbed out of the bus and I expected to see a dark, dank muddy swamp befitting the name "Dead Sea." The guide was still going on in a discussion of potash, sulphates, bromates, and other salts as he walked toward the tourist haven, refreshment stand, and restaurant near the waters. As I approached the waters, chatting now with one of the women from the bus, I stood amazed and shocked as I peered at its waters. It was absolutely crystal clear and beautiful despite its thirty percent by weight mineral content. Though out of every cubic foot of this water weighing approximately 65 pounds there is about 19.5 pounds of mineral salts, yet the water is clear as glass! (Try pouring two one-hundred pound bags of salt into your full bath tub when next you bathe, and I guarantee that you will never again in your life forget what this is like!)

"Taste it," smiled the attractive, about-forty-five lady at my side. "Dip your finger in and lick your finger. Do it; you'll find it interesting." I co-operated and, "Ug-g-g-g-g." The taste burned my tongue and it had an unforgettable awfulness in its supersaturated, supersalt flavor. "Now listen," spoke my companion at the brink of this sea, "what do you hear?" After a long pause, I replied, "Nothing; absolutely nothing." She gave a knowing smile, saying, "Of course. You heard nothing because this is the 'Dead Sea.' There are no fish in the water so you cannot hear one occasionally leap out of the water and make a splash. No frogs can be heard croaking here. Look and see; there are no birds flying above the waters and chirping. All is absolute silence. Even its diamond clearness, its crystalline beauty, is due to its complete lack of algae which would cloud it. This is the *Dead Sea.*"

It was an eerie calm that pervaded this shore. Time did not permit me to swim and to test the buoyancy of the water which is known to be amazing, but I did at least try to let my arm "float." According to Archimedes Principle a body submerged or partially submerged into a fluid is buoyed up by a force equal to the weight of the volume of fluid displaced. Thus here a 160 pound person *with a volume of three cubic feet* will begin to sink into the water, and as he does so his body will displace some of the sea water. When this man has reached the point where 2.46 cubic feet of his 3 cubic foot volume is under water he will suddenly find himself floating. This is because he is now buoyed up by a force equal to the weight of the volume of water displaced. He has displaced 2.46 cubic feet of water by putting that much of his body under water, and 2.46 cubic feet of water weighs exactly 160 pounds (2.46 by 65 lbs/cubic ft. of Dead Sea water=160 lbs.). Thus his weight pushes downward with a 160 lb. force and the water buoys him upward with a 160 lb. force; he is in equilibrium with 2.46 cubic feet of his volume under the water and with 0.54 cubic feet of his body above the water. Thus he floats. Of course, it is up to him to paddle a bit so as to make sure that the 0.54 cubic feet of his volume above water includes his head!

As we walked away from this silent crystal sea my arm which had been put into the water was now extremely sticky. Once the water had dried off of my arm, that is, once it had evaporated, it left this sticky salt residue which was pasty in texture. I was quite relieved to find a fresh water faucet at the restaurant, and I promptly washed away the sea salt from my arm and hands.

It was a disappointment to hear from the guide that because of a recent border incident we would not be able to risk traveling to the traditional spot identified as the place of Jesus' baptism. This location is five miles north of the Salt Sea on the bank of the Jordan River. Though saddened, we, as all people blessed of God, yet had to be thankful for the many privileges and gifts that God had given us. Eyes lingering too long on a disappointment partake of ingratitude—so we raised our heads and set our faces with joy toward our next destination, Jericho.

ANCIENT JERICHO

Our map showed us that Qumran was only four miles to the south on the western side of the Sea, but time did not permit us to make a run for it. Then after lingering at Kal Ya for a short time longer, we were dispatched another eight miles, this time to the north, and amid the dry Judean Desert a green citrus-tree oasis leaped into view, which was Jericho. Here the trees and the low elevation, 835 feet below sea level, combine together to make this "city of palm trees" a cool resort area while other nearby cities swelter in the desert heat. Now, however, it is January, and we are perfectly comfortable lightly clothed. We climb out of the bus beside the mound of ancient Jericho and on the other side of the road is a surprisingly expensive-looking restaurant. Yet the modern town has over 41,000 in it today, so a fancy dining place for so noted a resort area and historic site is perhaps to be expected. At present, since June 1967's struggle, Jericho lies in the possession of Israel. Yet here we did not see soldiers on this day.

We were a mile north of the modern Jericho, and the name for the mound which we were now climbing, Old Testament Jericho, we were informed was *Tel-Es-Sultan*. Not far away, to the southeast, is the mound of New Testament Jericho. On this latter mound is the remains of Herod's Winter Palace famed for its 330-foot-long facade. Herod's Hippodrome was also uncovered there. That site is further known for its aqueduct which brought to it the fresh water of the Wadi Kilt. This wadi, or river-stream, flows west to east into the Jordan and it is located about two and a half miles to the south.

As we reached the summit of the pear-shaped mound of Old Testament Jericho, all of our party marveled in incredulity that we were really here. Our guide somehow became separated from our group, but in this case we did not suffer for a professorish looking man about fifty-five began to explain everything to his young feminine companion, probably his daughter, and some of us listened in and he cordially included us into the audience. We never learned his name, so I do not know if he was the world's leading archaeologist, a well-read person, or what. Nevertheless, later study seemed to confirm his talk and it went somewhat as follows, as I recall:

The Gentleman: "This mound was excavated in 1868 by Charles Warren and in 1907-11 by Ernst Sellin. In 1929-36 a more thorough excavation took place under the direction of John Garstang.

"When Joshua took Jericho he took one of the strategic cities of Canaan. Because of its central position all of the Canaanites would soon hear of this and many would lose their will to resist the God of Joshua (Joshua 2:9-11). The falling of the high walls would also give Israel confidence in the power of their God to vanquish their taller and stronger foes who inhabited walled cities such as their eyes had never beheld.

"Jericho was also important because it was situated at a commercial crossroads. It was located at one of the ideal places to ford the Jordan, and merchants as well as armies wishing to make an east-west passage would have their way blocked by the forty-eight miles of the Dead Sea until they came to Jericho's ford. From here the traders went north to Shechem, west to Jerusalem, and south to Hebron.

"As you can see, the mound is somewhat pear-shaped and it appears to be less than a quarter mile long. It is an eight-acre mound. In times of siege all of the people who farmed the surrounding oasis would come to live within the walled city and, though it was small by modern sizes, yet it would be then crowded with people from all the surrounding friendly country. It was one grand fortress built upon a hill, and, properly provisioned, its walls could keep out invaders for years. Thus when the spies were first sent out from Kadesh-barnea, they, not trusting in God's power, complained that they could never conquer such strong people who lived in cities with walls so high (Num. 13:26-33)."

Steve: "But from being here, I can now see how the whole army of Israel was able to walk around this city seven times on the seventh day. The city is just not that large, I'm surprised."

Arlene: "How old is the oldest civilization found here?"
Gentleman: "Some say a stone age culture, neolithic, dating as far back as 6000 B.C. This date is based on Carbon 14 dating, but there is much debate over this figure. Few are certain.

"Garstang's fourth occupational level was labeled 'City D.' This level he later identified positively as the Jericho of Joshua's day. He identified it as such on the basis of an examination of 100,000 pottery fragments, which included 1500 unbroken pieces. Many other finds including 80 scarabs were also unearthed.

"He found that the walls had been in the shape of two concentric circles going around the top of the mound. The walls were composed of sundried bricks three to six inches thick and running in length from one to three feet. Look over there and there, you can see such brick walls all around. Garstang discovered the walls to have been about thirty feet in height from their bases at the top of the mound. The inner wall was about twelve feet thick and built upon the foundations of an earlier wall. The outer wall was about six feet thick. Between the walls there was a space from twelve to fifteen feet which was interrupted periodically by cross walls which joined the outer and inner walls.

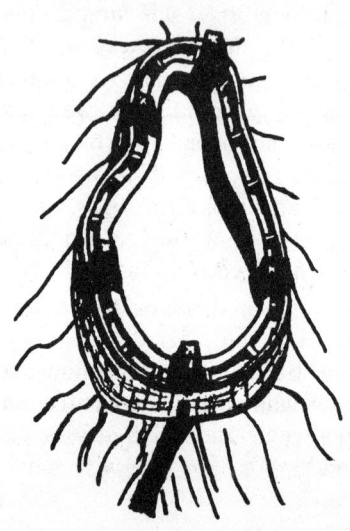

"Garstang reported that the outer wall had fallen outward down the slope and that the inner one had collapsed into the interwall space. Only where the walls joined a tower did they remain. The remnants of houses which once stood between and atop the walls were found also. It appeared to the archaeologists that the city was destroyed suddenly, and not after any prolonged siege. This was because they found ample food provisions left and even bread still in ovens—as in Pompeii which was suddenly and quickly ashed and gassed to death by Vesuvius erupting in A.D. 79."

At this a lady called this man who was speaking, and he nodded and departed.

Arnold: "What about the story of Joshua and the Battle of Jericho? Do you believe that the walls fell down miraculously? I guess that you do since you believe the Bible. It struck me that the fellow who was giving us the lecture a few minutes ago also believed it. He seemed to know what he was talking about. Well...do you think that it was God who pulled down the Jericho walls of Joshua's era?"

Prof. Cohen: "Yes, we do. Do you know that the description of the fall of Jericho in Joshua 6:20-25 and 2:15 specifies that (1) the walls fell down miraculously, (2) they fell down flat, (3) but not all of the walls fell because Rahab's house was on the wall and it remained standing, and (4) the city was burnt by fire."

Arnold: "Very good, but what is the real significance of all these specifications?"

Prof. Cohen: "The significance lies in the fact that when John Garstang, Pere Vincent, and Clarence Fisher excavated the site of Jericho in 1930-1936 they found walls which had fallen down; which had fallen outwardly; and that not all of the walls had fallen. They also discovered an ash layer and charred timbers indicating the city to have been destroyed by fire. This is remarkably similar to the details as described in the sacred narrative."

Arnold: "But didn't I hear somewhere that a Miss Kathleen Kenyon conducted an excavation here in 1952-1956 and questioned Garstang's conclusions?"

Prof. Cohen: "Yes, but remember that the expedition years later could not redig up the late Bronze levels which the earlier excavation had already unearthed. Also note that certain physical facts cannot easily be disputed, namely, the fallen brick walls, the inner walls with lower portions still standing, the fact that there were ruins of wall dwellings, and the fact that the city had ash layers from fire. All of these at least present a prima facie argument against anyone merely reading the Bible story and scoffing it away by saying that such events and circumstances as described in Joshua 6 are purely imaginary and could never have existed at Jericho.

"Although Jericho is one of the most argued over *tels* in all of Palestine, many archaeologists of note concur from Jericho's pottery remains that the Canaanite city destroyed in Joshua's time fell at least somewhere between the years 1200-1500 B.C. Garstang, writing years after his original excavations, objected to even the placing of the date of the fall of the Canaanite city to the Hebrews in the 'doubtful category.' He strenuously held to his original 1400 B.C. dating and maintained that at this time the walls fell outwardly and that the city was burned over by an intense fire. It was his belief that except for the fact that certain archaeologists had axes to grind concerning the date of the exodus, his 1400 B.C. date would have gone unchallenged. Aside, however, from this controversy the mere facts of fallen walls, houses on the wall, and ash layers being found at Jericho's site ought to make many think twice concerning the trustworthiness of the Biblical record. Read Joseph P. Free, *Archaeology and the Bible History*, 5th edition (Scripture Press, Wheaton, 1956).''

Howard Carlson: "The current line put forward by the Hebrew University is that when it comes to argued-over-Jericho, 'the only thing that anyone is sure of is that not too many are sure of anything.' "

Prof. Dunzweiler: "One must certainly be careful as to what he gives credence to, but there are certain things that we can be sure of. Permit me to underscore that last clause. From both the Bible and the archaeological excavations upon this mound we do know certain definite pieces of information, though much else may be beclouded by doubt."

Howard Carlson next showed us two incredibly deep, four-sided, square excavation pits which were dug deep into the mound. Their size, to my rough estimation would be each 40 by 50 feet by 70 feet deep, though one was a bit larger than the other. In one was a stone Canaanite tower which looked to be about fifteen feet in diameter and perhaps thirty feet high. We had to peer off of the edge of the unfenced, squarely cut hole to see it below. How old was it? Perhaps from 4000 to 6000 years—I do not know for sure. But obviously they did not dig a hole and then build it inside—at least the burden of proof would rest on anyone advancing such an hypothesis. When that tower was first built the *tel* was much lower. It is in excellent preservation, having been buried in the mud for millennia, and it stares at the onlooker and in silence it cries out its antiquity.

Marveling that no one had yet fallen into one of the two pits and sued the city—or is this the way that only Americans speculate—we posed for pictures atop its crest. We then saw much of our tour absent, and so hastened to the bus and the anxious guide.

Guide: "Do all of you see that high peak over there to the north, towering over Jericho? Can you see the Greek Orthodox monastery at the peak? That is the Mount of Temptation where tradition says that Satan took Christ to show Him all of the kingdoms of this world, tempting him, that if he would but worship Satan they could all be His (Matt. 4:8)."

Florence: (in low tones): "What about that?"

Prof. Cohen: "We believe the Biblical account to be true; but it nowhere identifies or describes the mountain except to say that it was 'exceedingly high.' In fact, from the Biblical account we cannot be absolutely sure that Christ was transported *bodily* to the mountain. This Mount of Temptation fits that part all right—look at it. You can see Mount Hermon away up in Syria from its top. The Bible, however, simply does not name the mountain. This peak here is just a guess; we are in no way obliged to agree. The Bible just doesn't say."

AT HISHAM'S PALACE

We drove a short spell northeast as the guide told of the bananas, apples, dates, and citrus fruit grown at Jericho. He said that the snow of two weeks before which so devastated so many of the trees of Jerusalem also hit Jericho, and he asserted that as far as he knew it was the first time it had snowed in Jericho in all of recorded history!

We climbed out of the bus and were each handed a circular entitled, "National Parks Authority—Hisham's Palace, Jericho." It continued:

"This palace, dating from the times of the Omayyad dynasty (early Moslem era), is built on a site known as Khirbet Mafjar.

"Inscriptions show the building was begun by the Caliph Hisham Ibn Abd el-Malik in 724 and continued until 743 C.E. (A.D.).

"Hisham, whose main residence was in Damascus, was much impressed by Jericho's equable climate, and he built this as his winter palace. However, only four years after its completion, it was destroyed by a severe earthquake. Apart from some primitive settlement on the site in the 12th century, it was never reoccupied."

We were then taken through the ruins of this palace. Over a large area the remains spread with cut stones which were many and quite sizable. Its stone baths and their detailed, well-preserved floor mosaics were indicative of the fineness of its construction and of its lavish ornamentation. It was difficult to comprehend that once not long ago life flourished amid these large, dim, yellow-brown, stone slab ruins. Steam rooms (!) and animal decorations took up the majority of the remainder of our guide's explanation. The water, it had been explained, was traversed to this palatial estate by a four-kilometer aqueduct running from Ein-Dug to the west to here. Then it was artificially heated and the steam was channeled through stone passages and windows into the steam room. We walked by the Ornamental Pool, and then again filed into the bus.

In the bus our guide was saying, "...destroyed only four years after its completion, it lay hidden until in 1931 a British military officer rediscovered it. It was the king's winter resort. This is so because in the summer Jericho becomes excessively hot. Jericho gets only about 70 millimeters of rain annually; and this falls in the winter. At other times of the year this lowland has such a heavy dew, that this, along with its water system, springs, and wadis, enable its crops to grow well."

Since this was the palace of a Moslem ruler, one of the people on the bus asked the guide about some of the practices of Islam. Among other things, the guide related that, to become a Moslem, one had to say aloud three times the declaration, "I am a Moslem," and it was done. To divorce, he asserted that one had to say three times, "I divorce you." These were probably somewhat oversimplified by the guide, thought I, but nevertheless significant. He stated that to cease being a Moslem there was no handy recitation, for the penalty for apostasy from Islam was death. This explained why Christian missionaries to Moslem lands often see so little outward fruit.

THE SYNAGOGUE

We soon arrived at what appeared to be an Arab refugee camp. All looked peaceful and I did not see any soldiers around. The men were not well dressed, yet neither were they in rags. "Old clothes" would be the proper description. Within this setting we were taken to what was still standing of a fifth century A.D. synagogue.

As we walked toward it, I was explaining to one of our companions that the word *synagogue* was a Greek word–not a Hebrew word at all—which came from *syn*, meaning "together" or "with," and the verb *ago*, meaning "I am leading." Thus *synago* is the Greek verb for "I am gathering together"; and the noun *synagogue* thus came to mean "a place where people gather together (for religious worship)."

It came into vogue as a Greek word rather than a Hebrew. This was because, after the start of the spreading of the Greek culture through the world by the conquests of Alexander the Great (336-323 B.C.), the civilized world began to speak Greek more and more. This process known as "Hellenization"—which the Herodians of the New Testament supported and the Pharisees detested—also affected the Jews. The Jews of Palestine were greatly affected, but those of the *diaspora* more so. These latter "scattered ones" lived in a Greek world for the three centuries which preceded Christ, and being far away from their Jerusalem Temple they "gathered together" (they *synagogued*) for worship in houses and other places where they were. Hence erupted forth both the entity and the name *synagogue*.

The real beginning of this institution, however, apparently was initiated immediately after the deportation of the Jews from Jerusalem into Babylon. This deportation began at c. 606 B.C., with Jerusalem and the Temple being destroyed in 586 B.C. With the Jerusalem Jews in Babylon, and with the Temple no more, the synagogue became a necessity and evolved at once.

The following mosaic appeared on the floor of the fifth century synagogue as I have sketched it below.

CHAPTER XXI

CROSSING THE OCEAN

Wednesday, *January 24th,* streaked by for everyone as all consummated their final visits, purchases, and farewells as we readied to depart in the afternoon for Tel Aviv. All of us say our adieus to different names, but alas, the tears so often cannot help but run down the cheek.

It is late afternoon and sixty-five kilometers lay between us and Tel Aviv's Dan Hotel. The darkness comes upon us quickly as our journey west commences and the rain begins and gets stronger with each kilometer. The thumping, thudding of the water upon our moving roof and the utter blackness before our headlights makes movement slow. This road is a main artery but it is not like the American turnpike and we do not see friendly rest stops and restaurants every few minutes. Fortunately, everyone has filled up the benzine tanks before we launched out into this water channel.

At 8:10 p.m., though the darkness of our trip made it seem as if it was 4 a.m., with pleasure I turn the key of room 766 in the Tel Aviv Dan Hotel. It is a beautiful room. Thanks to road signs (not too many), and to our map (not too good,), and to my compass (this made the difference) we arrived without the usual procedure of getting lost. We praised the Lord for His safe keeping, for when we were only blocks away from our goal an auto immediately in front of us slammed straight into a large traffic light post. The post was in the middle of one of Tel Aviv's complicated street forks. No one was hurt, but the man's auto was utterly smashed and pushed in at the front. And all this with a policeman watching only a few feet away.

RACING TO LOD FIELD

Thursday, *January 25th*. Up at 6:15 and then breakfast. The *mel-tzar* (waiter) greets us with a respectful *boker-tov* (good morning), and we order. Professor Dunzweiler, after consuming no small time with the menu decides upon a *bay-tsah* (egg) scrambled as is his unvarying habit.

Our plane departs at nine o'clock. Owing, however, to poor road signs (almost invariably written in Hebrew) and to a map which did not indicate one-half of the curves and traffic circles, it appeared that we were not going to make the plane. At least with the compass, when in doubt, we always made a turn toward the general direction to which we were heading. Our difficulty no doubt was also due to the misapprehensions of our foreign conceptions. We had been told in the States that the Lod Airport was the "Tel Aviv Airport." This was a misconception, as the shortest route is thirteen miles through mostly urban traffic in a strange land via the Tel Aviv maze street grid. For us it meant twenty miles. Had we realized, we would have encamped that night in a hotel at Lod near the aerodrome; but in our abysmal ignorance we drove from Jerusalem right past Lod and back into far away Tel Aviv.

We had stacked the cards against ourselves, geographically speaking. Yet our American grit and drive, and the compass, delivered us to the airship in time after all. The TWA agent personally rushed us to the plane which was with its steps up about to begin its taxi to the runway. . . . Perhaps we should have started earlier???? Fortunately we made it and all wore smiles. I must candidly state that I, as many of my fellow Americans would have, smiled through it all, knowing that there would be other planes after this one. Some however, as in any crowd, wore deep frowns and somber looks in a sour fashion when the score was going against us. . . . Perhaps we should have started earlier???

HIJACKED TO GENEVA???

It is 9:07 a.m. and we are aboard a Boeing 707 Starstream jet liner on Flight 883 to Athens, Geneva, and New York. As we fastened our safety belts, Mr. Dunzweiler states that we will be going to Athens, Frankfurt, and New York. I mused to myself, "I thought it was... Geneva...." Bob Dunzweiler explains how he had promised to bring his special lady friend some figurines from Frankfurt, Germany. He said that these figures were known as "Hummels."

Soon we are airborne and our dazzling silver comet is streaking through the clouds in its wild climb skyward. The voice of the Captain greets us in English tones and when he pronounces the word "Geneva" Professor Dunzweiler makes a sour face and moans. I summoned a stewardess—for had I not an air sick passenger with me?—she explains that two flights would depart in the morning from Tel Aviv to New York. Both would stop at Athens and one would stop at Geneva while the other would fuel at Frankfurt. Disappointment rides upon Professor Dunzweiler's brow, and he moans, "I wish we had missed this plane after all;...and had made the Frankfurt one later in the day." After a brief inquiry about a parachute's availability, which the stewardess termed as "somewhat irregular" he settled down into a cherry melancholy stupor. He referred to the air company as "Dirty Rotters"—but said it with a smile bearing them no ill will nor grudge. I attempted to take his mind from the subject by discussing the possibility that TWA, Trans World Airlines, really had originally stood for its Chinese millionaire owner, a Mr. Twa. Finding this not to be germane, he returned to the Frankfurt territory.

Our distances were to be as follows: Lod to Geneva, 1750 miles; Geneva to New York, 3862 miles, totaling 5612 miles from Lod to NYC. The trip coming via Athens was slightly longer, so our total air mileage from New York was about 11,500 miles.

On this leg of our journey, from Tel Aviv to Athens, our plane is less than one-quarter full. We count only 12 of the 114 economy seats to be occupied, and only two of the thirty-one first class seats. With such absenteeism it is obviously difficult for air companies to make five-million-dollar Boeing

707's or Douglas DC-8's, or Lockheed Electras, pay for themselves ... And the $20 million Boeing 747?

To the right we see many high, snow-capped mountains which, according to the pilot's announcement, are the peaks of Turkey—the "Asia" through which the Apostle Paul traveled in order to bring them the Gospel... From Tel Aviv to Athens we will traverse 753 miles. It is now 10:30 a.m. Israel time, and below with one hundred percent clarity I can spy the Greek Sporades Islands in the Aegean. The orange-colored isles below in the midst of the dark blue Mediterranean appear to be peaked orange flat clouds themselves also flying through the air. They strike one's visual senses as themselves being elevated far above their dark surroundings . . . . Now the Cyclades Islands of Greece in the South Aegean are floating by. We are able to discern roads between the jagged crags of the isles.

We are descending now into Athens, and bright green vegetation in the water—an algae—surrounds the coastline, and serves as a buffer between the brown of the land and the blue of the ocean. As we lose elevation and come in over the sea our eyes now can see white spots of breaking waves dotting the sea beneath. Lower still and the mountains are now to our right and their heights loft higher than our plane. They are enormous. The gigantic city of Athens is to our immediate right as we now skim over the water.

Our landing time is 10:55 Israel time, but the Athens airport clock reads 9:55 a.m. I am in the Athens airport; Professor Dunzweiler elected to remain in the plane. His missing Frankfurt is somewhat of a Jonah's gourd to him; but in his case it is a disappointment not with reference to his own pleasure, but with reference to his desire to please another. And assuredly this latter type of miff is acceptable.

LIFE JACKETS AND MOUNTAINS

As the plane lifts for Geneva, the stewardess again gives her demonstration of how to put on the life jacket which is under each passenger's seat. It is difficut not to chuckle, for, as we watch, she fails to get the straps on twice in a row. At last on the third try she makes it. The men uniformly find this funny; but the women aboard glare a disgusted look toward the stewardess. She smiles at the men, and looks all business at the women. This goes on at least until the life jacket ceremony is out of mind.

The Captain announces that Geneva is 1000 miles away and that our flight time should be two and a half hours. I pray that, if it be His will, God might deliver our plane home safely (Jam. 4:13-15; Acts 27:24).

It is now 10:50 a.m. Athen's time (11:50 Israeli time). We are being served a luxurious dinner. It begins with shrimp cocktail. Next there is a fine turkey platter, and for dessert an apricot fruit tart. Professor Dunzweiler and I discuss the nicety of the Arabic custom of calling a man "Abu" plus his son's name. Imagine, think we, referring to our sixteenth President as "Abu-Tad." . . . Below, the Italian Apennine mountain chain, which runs the length of the peninsula, is stretching its creviced and jagged brown and snow-capped points before us as rows of buckled contruction paper. Only dryness and desiccation lie below; there is no green at all. Perhaps there are green fir trees amid the acres underneath; but at this altitude, if they are there, they cannot be discerned. The watch here reads 12:20 p.m. , Athens time.

The Captain unexpectedly comes in voice and we hear, "We will soon leave Italy and fast approach the Swiss Alps. We shall fly between Mt. Blanc, the highest peak in Europe, 15,781 feet; and the famed Matterhorn, 14,691 feet, which marks the border between Switzerland and Italy. We have not yet, however, reached these peaks. The French Riviera is now below and to our left; and the Italian Riviera is to our right." 12:40 p.m., Athens time.

The Captain walked by and I showed him my compass with which for my own pleasure I monitored the plane's course. I offered it to him if he needed it. He gave a jovial grin and responded, "Good. I'll come for it if necessary. Now I know where to find it." He started to walk off, and then leaned back and said, pointing out through the window, "Say, also watch that wing out there for me, and call me if it starts to come off." He had everyone around laughing. However, I did note that Professor Dunzweiler tightened his seat belt—or at least it appeared so.

The mountains before us are the Alps, and they, being

higher than the brownish mountains of Italy, are much more white-capped. As we approached Mt. Blanc, we come into what seems to be grasping distance of the immense and razor-sharp Alps below. "What an impassable barrier to land armies," I think. The air currents are now giving the plane turbulence, and a few on board now look flushed and slightly airsick. . . . Now we have entered into the clouds and all below is cottony white, and out our windows the scene is wispy, whitish.

GENEVA

It is now 2:15 p.m., Israeli time; 1:15 p.m., Athens time; and 12:15 p.m., Geneva time, and it is announced that our plane is beginning to make its landing run over the water of Lake Geneva (or "Jenev" as they would pronounce it). The Captain declares the Geneva temperature to be one degree centigrade or thirty three fahrenheit. As we race over the water of the lake we see the ground all around covered with snow except for the trees which lift their heads haughtily above the white blanket that covers all else. Single houses, trees, forests, hotels, and snow below—it is beautiful.

In the Swiss airport of Calvin's city we found a host of shops, and an especially large wristwatch display. As we sauntered over to it, Professor Dunzweiler suggested that we purchase Swiss watches from Switzerland as a present that some loved one would treasure. He said, "They must be cheap in price at least here." We received, to our dismay, somewhat of a jolt when we gazed at the prices. I could not spy so much as even one low-priced watch out of the hundreds before us in the mammoth selection offered. I noted one for 3400 Swiss francs. This caused me to stare toward the money exchange booth and to note its sign stating that one American dollar was equivalent to 4.33 francs. This made the 3400 franc watch cost $786 which was more than the trinket and bauble I was hunting.

When one of the many ladies behind the watch counters approached me, seeing the prices of the watches, I asked, "Does everyone in Switzerland speak French as you do, Mademoiselle?" She smiled and replied, "Here in *Jenev*, part of French Switzerland, they speak French; but in Zurich, which is in German Switzerland, they speak German. Italian is spoken in some places next to the Italian border."

For thirty-one francs I secured a silk Swiss blue flowered head scarf as a gift for someone special. Another American whom I met at the counter said that he wished an all white one for his wife, but alas, they had none. I related to him how she would love a blue one purchased in Switzerland. He looked at me sternly, and countered, "Look, you may like a blue one; the one for whom you are buying may like a blue one; but I know my wife and she said, 'white,' 'pure white.' I'll wait until I get home to get one."

One hour and fifteen minutes later we were taking off again with 3862 miles from Geneva to New York before us. The Captain's voice now comes over the speaker system, saying, "Our Flight, 883, Geneva to John F. Kennedy Airport, New York City, should be in transit seven hours and forty-eight minutes, and we ought to arrive at 11:30 p.m. Israel time, for those of you who boarded with us at Tel Aviv. The time of arrival, Eastern Standard Time, is actually scheduled to be at 4:30 p.m. We will be flying west at 35,000 feet, high above any turbulence, and so we anticipate a very smooth flight. Let me welcome all of you aboard, especially those of you who have recently joined us at Geneva."

After a time, through the window we note a plane flying directly east at 9 o'clock high. Its white vapor trail follows it like a deer's tail. Now out of our windows we observe a clear light blue sky above the far horizon, and below there is a solid blanket of white ermine fur composed of clouds. The pilot, a Captain Flanigan, just stated, "We have been vectored somewhat off of our course," and that we are now slightly north of our intended route. After a period of time elapses, he comes on over the speaker again informing us that we are at this moment over Paris. Our new course, he explains, should be at 270° due west at 48° north latitude. From the map, I noted that Paris is at 48°52' north latitude. Later we will have to head a bit south as JFK is at about 40°40'.

The Captain next remarked that "soon" "we will *probably* go over the ocean." Prof. Dunzweiler jumped forward, exclaiming, *"Probably!*—Please inquire for me just how one goes about making parachute and lifeboat arrangements!" We laughed—although, as I have oft stated before in a more serious vein, we never flew except that we asked the Lord to deliver us on our journey.

It was next reported over the speaker, in a cordial way, "Our stewardesses are here to help you. Their names are Trixie, Bubbles, Che-Che, and Ginger." The plane was now filled to about fifty percent of its capacity. I have never realized before, quite to this extent, that the undertaking of flying regularly scheduled flights involves planes frequently flying with numbers of empty seats, often at a financial loss.

It was 4:30 p.m. according to Mr. Dunzweiler's Tel Aviv Starting-Time-Chronometer, and we are being served a steak dinner with vegetables, salad, juice, and an apricot fruit tart for dessert; coffee and rolls, also. Since previously at 12:15 p.m. Tel Aviv time a sumptuous luncheon had been served us, now only four and a quarter hours later it is impossible for us to finish all of this splendid dinner. Someone, walking by, calls the stewardess's attention to my having inadvertently poured my small container of white salad dressing into my coffee. "Did the cream taste strange?" She asks with a giggle. The stewardess's eyes, however, suddenly noticed something beside me, and she put on a frown and scolded my professor companion, saying emphatically, "Shame on you for eating your dessert without finishing your vegetables."

A motion picture in color is now being shown as we dart westerly over the cloud beshrouded icy Atlantic below. The earphones were again rented at $2.50 per set for those who wished to hear radio music or the sound track of the picture.

JUMPING ACROSS THE OCEAN

As we fly I soon find myself chatting with a handsome, gray-haired lady who had been seated across the aisle to our right. She is returning home to the United States from Geneva where her daughter is temporarily studying. She explained that her daughter had been heartbroken when she found that her boy friend of some years was taking drugs. Therefore, it seemed best for her daughter to spend a semester in Europe at this time. She advised, "Parents ought to enjoy their daughters while they are tots, because when they get older the problems become more intense."

This brought us into a discussion of sin being in the world. I likened the ocean below us, an endless separation between two continents, to the chasm between God and man caused by sin. William R. Newell, who wrote the hymn, "At Calvary," in his commentary on Paul's Epistle to the Romans told an interesting story on this very point. He compared a person's trying to become righteous in the eyes of God to a group of people attempting to jump across the Atlantic Ocean. Oh, yes, some leap farther than others. The elderly lady may run and splash into the water only three feet from the eastern shore of the U.S., while some great athlete may bound as far as thirty feet out into the waves. But, you see, even the best comes nowhere near jumping across the Atlantic on *his own power*. So it is with all who attempt to save themselves in the eyes of God by doing good deeds, going to synagogue or church, being baptized, et cetera. This is what Romans 3:20 means when it declares:

> "Therefore by the deeds of the law (that is, by attempting to fulfill the law) there shall no flesh be justified in his sight."

Yet how thankful we can be that there is another way, the way of faith. When we acknowledge our sinfulness and fall at the foot of the Cross by faith in Christ, God counts Christ's death as sufficient payment for our sins, and we are saved. Christ's righteousness stands instead of ours, and we are born again with a hope that awaits Christ's coming from Heaven and which goes beyond the grave. So Romans 10:9-13:

> "That if thou shalt confess with thy mouth the Lord Jesus, and shalt believe in thine heart that God hath raised him from the dead, thou shalt be saved. For with the heart man believeth unto righteousness; and with the mouth confession is made unto salvation. For the scripture saith, Whosoever believeth on him shall not be ashamed. For there is no difference between the Jew and the Greek: for the same Lord over all is rich unto all that call upon him. For whosoever shall call upon the name of the Lord shall be saved."

A Pan American jet liner has been flying parallel to us for the last two hours of our flight. One could constantly see it when he looked out yonder through the plexiglass windows.

We are coming in for a landing at John F. Kennedy Airport,

New York. Our landing time will be 11:16 p.m. Israel starting time; 4:16 p.m. Eastern Standard Time. It is announced that the temperature is 20° at JFK, and that there are snow flurries expected. This is quite different from the warm Palestine which we had left this morning.

As we disembark from the plane we spy the welcoming faces of friends and loved ones. The woman at customs looked through my suitcase, and this is the first that this has been done during our entire trip. She asked me if my bags contained any fruit....She apologized as my four Jericho oranges were confiscated.

We thanked God for our safe return, and for the privilege we had been afforded. We had seen the land of the Bible; we had participated in an *Israel Safari*.